DATE DUE FOR RE

ON EX

MARTIN CLASSICAL LECTURES
VOLUME XXX

The Martin Classical Lectures are delivered annually at Oberlin College on a foundation established by his many friends in honor of Charles Beebe Martin, for forty-five years a teacher of classical literature and classical art in Oberlin.

HOMER *and the* NIBELUNGENLIED

comparative studies in epic style

BERNARD FENIK

Published for Oberlin College by
HARVARD UNIVERSITY PRESS
Cambridge, Massachusetts, and London, England   1986

This book is printed on acid-free paper, and its binding
materials have been chosen for strength and durability.

LIBRARY OF CONGRESS CATALOGING-IN-PUBLICATION DATA

Fenik, Bernard.
  Homer and the Nibelungenlied.

  (Martin classical lectures ; v. 30)
  Bibliography: p.
  Includes index.
  1. Epic poetry—History and criticism.
2. Homer—Criticism and interpretation.
3. Nibelungenlied.
I. Title.   II. Series.
PA25.M3   vol. 30   [PN1303]   973 s   [809.1'3]   85-16330
ISBN 0-674-40608-7 (alk. paper)

329960

*To the memory of Ingeborg,
who persuaded me to attempt this*

Acknowledgments

A PROPER ACCOUNT of what this study owes to Hans-Georg Richert, Professor of Germanic Languages and Literatures at the University of Cincinnati, would exceed my capacity to describe and his to endure. This sparest of acknowledgments must therefore serve to hint at the enormity of my debt. I welcome this chance to thank also Robert Lewis, formerly of the German Department at the University of Cincinnati, who read the manuscript in an early form. He corrected many mistakes and suggested even more improvements. My thanks as well to Professor Burghart Wachinger of the University of Tübingen. He also read the manuscript in its beginnings, making useful suggestions and helping me more than he knows. It is a special pleasure to acknowledge the generous support I have received from the Classics Fund of the University of Cincinnati established by Louise Taft Semple in memory of her father, Charles Phelps Taft. One full quarter of academic leave was paid for by that fund, and other grants were made from the same source for earlier study and the final writing. Appointment as Martin Lecturer in 1983 was a privilege and an honor. I am grateful to the Classics Department of Oberlin College for inviting me to participate in that distinguished series and for their encouragement of an enterprise that was, from the start, experimental and tentative. My debts run deep to those who helped sustain me in the days of turmoil and sorrow: to Getzel Cohen, for unwavering personal and professional support; to Eugenia Foster, for steadfast friendship; and to my wife, Mary Chotard Doll Fenik, for guidance into wholeness and for more besides than she would want me to say.

Contents

Preface

I NEED to say at the start that this is not a book about oral poetry. Nor will I enter into the question of whether the *Iliad* and the *Nibelungenlied* are oral or literate forms, or the products of some process of transition between those two modes. This is, instead, a study of certain kinds of artistic design shared by the ancient Greek and medieval European epic, and indeed not just by them but by much other literature as well. The question of orality or literacy will therefore be kept from the foreground of discussion. The reason is this: I offer analysis of how the epics work at certain levels of narration and I argue that they show close organization and high refinement in the short to intermediate blocks of composition. I do not believe that this answers the question of how they were composed, although I would like to believe that the findings will need to enter into any solution arrived at in the future and by others.

The fact is that oral poetry has become a discipline in its own right and most of us on the outside know about it only what we read. Some excellent introductions and surveys have appeared, offering definitions, examples, and a theoretical framework,[1] but few substantial texts to work with and little in the way of empirical, side-by-side comparison with stuff of the written variety.[2] Thus the qualitative limits of oral poetry have yet to be established, and the ancient and medieval materials, at least, tend to be viewed through the glass of theoretical bias. My effort is therefore to get back to practical criticism without commitment to a theory of origins, to look hard at the texts and to leave the implications to fall out as they may, to be thought through to the end by others who bring more to the task than second-hand knowledge of oral poetry. My concentration on the texts is not so much an effort to avoid controversy (an impossibility in this field of inquiry) as to force attention back to the poetry itself, which easily becomes neglected or tendentiously excerpted in the war of hypotheses.

Milman Parry argued that the *Iliad* and the *Odyssey* are so unlike poetry of the written word that different standards are needed to interpret them.[3] His attention and assertion were directed mainly to the epic diction. Homer's formulas set him apart from writing authors who choose and refine their expressions according to circumstance. Parry's demonstration of large formular systems in Homer was absolute and final, as was his proof that repeated expressions in later authors (the tragedians, Theocritus, Vergil) are essentially different in nature and application. These demonstrations must be built as an irreducible ingredient into all interpretation of the poems.

Some of Parry's successors tried to extend his arguments beyond diction to the larger components of Homeric style, such as structure and characterization. It was asserted, for example, that Homer's persons are no more than collective types, generic profiles sprung from a vision bounded by the stereotype.[4] Others compared Homer's manipulation of themes to the routine of a player shuffling cards, or described his narrative as strung out in relentless parataxis with one episode lined up in rank and file beside the next.[5] The Greek epic was thus given over to the rule of formula at every level. Misled perhaps by the rigor of Parry's demonstrations, these critics extended his conclusions into areas not covered by his proofs.

The result was a distorted view. These descriptions of "Homeric style" are in fact little more than radical abstractions, theoretical constructs cut off from the living roots of the texts, hypotheses about what oral poetry should or must be like if Parry's conclusions allowed indiscriminate extension.[6] But we should not be so quick to discard the experience of countless generations of readers who found qualities of beauty and imagination in the *Iliad* and the *Odyssey* that give them a special place in the world's literature. Indeed, close analysis reveals more to refute the extreme formulists than to support them. That is one of the efforts of this book. The interpreter of Homer thus faces an apparent paradox. Dictional formulas and type scenes carry an air of automation and pre-stamped design. On the other side, Homer's artistry transcends the sheer mechanics of his verse technique.[7]

There is a growing consensus in some quarters that the Greek epic belongs to a period of transition from oral to written composition.[8] We will see later that something similar is claimed for the *Nibelungen-*

lied. The theory takes its start in the double nature of Homer's style just described. There is powerful evidence of orality in the texts, namely the formula systems that seem to exist only for and in real oral practice. It seems doubtful that a person literate from the start could ever learn them perfectly, for mastery surely required years of apprenticeship and constant practice. This is not something one learns from written exemplars or picks up casually. Then, again, nothing made known to us as real oral poetry remotely approaches the quality of the *Iliad* and the *Odyssey*, and these simply cannot be accounted for on the basis of improvisation. Yet is improvisation necessarily a dominant ingredient of oral composition?

The dilemma stems, in any case, from what appears to be contradictory evidence in the poems themselves. This creates a temptation, and we must be wary of it, to cover half the picture. One can, for example, simplify things considerably by equating Homer's formulas with the sort of repetition most literature conventionally traffics in. The Greek epic will thus not be generically distinct. Those committing this error have failed to grasp how much of Homer's diction is reduced to astonishingly rigorous systems—not to mention Parry's demonstration that even programmatic repetition in other authors is different. On the other side, hard Parryism (as it is called) tends to ignore anything not explainable in terms of formula or type. In the end, the epics provide plenty of evidence for both points of view: for orality at the level of diction and for something else in the larger strategies of composition. To place Homer in some kind of transition between the two seems to account for both.

Unfortunately, that solution does not take us very far because there is still too much that we do not understand. The modes and circumstances whereby the *Iliad* and the *Odyssey* could have been assembled and written down remain obscure. We have no model to demonstrate how a language that formulaic—so perfectly and consistently systematized over large stretches—could maintain its integrity in the service of written composition, or how oral practice could produce something that good or transmit it reasonably intact. On the other hand, our knowledge is disquietingly spotty as to the general formulaic content of Homeric verse. The samples actually tabulated in detail are disquietingly small.[9] We know next to nothing about the relationship of the Homeric poems to antecedent and contemporaneous epic. We do not even understand the meaning of the words we use. There is still no scientific definition of "oral style" as opposed to "written style." Finnegan and Zumthor have shown that the line dividing them is exceedingly hard to draw. In fact, it all but disappears in the welter of transitional examples.[10] "Oral poetry" is not a defined quantity, much less a fixed measuring device.[11] Finally, I remain unconvinced that we know or can even reliably surmise the artistic quality that oral poetry might achieve under ideal conditions. Maybe the modern examples delude us in this more than they help, and maybe not. In any case, "oral style" and "written style": the sharp articulation of the terms disguises a nebulous and fugitive content.

I believe, in short, that we are not yet equipped to solve the question of how the Homeric poems were composed. To call them transitional pieces means recognizing apparently contradictory signals from the texts and concluding that somehow different styles are represented there. But our definition of these so-called styles is imprecise and maybe fallacious. Hence we cannot picture an actual process, the flesh-and-blood event. "Homer the poet of transition" is only another abstraction among many. Still it is a useful concept, more so than many of its rivals, because it at least emphasizes all aspects of the texts and helps to keep us honest in the face of a complicated and confusing reality.

There is, in fact, no incompatibility between Homer's formularity at the level of diction and his poetic vision. We establish this simply by our experience of the *Iliad* and the *Odyssey* themselves. Brian Hainsworth writes:

> Their [the poems'] oral origin is a point that enters criticism at a lower level, for it refers to the means available to the poet, not to his end.
>
> Our judgment about the use of a given epithet for a hero at a given point is inseparable . . . from our theory of the poem's mode of composition. But the conception of Achilles or Odysseus has very little to do with the question whether their creator composed by word of mouth or pen in hand.[12]

Still one would like to understand the totality of Homer's style under a single dominant perspective, and recent studies have attempted that. The most notable are by Michael Nagler and Gregory Nagy, who have tried to transcend the dichotomy of formularity/creativity with new definitions of "the formula" and "the tradition" respectively.[13]

My own effort will be to study the artistry of the epics at the level of scene and episode, that is, to describe how the story is shaped and articulated over short to medium-sized episodes. All these poems deal heavily in narrative formulas—that is, repeated actions and clusters of detail that have something of the same permanent definition as the verbal formulas and their same ability to enter numerous combinations.[14] The advantage of working with narrative formulas is that we have in them something heavily stylized, a compositional unit just several steps larger than the dictional formulas, and as much a pure-blooded product of the oral manner as they (I assume this as a given).[15] At the same time, there was more freedom for the composer at this level, more room for variation, more space for effective placement, more opportunity to create by means of repetition a dense and transparent narrative. Homer's artistry reveals itself best, I think, at this level. At the least, this is where we can best define and measure it because it is here that we can establish both formularity and variation.

My emphasis, then, will be on the fixed orderings and recurrences of epic. These lie at the heart of its style and they were traditional. My effort, however, is not to chart type scenes but to study composition; to explain narrative structures as vehicles of emphasis, pace, shading, and implication—in short, as form creating meaning.

Narrative formulas, like formular diction, will have been inherited and learned by each practitioner. They were, of course, an aid to composition but, cast as they were along traditional lines, they also served as filters and molds reducing experience into meaningful categories and serving as a language of stylized communication between poet and audience. I shall try to show that these systems of narrative formulas were a live instrument, endlessly variable and responsive, subject to constant evolution and renewal. In sum, my aim is to define techniques of composition that belonged to traditional practice and to study their artistic use.

Several considerations recommend a comparative approach. First, I believe that ancient and medieval epics are much alike in the way they shape narrative at the level of scene and episode. It is useful to study these techniques because interpretation can build on them. Second, these shared features might eventually shed light on origins. Third, I think the time is ripe for a comparative study of both Homer and the medieval epics that takes us back to the texts instead of away from them, one that does not lose itself in formula counts or debate about definitions or in hypotheses concerning origins where evidence fails and speculation hangs in the air. More actual comparison of texts will take us further. Fourth, it can only help to widen the comparative base for all the epics in question. Finally, I hope my procedure will help to refine our understanding of epic style generally. To anticipate a general conclusion now, I believe that Homer's otherness has been exaggerated and that those who, from antiquity, read the *Iliad* and the *Odyssey* like any other literature were closer to the truth, for all their mistakes, than those who claim they are accessible only to radically different modes of interpretation.

Note on Texts

Iliad: D. B. Munro and T. W. Allen (Oxford, 1920)

Odyssey: P. Von Der Mühll (Editiones Helveticae, Basileae, 1962)

Nibelungenlied: (1) H. de Boor (nach der Ausgabe von Karl Bartsch, 20. Auflage, Wiesbaden, 1972); (2) U. Hennig, *Das Nibelungenlied nach der Handschrift C* (Altdeutsche Textbibliothek Nr. 83, Max Niemeyer Verlag, Tübingen, 1977)

Lamprechts Alexander: nach den drei Texten mit dem Fragment des Alberic von Besançon und den lateinischen Quellen, K. Kinzel (Halle, 1884)

Henric van Veldeken, Eneide: G. Schieb and Th. Frings (Deutsche Texte des Mittelalters, Band LVIII, Berlin, 1964)

Kudrun: Karl Bartsch, 5. Auflage, überarbeitet und neu eingeleitet von Karl Stackmann (Wiesbaden, 1965)

Das Rolandslied des Pfaffen Konrad: C. Wesle, 2. Auflage, besorgt von P. Wapnewski (Tübingen, 1967)

The Song of Roland. An Analytical Edition: G. J. Brault (University Park and London, 1978); vol. 1, Introduction and Commentary; vol. 2, Text and Translation

Ortnit: A. Amelung and D. Jänicke (Deutsches Heldenbuch, dritter Teil, 1871; repr. 1968, Weidmann, Dublin/Zürich)

Wolfram von Eschenbach, Parzival: A. Leitzmann (Altdeutsche Textbibliothek, Nr. 12–13, Halle a.S., 1912 and 1913)

NOTE: I have taken the liberty of normalizing slightly Wapnewski's text of the *Rolandslied* by inserting vowels in place of ligatures and lowering superscripts into linear spellings. Proper names are used as they appear in the work under immediate reference. Thus Charlemagne is Charles in the *Chanson de Roland* and Karl in the *Rolandslied;* Parzival's adversaries outside his lady's city are Enguigeron and Clamadeu in Chrétien, Kingrun and Klamide in Wolfram. Other characters are also given their French or German names as reference is made to the pertinent texts.

— I —

HOMER

Introduction

THE THREE CHAPTERS on the *Iliad* that follow try to unravel the interplay of formularity and artistic design. They represent a development of my earlier book on the battle scenes. I have chosen to work with them once again because their heavy stylization makes them ideal for the experiment as defined. They also allow some of the best comparisons with the *Nibelungenlied*.

The *Iliad*'s battle scenes are made from conventional action sequences. Certain single events or groups of events occur repeatedly and in different fixed combinations. Careful study reveals a large repertoire of narrative formulas, a stockpile of movable segments. These enter into various combinations to create standardized encounters. The battle scenes are "typical" in that they, like many single lines, are built of separate, definable ingredients that appear elsewhere in the same or other combinations. Scene composition thus reveals itself as analogous to verse construction—not so rigorously systematized as the latter but a product of the same compositional habits and circumstances. I take that as a given not requiring further demonstration.

My effort in that earlier study was to demonstrate the existence and basic operation of narrative systems. The emphasis was on the morphology of the stereotype and on the mechanical aspects of composition, not on originality and design. Yet it must be the final goal of all such studies to discern the controlling will behind the manipulation of formular blocks, and that is the kind of question asked and answered in the following chapters: Homer, like any great artist, was born into a tradition that he simultaneously absorbed and recast.

It turns out that the composition of the battle books is uneven in the sense that some are profound and disturbing creations; others remain on the surface, offering little more than one exciting fight after the other. Books 11 and 12 fall into the first category, most of book 13 into the second. Interestingly, the basic techniques for organizing the narrative and holding it in orderly disposition remain the same throughout. Book 13 shows the same careful organization as the others, but the devices employed to that end do not become the stuff of great poetry. No drastic conclusions should be drawn from this in the direction of single or multiple authorship, or of the genesis of the *Iliad*, but I believe these are still legitimate questions that might be fruitfully pursued by more study along the same lines. I want to emphasize that my interpretations of books 11, 12, and 13 are made with only sporadic reference to the *Iliad* in general. They need ultimately to be tested against that broader base.

Many readers will find my interpretations of Homer unconventional, even radical. I believe, for example, that the Achaean heroes are sometimes drawn in sharply negative portrait—and not just Agamemnon but also Menelaos, Idomeneus, and even Diomedes (to mention only those dealt with here). Both armies are distinguished by individuals whose persons and fates illuminate the great issues of warfare and human life, of suffering and excellence, of heroism and folly, grandeur and pettiness, elevation and fall. Some of the most penetrating characterization and thought emerge from the headlong carnage of the battle scenes. On the other hand, my view of Homer's poetic technique is conservative: those features of his style that set him apart—the "oral" qualities of formularity and deep stylization—are used in the service of a composition much like what is found in all serious literature. It is my opinion that Homer assembles his story in many of the same ways and to the same ends as the authors of the medieval epics and indeed all composers of integrated narrative. My aim is not to obscure Homer's distinctiveness, but to follow the path of empirical observation to a balanced understanding of the workings of this enigmatic and magnificent poetry.

Iliad 11

> We . . . perceive immediately the hand of a poet who designs,
> articulates, constructs.
> —Wolfgang Schadewaldt

THE FIGHTING in book 11 of the *Iliad* (67–595) comprises a single block of narrative and falls into four natural divisions: I, the aristeia and wounding of Agamemnon (67–283); II, the brief success and wounding of Diomedes (284–400); III, the isolation and wounding of Odysseus (401–488); IV, Aias' counterattack (including the woundings of Machaon and Eurypylus) and his retreat. The combats are highly conventional, from small details to entire sequences.[1]

The introduction previews symmetries to follow as an opening deadlock (67–73) and eventual Greek breakthrough (84–91) are set in a balance of 7 and 7½ lines respectively. The first contains a simile (67–71) corresponding to the elaborate and simile-like designation of time in the second (86–90).[2] They also echo each other inwardly: reapers in grain and a woodcutter felling trees; a grim similarity between subject and carrier in the first (cf. 19.222), an arresting difference in the second—when the woodcutter is already tired and takes his ease, then the slaughter begins in earnest. Lines 74–83, falling between the two, might be interpolated but they do not touch the issue.[3]

Agamemnon

Beginning at line 91 Agamemnon slays three pairs of Trojans in a row. Then he drives all the enemy before him in a great charge (148–217) before finally encountering one last pair of opponents. Thus all his single combats are with sets of twos. There are no exceptions. The same will be true for Diomedes and Odysseus (below). To repeat: Agamemnon meets three two-man Trojan teams; next he sweeps the field clear; then his day ends against a fourth and last pair. This is the shape of his aristeia. One other detail to bear in mind: two brothers make up every set of opponents except the first.

The repetitions are obvious and an unpretentious symmetry naturally attaches to them. Do they mean anything? Or are they no more than a semiautomatic formular string? Maybe the poet got the notion of brothers fighting by twos and followed the path of least resistance by lining them up one after the other. The slaying of brother-pairs is a common thing in the *Iliad*. Diomedes and Odysseus will do it later in this same book. There is another series of them dispatched by Diomedes in book 5 (9, 144, 148, 152, 159), and Hector and Aeneas do away with Greeks in the same way (5.608, 541). In short, did the poet reach here for a free-floating typos and then compose the rest of the way by free association? Or, at a somewhat higher level, are these repeats a convenient storytelling device, a means to impose some order on an otherwise unarticulated surge of events? A line of signposts for the poet to steer his course by? Or perhaps there are finer connections, too. Can we speak of leitmotif and theme?[4]

The first two victims are only names, appearing once and vanishing forever in the space of a few lines (91–98). The details of one death are conventional but ugly: Oileus is struck in the forehead and his brains pour out.[5] This sets a tone and anticipates things to come.

Leaving them, Agamemnon moves on to bigger game, two sons of Priam (101–21). The combat itself is of no consequence since both are quickly disposed of. Two other things set the incident apart, its anecdote and concluding simile. I postpone the simile until later. The anecdote tells us this: Achilles had once captured these same two youths by falling upon them as they tended sheep.[6] Then he released them for ransom. No such luck this time: Agamemnon destroys them like a lion crushing the young of a deer (113). This is Agamemnon the avenger, his familiar and self-adopted role in the *Iliad*.[7] The simile wins the two our sympathy, but grace is denied. Agamemnon had made it clear long since that all Trojans have to pay. We recall his sentence on the Trojan Adrestos in book 6, pronounced with raving enthusiasm (57):[8]

> Let none of them escape abrupt destruction
> at our hands, not even the one his mother
> still carries in her belly, not even him . . .

For Isos and Antiphos, then, fate had this in store: first, good luck of sorts, Achilles captured and delivered them; then calamity at the hands of Agamemnon. The contrast with Achilles is underlined by the remark that their slayer recognized them from their earlier captivity (111).

This difference between the two men is stated and sustained in the *Iliad*, directly and by implication. The son of Peleus had once been a man of mercy. His chivalrous treatment of Eetion is set off in that same sixth book against Agamemnon's dark pronouncement on Adrestos and all Troy with him. We hear twice about Achilles sparing captives in the days before his grief (here and 21.34). Agamemnon will encounter suppliants twice and execute them all because of their city's crime (6.55, 11.131).[9] Achilles turns into a relentless avenger only in self-torment and with his own mortality in mind. This is how he pronounces sentence on Lykaon, another whom he had once captured and sold for ransom before catching him a second time (21.106):

> But die, my friend, you too. Why this lamentation?
> Patroclus also died, a far better man than you.

Lykaon is elevated by his slayer. He is a pathetic figure, helpless and weak, but his death is set against the fates of better and more important men. It becomes more than a case of random bad luck. It acquires context, definition, perspective, and a somber illumination from the heroic code and destiny. For Isos and Antiphos death brings nothing of the sort. Weakness is simply devoured by strength (113):

> As a lion seizes the helpless young of a swift deer
> in its powerful teeth and breaks them easily,
> having come upon their lair, and takes away their tender life.

The spirit in which Agamemnon and Achilles refuse mercy sets them profoundly apart. These few details in book 11 belong to a consistent portrait of the Greek general and to a dominant theme of his aristeia.

The motif of suppliancy was only hinted at with Isos and Antiphos by the implied comparison between their first and second captures. But that motif now receives full development as the first part of Agamemnon's aristeia reaches its climax with Peisandros and Hippolochos, two sons of the villainous Antimachos (122–47). This Antimachos was a henchman of Paris, sustained by bribes, who obstructed the return of Helen (123–5) and, with that, a peaceful end to the war.[10]

Worse yet, he had conspired to engineer the murder of Odysseus and Menelaos years before during their embassy to Troy (139–41). The youths plead for their lives but make the mistake of revealing their father's name. That seals their fate. Agamemnon, forever solicitous of his brother (4.148, 7.103, 10.233), metes out a fearsome penalty: Peisandros is killed outright; Hippolochos has his head chopped off, then his arms too, and his mutilated trunk rolls through the ranks "like a mortar."

The three sets of slayings build by stages to a crescendo. Specifically, they become increasingly elaborate and hideous (95–98, 113–21, 145–7), and the victims' lineage acquires immediacy and pertinence. No parents are named for the first. Priam is the father of the second pair, Antimachos of the third, and here family becomes an explicit issue. The slain are helpless prey: Bienor and Oileus felled in a single rush; Isos and Antiphos like fawns in the jaws of a lion; Peisandros and Hippolochos cowering in the chariot and supplicating with tears. Thus: a continuum of brother-pairs, increasingly detailed and grisly killings, growing emphasis on the families of the slain.

At this point single combats give way to a scene on the large scale: the Trojans break into full retreat with Agamemnon and his army at their heels until Zeus (through Iris) makes Hector stiffen his ranks (148–216). Certain symmetries here were already emphasized by Wilamowitz; for example, the first description of Agamemnon's charge (148–62) begins with the Greeks and ends with the Trojans, with a simile in the middle.[11] That does not take us very far, but Schadewaldt refined and elaborated, showing how a firm order controls the section from start to finish:[12]

A. General description (more from the Greek side), 148–62 (16 lines),
    simile (Agamemnon—fire), 155–7 (3 lines),
    Zeus rescues Hector, 163–4 (2 lines).

B. General description (more from the Trojan side), 165–80 (16 lines),
    simile (Agamemnon—lion, Trojans—cattle), 172–5 (4 lines),
    Zeus rescues Hector, 181–216 (36 lines).

These architectonics match the symmetries of the single combats before and after. The two rescues of Hector—first a bare notice and then full development the second time around—are also in regular Iliadic style.[13] Worked through both sections is the refrain of Agamemnon's pursuit (153, 165, 168, 177). Field position is exactly noted: past the tomb of Ilos, by the wild fig tree, close up to the Scaean Gate and the oak.

Agamemnon's aristeia ends in his confrontation with two sons of Antenor, Iphidamas and Koon (221–63). He kills them both but is wounded by Koon and forced to leave the fight. Antenor stands as the opposite of Antimachos: a great and good man; husband of the priestess Theano (a person of eminence and kindness in her own right);[14] outspoken advocate of surrendering Helen (7.347) and hence opponent of Paris; the host long ago for Odysseus and Menelaos in Troy (3.205) when Antimachos plotted their murder. His pro-Greek sentiments assured his survival in the later tradition after the city's capture and that of some of his family as well.[15] Antenor stands high in the city. He is on the wall in book 3; he is singled out to accompany Priam to the site of the duel; marriage connects him to the ruling line of the royal house (3.121), and he maintains friendly relations with the collateral branch as well. His sons are often to be found in the company of Aeneas and also of Poulydamas, Hector's wise and unpopular counselor.[16]

It is no surprise, then, that Iphidamas and Koon fight well, unlike the offspring of Antimachos. Iphidamas charges Agamemnon head on, and Koon manages to disable him. Still, they die along with the rest. Both earn our sympathy and not just because of their father: Iphidamas because of a promising youth cut short and a splendid marriage brought to naught, for which he had given much and promised more (241):

> And so he fell and embraced the iron sleep
> in piteous fate, defending the city and far from his bride,
> his wedded wife. He knew no joy from her, yet had given much to
> win her.

Koon dies defending his brother and suffers mutilation for his pains (261). Agamemnon chops his head off, a ghastly abuse and unusual in the *Iliad*. It happens only four times and the Greek general does the honors in half of them: here and just before with the sons of Antimachos.[17]

Our passage thus repeats, shapes, compares, intensifies. Three pairs of Trojans are slain in single combat; then, after Agamemnon's sweep across the field, one last pair joins the rest. The focus is on youth, parentage, vengeance.[18] Sons are slain, but it is their parents who provide the issue and supply the commentary: Priam, Antimachos, and Antenor. Priam is treated with sympathy in the *Iliad*. No guilt attaches to him for the abduction or retention of Helen. His response to that act and all its consequences is to accept the gods' will in measureless sorrow. The question of why he (or Hector, for that matter) allows Paris free rein is never allowed to surface. It becomes explicit only in the characters and fates of single persons. Priam stands at the head of suffering Troy as Paris and Antimachos typify Ilium the transgressor. Two sons of Priam fall, then two of Antimachos, finally two of Antenor. Sons of the good are exterminated just like sons of the bad. Agamemnon, executor of judgment, makes no distinctions. A son of Antimachos is hacked to pieces, a son of Antenor is beheaded. We are denied satisfaction from retribution on the house of Antimachos. Peisandros and Hippolochos cannot even resist. They plead for mercy and offer ransom; death and dismemberment are what they get. Near the start of it all the poet casually mentions the previous capture of Priam's sons, their survival and deliverance—a reminder that Achilles had other notions of Trojan guilt and the conduct of warfare.[19]

A steady pulse of repeats and the formal pairings shape the passage and lend it a firm definition. But these also make emphases and carry meaning. The theme of sons and fathers raises the question of Trojan guilt, then quickens it with the shocking manner of its expiation. Agamemnon imagines himself the arm of retribution, defender of the right, avenger of wrongs. But his actions and victims combine to tell a different story. The sons of Antimachos carry the burden of inherited guilt, to be sure, but their punishment brings us little satisfaction and no glory to their slayer. Their stature and performance deny him that.[20] More to the point, their fate is no different from that of the sons of Priam or the sons of Antenor, the Greeks' best friend in the city. Here is a grim and compelling disorder: guilt and innocence, bravery and cowardice, reprisal and atrocity. Agamemnon's charge across the field, held to its own meticulous order, brings variation and overview before the final, emblematic killing: two offspring of an excellent nobleman follow into Hades the sons of the tormented Priam and the criminal Antimachos. The poet bids them farewell with a grave and spare summation (262):[21]

There the sons of Antenor, fulfilling the lot assigned them,
at the hands of Agamemnon the king, went down to the house of
   Hades.

The battle account here is heavily conventional and proceeds along
well-worn paths. But that nowhere deteriorates into a wooden regularity. Nor are the single incidents leached of their content by exact
repetition. Every pair of fighters Agamemnon meets is different. Together, they lay bare the disquieting ambiguity in his acts of retribution.

Fathers and sons are important in the *Iliad* generally.[22] Sons are an
extension of the parent and embody his qualities. One thinks of the
exchanges between Tlepolemos and Sarpedon on the subject (5.633)
or between Achilles and Asteropaios (21.153), between Diomedes and
Glaukos (6.123), and the importance of Tydeus in securing respect
for Diomedes (14.110). A fighter's death often receives rank and definition from his father's grief, as in the case of the seers whose skill
does not save their sons' lives (5.148 and 11.329), or young men like
Simoeisios (4.473), Satnios (14.442), Aisepos and Pedasos (6.21), and
Iphition (19.382), whose deaths become more poignant through stories about their mothers. Again, the slaying of opponents in pairs is
not unusual. Hector kills two Greeks together in book 5, and so does
Aeneas (608, 541). The last is an event of pathos with a memorable
simile. There is even a series of pairs attacked by Diomedes in book
5 at lines 9, 144, 148, 152, and 159, and the victims' fathers figure in
some of the anecdotes. But those fathers and sons are set in much
weaker thematic relation to each other, nor is Diomedes cast into the
same lurid twilight as Agamemnon. Again, book 11 is not the only
place where the slain are drawn together in contrast. In the aristeia
of Idomeneus, for example, Othryoneus (14.363) and Alkathoos
(14.427) are set in sharp polarity. Both are slain by Idomeneus. The
first is a presumptuous braggart who promised to drive the Greeks
from Troy in return for the hand of Cassandra. The second is an
admirable nobleman and son-in-law of Anchises. Character, marriage
anecdote, and boasting by the slayer connect and set them in opposition.[23] The poet works with familiar things here in book 11, but
the combination and effect are singular.

The similes conform, placed as they are at the regular and pre-
dictable junctures, and all but one making standard comparisons:
lions, fire, flood, and so on.[24] But they also carry the theme of off-

spring. To remind ourselves again: Agamemnon has no chance to mete out penalties on perpetrators or leaders, only on their children. The content of the passage derives from that.[25] The two sons of Priam perish like fawns in a lion's maw. Not without reason, the mother doe receives the most attention (113):

> As a lion seizes the helpless young of a swift doe,
> in its powerful teeth and breaks them easily,
> having come upon them in their lair, and takes away their tender life,
> and the mother, even if she be hard by, cannot
> ward off the evil, for a fearful trembling masters her.
> With speed she darts through dense thickets and timber,
> headlong and sweating and away from the pounce of the mighty beast.

Before continuing, a few more words about narrative formulas. Lions, deer, and fawns are common in the *Iliad*'s similes, however unique their combination here.[26] The comparison is conventional in still other ways. The lion is Agamemnon, the fawns the sons of Priam, the doe stands for the Trojans in retreat. As often, a simile describes a mass movement, here a shift along the entire Trojan front.[27] It also anticipates or leads the narrative, for the retreat is actually mentioned only after the simile ends. This is also regular Iliadic technique. A Trojan fallback all along the line will occur right after Agamemnon's next single encounter. This reverse is first sounded in the simile and reemerges shortly thereafter in full-scale elaboration. The lion returns in a few short comparisons through the following encounters (129, 239), including the next one with the sons of Antimachos—another link between them and the sons of Priam just before. There is also an extended lion simile at 172 during the great charge.[28]

In short, we can explain very much about the similes here on the basis of conventional narrative modes—except what is most important. These similes build in strings here and supply a commentary. The last puts its seal on Agamemnon's performance after he is wounded by the Antenorid Koon. He fights on for a while, but then the wound dries and he suffers the pains of a woman in labor. His physical torment is emphasized. The simile is striking and without parallel (267):

> But later, when the wound dried and the blood no longer flowed,
> sharp pains penetrated Agamemnon and loosened his strength.

Like the sharp pain that grips a woman in labor,
a piercing hurt, and the Eileithuiai send it, daughters of Hera,
dispensers of birth in suffering, mistresses of the wrenching
   contractions,
so sharp pains penetrated Agamemnon and loosened his strength.

This simile, consummating the sequence, puts a definition on Agamemnon and his work. How shall we define the association between
this ravager of young men and the woman in childbirth? Caution and
precision are required. The feasting lion, the helpless dam, the slaughter and mutilation of men's sons, the woman wracked by birth pangs—
these comprise no tidy symbolic code. The combination suggests; it
is not literal and prescriptive. It would be wrong to interpret like this:
"As Agamemnon robbed men of their sons, so he is punished by the
pains it cost to bear them." There is no sentimentality, no sure equiva-
lencies, and no moralizing. In Agamemnon's deeds clarity and principle are swallowed up in an ugly muddle of guilt and innocence,
redress and outrage, atonement and abuse. The enigma lurks on the
other side of fixed definition, resisting articulation as a trim paradox.
The issues are clear only to Agamemnon. He fights hard to set things
right, but the evil he attacks eludes him and multiplies. And it draws
him into the world he contends against. He is made to share pain
and guilt, but darkly, without resolution or enlightenment.

Diomedes

Hector sees Agamemnon leave the field and knows the moment to
follow Iris' instructions has arrived. He fires his troops and leads a
successful charge (284–309), described by a string of three short similes (292–8). In the first, he drives his men against the enemy like a
hunter setting his hounds on a boar or lion. That subject is resumed
and reversed at 324 when Diomedes and Odysseus counterattack like
two boars scattering the hunting dogs. Later (414) Odysseus will be
surrounded and pressed hard like a cornered boar. The precise and
sustained use of similes from Agamemnon's aristeia thus continues.[29]
   Similes also chart Hector's assault within a smaller space. The first
series (292–8) ends with him falling on the Greek ranks like a hurricane
churning the ocean (297–8):

> And he fell upon the fray like a fierce blast of wind
> that sweeps down on the dark blue sea and heaves it up.

A slaying catalogue follows and issues into a full-scale variation of the same subject: Zephyros falling on the sea, swollen waves, scattered foam (305). That is, the first storm simile is resumed and intensified by the second:

> As when the west wind strikes in a heavy blast, driving into
> the clouds of the south wind, the bringer of bright skies,
> one swollen wave rolls after the other, and the spume
> is flung high by the rush of the far-sweeping wind.

Similes thus frame Hector's charge and establish an escalating continuum. We recall that Agamemnon's sweep across the field is also charted by similes at structural mark points.[30]

A wholesale flight to the ships is averted only by Odysseus' call to Diomedes to make a stand. This summons, and Diomedes' reply, are set off in paired three-verse speeches (313–15; 317–19). The two men turn on the Trojans and fight together briefly as a pair, but each then dominates alone in successive aristeiai. Odysseus, who stopped the retreat, immediately takes a back seat as Diomedes steps to the fore by slaying Thymbraios. The man's attendant falls to Odysseus (320). Diomedes' next two victims are sons of Merops the seer. Their father's useless warnings are elaborated in a moving anecdote (328). Odysseus also kills a pair, but they are mere names in a single line. He now drops from sight, except as object of a short address (346), as his partner faces Agastrophos, Hector, and Paris. The first is only a transitional figure: his death inspires Hector to intervene, and that brings Diomedes' entry here to its climax.

Looking forward and backward, we observe that the slaying of pairs has continued: first Thymbraios and his attendant, then the sons of Merops. Agastrophos dies alone, but Hector and Paris now meet Diomedes in turn. They do not fight as a team, but they are a pair nonetheless. Agamemnon managed to kill both of the last brothers he faced, but a wound from the second forced him out of the fight. Diomedes will hurt Hector badly, only to be shot by Paris and driven from the field in pain. Odysseus will end his day against a pair of brothers too, slaying both but suffering a disabling wound from the second. All three Greeks leave by chariot. The refrain is obvious and insistent.[31]

Hector's charge arouses fearful suspense (347) but the fight ends abruptly and is entirely one-sided. Diomedes almost kills him with a single stone throw and pursues him with derisive threats (362):[32]

> You escaped your death once more, you dog. But the evil
> just missed you. This time it was Apollo who saved you—
> I suppose you pray to him on your way to where the spears fall heavy.
> But I'll dispose of you for sure the next time we meet,
> in case there is also some god to stand by me.

This stands parallel to the next encounter: Paris wounds Diomedes in the heel and gets an even worse tongue lashing (385):

> You scurrilous bowman with your pretty locks, eyeing the girls,
> if you tried meeting me in armor, face to face and in close,
> your bow and quick arrows wouldn't protect you.
> Now you scratched my heel and brag for no reason.
> I don't care—it might as well be a woman or silly child that struck
> me.
> A futile missile from the hand of a feeble good-for-nothing.

Diomedes meets the two unlike brothers in succession. He beats one, is wounded by the other, and insults them both. Structure and details draw the two encounters together.

The similarity of Diomedes' wounding here to the death of Achilles in the epic cycle is considerable (a heel wound inflicted by Paris), and speculation about a connection with the *Aithiopis* has flourished accordingly.[33] We recall that Achilles slew Memnon in that poem and died at the hands of Paris. In the *Iliad* he kills Hector under the same circumstances as Memnon in the cycle, in vengeance for the death of his best friend. Achilles' own death lies beyond the *Iliad*. It is an important theme there, but the manner and perpetrator remain undisclosed. The humiliating paradox of Achilles' (cyclic) fate is attached here to Diomedes. Intolerably, Paris succeeds where Hector fails. The best fighter on the Trojan side yields in accomplishment to the most despised. Abnormally, the bow is mightier than the sword.[34]

The motif-transfer is not without point. Diomedes is a man of con-tradictions. He agreed to face Hector with bravery and resignation (317):

> All right, I will make a stand and endure it. But we'll have
> little pleasure in it, since Zeus the cloud-gatherer
> wants to give the Trojans success instead of to us.

His tone stayed the same under attack (347):

> Here comes a disaster rolling upon us, brutal Hector.
> No matter, let us stand firm, stay to meet him and defend ourselves.

But success brings a change. The easy victory seems to surprise and elate him. He swells with disdain and menace, sure that he has been cheated by Apollo (363). And so he has (353), but there is even worse in store, an arrow in the foot from Paris.

Like Hector, Paris draws a stream of abuse. But now it degenerates into vituperation and bravado. "Useless boasting, just because you scratched my heel! I take no notice, it's like the blow of a woman or child. A futile missile from the hand of a feeble good-for-nothing!" Wilamowitz admired this "indomitable spirit" (196), but the harangue miscarries. Let the facts speak for themselves. The arrow does more than scratch him: it pins his foot to the ground (377) and Odysseus has to pull it out (396). Does he take no notice? The wound is extremely painful (398, 400) and forces him to the rear. Paris continues to fight and soon puts Eurypylus and Machaon out of commission. Even Diomedes' taunts about Paris' useless boasting miss the mark. Paris makes no boasts at all. He laughs, is glad, and wishes he had inflicted a mortal wound, no more. Diomedes is the loser here in every respect. He is disabled by a despised opponent and throws away his dignity in frustrated invective. *Cesserunt prima postremis:* Diomedes' grand start degenerates into a dismal finish.[35]

He vacillates between extremes and gave evidence of the same tendencies earlier. For example, he made a fine impression in book 4 (370, 412) by holding his temper in the face of provocation from Agamemnon. Sthenelus, his charioteer, came off badly in comparison with his bragging and arrogance. Later, when the two of them faced Aeneas and Pandaros, Sthenelus showed what his conceit was worth and Diomedes was vindicated (5.252). But accomplishment went to his head there too. Wounding Aphrodite was not enough. He allowed himself the same abuse against her that he flings at his human opponents in book 11. He even disregarded Athena's warning (129) and tried repeatedly to thwart Apollo's rescue of Aeneas (432). It took a direct rebuke from the god himself to bring the man to his senses. Diomedes is a brilliant warrior and excellent in council. He is without the profound and conflicting strains of Achilles or the complexity of Odysseus, but not without an ominous shortcoming: he cannot endure success.

In sum, Diomedes gives no edifying lesson in heroic virtue, and there is no celebration of the hoplite over the champion of the boudoir. Instead, there is contradiction and paradox, a sense of frustration, of lost footing and elusive mockery. Achilles' fate carried an insufferable irony: triumph over the best, defeat from the one respected least. Diomedes is made to share that. His disgrace is not as final as Achilles', and so is less terrible, but it is a sure defeat, disquieting and unwholesome. Like Agamemnon before him, Diomedes leaves the field having been put to an inward test and having failed it.

Odysseus

This episode is controlled by a close symmetry:

1. Odysseus, suddenly alone against the Trojans, ponders whether to stand or flee. He decides to stand, 401–10.

2. *Simile: he is like a boar holding hounds at bay, 414–20.*

3. Combat, ending in the slaying of the two sons of Hypasos and the wounding of Odysseus, 420–58.

4. Odysseus alone and pressed hard: he calls for help, Aias and Menelaos rush to the rescue, 459–73.

5. *Simile: he is like a wounded stag set upon by jackals, 474–84.*

6. He is rescued by Aias and Menelaos, 485–8.

The scene of Odysseus alone against a horde of the enemy is painted twice. The first ends in single combat, the second in rescue. Similes articulate the sequence, marking the circumstances exactly and maintaining themes of the scene at large. Odysseus is a boar holding his own in the first, a wounded deer falling to predators in the second. The first continues the boar/lion/dog series from earlier. The second resumes details from the wounding of Agamemnon: the man fights while blood from his wound runs warm; when it dries he begins to fail. Compare 264–8 and 476–80.

Odysseus' aristeia culminates in his combat with Sokos (number 3, above). That shows a strong regularity of its own:

A. 1. Sokos threatens: he will avenge his brother or die beside him, 430–3 (4 lines).

   2. He wounds Odysseus, 434–8 (5 lines).

B. 1. Odysseus threatens: your doom is sure. Today you will give glory to me and your soul to Hades, 441–5 (5 lines).

   2. He kills Sokos, 446–9 (4 lines).

C. Final speech by Odysseus, 450–55 (6 lines).

Events pass by at a measured pace, in equal blocks of action and time. Just before facing the sons of Hypasos, Odysseus had pondered the heroic code:

> I know that cowards shrink from the conflict.
> But whoever is among the best in the fight, he has to
> stand his ground with might, whether to be struck himself or to strike another.

This is a somber heroism—articulate, understated, introspective. The duel with Sokos is held to the same tenor. Both men fight with their own deaths in mind (431, 455). The rewards and terrors of their fierce ethic are expounded by the victor: no grave for Sokos, birds will make him their food; Odysseus will some day be buried by his comrades. Victory or defeat, renown or oblivion, corpses interred or torn by animals: these stand opposed. No ugliness or rancor mars the words of either man. Odysseus addresses his adversary with respect, with distant pity, and without mercy (441–5, 450–5). No other exchange between enemies in the entire *Iliad* carries this high tone. Odysseus is free of the excess and frenzy that disfigure the accomplishments of Agamemnon and Diomedes. The shape of this great scene, with its fixed points and stately progression, reinforces its gravity and elevation. A stringent regularity governs Odysseus' entry from beginning to end, holding the spectacle to a solemn tread that seems to express in its own terms the abiding ordinances these men live by.[36]

Aias

It belongs to the manner of the *Iliad* that a string of similar events gradually changes in progress. This simple device gives even the most repetitive sequences variety and life. Here, for example, success ends for the first three Greek chieftans against a pair of brothers. Each wins that encounter but only at the cost of a crippling wound. Odysseus brings some new details: isolation against a throng of the enemy, a monologue, a call for help and rescue. Aias continues some of these: one man against many and eventual retreat to safety. I have compared the performances of Odysseus and Aias elsewhere:

> The two consecutive scenes of a warrior's isolation and fallback thus stand in close correspondence: one against many, wounding of a Greek, retreat, call for help, rescue. But observe the changing distribution of constituent items. Odysseus is disabled by a Trojan and driven to retreat by human agency. It is he who calls for assistance. Aias is repulsed by Zeus; it is his rescuer, Eurypylus, who suffers a wound, who calls for help and is led off the field. Odysseus gives expression to the ordinances he lives by. Aias acts, nothing more. In short, the variation is not random. The character and strength of the two men are precisely registered. Aias, at the end of the series, also stands in contrast to the entire three. Unsurprisingly, he is the mightiest and least colorful of them all: ferocious, stolid, unyielding, more successful than the others even in defeat, but with no inner person emerging under the pressure of circumstances.[37]

Summary

Four major Greek warriors are wounded in succession. This makes a series by itself, but other repeated details conspire to draw them into interdependence. Odysseus is the main positive foil to the rest, with his restraint set against the zealotry of Agamemnon and the failings of Diomedes, in one direction, and his articulate intelligence against the silent might of Aias in the other. The four comprise a stunning tour de force at the level of character—and scene drawing. The Achaean defeat occurs at many levels. It lays bare the sickness in Agamemnon's crusade for justice. It exposes the shallow reserves of character beneath Diomedes' shining surface. It reveals the integrity of Odysseus in a beating and shows the animal force of Aias, even in these extremeties driven back only by Zeus himself. Here are the many faces of defeat. All this, to be sure, sets the stage for Patroclus' visit to Nestor and with that for the Patrocleia itself. But the poet's attention rests also on larger issues and on the exploration of character. The Trojans lose badly in most of the *Iliad's* fighting. Even Hector's triumphs are tempered with many setbacks and heavy losses to his men. The Greeks are always better fighters, and only Zeus's persistent intervention beats them. At this level Homer doubtless sailed in the mainstream of usage, in deference to tradition and his hearers' prejudices. But he holds himself to no patriotic stereotypes in the depiction of persons. His Achaeans are no gallery of heroic statuary held to conventional postures. The winners are drawn with the same merciless imagination as the losers.

The technique is simple: strings of persons and events are drawn together by common details amd implicitly compared. But Homer knows how to assemble tableaux of great richness and subtlety. Schadewaldt has delivered a splendid analysis of the device in book 6 of the *Iliad*.[38] Hector leaves the battle at the advice of his brother Helenus with instructions for the women of Troy: they should bring a gift to Athena in her temple and plead for the city. The mission is carried out, but the focus moves from that futile errand to three meetings Hector has in the course of it: with his mother, then with Helen and Paris, and finally with Andromache. Schadewaldt interprets these three meetings as a defined series, with each one drawn in relation to the rest. He calls the artifice "contrapost" and explains it as a bearer of meaning. Here are some excerpts from his analysis:

> We look first to the outer frame enclosing the action and sense immediately the hand of a poet who designs, articulates, constructs. The encounter with Andromache is the third and longest of the three "scenes" that comprise the "act" *Hector in Troy* . . . Hector with his mother Hecuba (6.242–85), Hector in the chambers of Paris and Helen (312–68), Hector and Andromache (369–502). This three-part sequence is introduced by a short prelude (237–41) and is followed by an epilogue (503–29) . . . The whole is a firm structure and yet seemingly uncontrived, as natural as a piece of life itself.[39]
>
> Hector meets Hecuba because he must arrange the formal entreaty to Athena. That is why he is in the city. But the scene delivers more. The heavy mood of alarm reaches new intensity in his mother's con-

cern (254): "My son, why did you leave the fighting and come here? Yes, I know, the Achaeans are wiping out our men, and so you wanted to raise your hands to Zeus from the high fortress. I will bring you wine, then, a libation for the god and to strengthen yourself." Another thing the scene does is this: the first meeting shows Hector as son; the second as brother and brother-in-law; the third as husband and father. Three grades of relation, three stages of inward connection. And in all three relationships Hector is the same: not lingering, driven to return to battle. The poet created a wonderfully simple token of this manly behavior: Hector refuses the wine offered by his mother, "that it not slow his menos and make him forget his might." In the next encounter, likewise, he will refuse Helen's friendly urging to be seated. And this resistance to women's concern will finally become deeper in the scene with Andromache.

That encounter is set in sharp focus by Hector's visit with Paris and Helen just before. Right in front of the main picture the poet sets its negative counterpart, thus bringing the central tableau into higher relief. Before Hector-Andromache comes another pair, Paris-Helen, in inverse relationship: the man of weak . . . and vacillating . . . will beside the strong woman, she conscious of honor and weary of her unworthy existence. Set against them are the hero with his wife . . . and son. Contrapost is one of the most effective artistic devices in the hands of this design-conscious poet. It forces the reader's attention in certain directions and spares the poet direct comment. And he controls the technique with such unobtrusive mastery that the artistic manipulation goes unnoticed.[40]

Three encounters, then, one after the other: Hector-Hecuba; Hector-Paris and Helen; Hector-Andromache. Simple details bind them, as three women bid him linger and he refuses because of duty. Each meeting is a mirror held up to the rest. Length and content gradually enlarge. Three relationships define Hector the man and reveal the war's consequences for himself and all Troy with him. The wounding of the Achaean chiefs in book 11 is done in the same manner: consecutive incidents are set in connection by shared details. Here the series is longer with more persons and a comparative welter of events, and because this is a battle book everything is more heavily formular. No matter—the style remains the same, only exercised this time at a longer stretch. It is less intense but more varied, less self-contained but more firmly grounded in the plot. In neither case are episodes strung together like beads. Interdependencies bind them. They are absorbed into overriding structures and play on our imagination as a set. We are invited to compare and infer, to ponder each event in relation to the rest.

Excursus: The Adrestos Incident

I SHALL USE *Iliad* 6.37–65 as a supplement to Agamemnon's portraiture in book 11. The scene is this: a Trojan named Adrestos is caught by Menelaos. He begs for mercy and offers ransom. Menelaos gives quarter, but his move to send his prisoner back to the ships is interrupted by Agamemnon:

> "Menelaos, my good brother, why do you concern yourself so
> for other men? Did you receive excellent treatment in your home
> from the Trojans? Let none of them escape abrupt destruction
> and violence from us, not even the one his mother still carries
> in her belly, not even him, but let all the people
> of Ilium perish for good, unwept and annihilated."
> Having said this, he changed his brother's mind,
> for what he said was fitting. And Menelaos shoved with his hand
> the hero Adrestos from him, and Lord Agamemnon
> stabbed him in the flanks. Adrestos twisted over, and
> Agamemnon braced his foot against the man's chest and pulled out
> his spear.

Everything fits: Agamemnon the relentless zealot, the same fixation on the young and innocent ("Let none of them escape, not even the one his mother still carries in her belly, not even him"). But then (61–62):

> Having said this, he changed his brother's mind,
> for what he said was fitting [*aisima*, "appropriate," or "prudent"].

Homeric usage makes the meaning of *aisima* clear; lexical contortion can therefore be dismissed from the start.[1] Nor should the words be interpreted as an ironic aside. The poet shows extreme reserve in making direct moral judgments and he is straightforward when doing so (e.g. 23.176).

Shall we therefore take the words at their face value, as Homer's own assessment of the act? I think that is impossible. Approval of the justice meted out to Adrestos is in disharmony with the treatment this theme receives on other occasions. It would also contradict the depiction of Agamemnon here and elsewhere and disrupt the tenor of book 6 itself.

Agamemnon assumes a familiar role here of elder brother and protector. But that relationship between him and Menelaos is often encumbered with damaging ironies. Three loci will establish the point: *Iliad* 4.155, 10.234, and 7.109.

4.155: Thinking that Menelaos has suffered a mortal wound from Pandarus' arrow, Agamemnon delivers a plaintive lament in which he condemns the Trojans' perfidy, invokes the justice of heaven, and deplores the risible collapse of his expedition. But all this melancholy misses the mark because the wound is slight—we know that from the start (4.127), and so does Menelaos. The result is the bathos of a mawkish and untimely threnody. Menelaos would have cause for alarm, like Priam in the face of Hecuba's premature grief (24.218):

> Do not become
> a bad omen for me in my own house.

Agamemnon knows that justice is with him and that the gods will see to its execution. The very thought revives his murderous obsession with the young and helpless (161):

> And they will pay at a great cost,
> with their own heads, and with their wives and children.

His predictions will come true, but not for the reasons he thinks. The events just before tell a different story. Pandarus was a fool for breaking the truce (4.104), but the gods used him for reasons of their own, and these are not explained or justified. Homer will not allow an event of such consequence to be sparked merely by the greed and stupidity of a single man. He gives it a supernatural dimension that neither we nor the actors fully understand. What makes the war go on is Hera's and Athena's hatred for the Trojans—a mysterious and relentless malice without pity or mitigation. There is no comforting ledger of crime and punishment (one thinks of Menelaos' frustrated incomprehension at the end of book 3 and at book 13, 620). The gods will destroy the city for reasons of their own, not because Pandarus broke the truce. He was seduced into committing the treachery because Troy's fate was already decided from above.[2]

Agamemnon thus understands nothing, for all his moralizing. He does not perceive the causes of things or their meaning, and even his grief is mistaken. Menelaos is not hurt badly, and Troy's women and children will suffer for reasons beyond Agamemnon's comprehension (and ours).

10.234: When Diomedes asks for a partner on his reconaissance mission six volunteers step forward, all anxious to join. Menelaos is among them. Agamemnon advises Diomedes to pick a man for his ability without respect to birth or station. This is practical generalship, but Agamemnon only wants to spare Menelaos (240): "He was afraid for blond Menelaos." Yet at line 120 of the same book he was excusing Menelaos' lack of enterprise on the grounds that he always awaits his brother's lead.

7.109: To the disgrace of all the Achaeans, none will answer Hector's challenge to single combat. Unable to bear the shame of it, Menelaos censures the entire assembly and prepares to face Hector himself. Agamemnon stops him in time ("It would be madness to fight Hector"), but other volunteers step forward after Nestor berates them for a second time.

Agamemnon's successful persuasion is signaled with the same 1½ lines as in book 6 where he turned Menelaos away from mercy for Adrestos (7.120):

> Having said this, he changed his brother's mind,
> for what he said was fitting.

I will return to the coincidence of expression below. Here the words fit much better, since nobody could take exception to Agamemnon's arguments: Menelaos would be overmatched, and there are other warriors on the Greek side to duel with Hector. It is not to Menelaos' discredit that he is willing to fight against the odds, nor can we blame Agamemnon for stopping him. Still the incident is humiliating for everybody: for the other Greek chieftains because they hold back; for

Agamemnon because of his protectiveness and for the speed with which he leaps to sacrifice appearances; for Menelaos because, despite his pluck, he is not to be taken seriously.

This relationship between the two sons of Atreus is flattering to neither, and it springs from a sustained conception—witness the consistency with which the poet depicts it. Add to all this the fact that Agamemnon has cut no splendid figure through book 6, and he does little better in what follows. Leaving aside book 1, where he causes all the trouble in the first place, his performance in book 2 is shabby and benighted. Book 4 brings more of the same, not only at the wounding of Menelaos but in the Epipolesis as well, where his pointless animadversions are rebutted and later remembered. When he later wants to run away (9.32, 14.83), Odysseus and Diomedes will remind him where the charge of cowardice belongs. To return to Adrestos, Agamemnon's curse on mothers and unborn young is inordinate by any standards. It was Menelaos who suffered the primary wrong, but he inclines to pity until Agamemnon expounds his doctrine of universal requital. And there is more than a touch of impiety in his taking it upon himself to kill another man's suppliant; indeed, it is an unheard of presumption.[3]

In short, there is nothing in Agamemnon's deportment in the Adrestos scene, or in his behavior before or afterward, to win respect or command our assent. If the phrase *aisima pareipon* signals the poet's approval, he has blocked the door to our own. His depiction of Agamemnon runs counter to his own assessment, if that is what it is.

The entire contents of book 6 confirm this. The episode "Hector in Troy," shows three meetings: with Hecuba, Paris and Helen, and Andromache and Astyanax. The internal contrapost of this series is matched by another that sets "Hector in Troy" against the fighting before it. Contrast and suggestion are everywhere. Agamemnon's sentence on all of Troy is tested in the second half of the book. His verdict is pronounced with raving enthusiasm—bad enough in context and much worse when the later scenes show us some of the people condemned. Nothing is as Agamemnon sees it. He imagines himself the arm of retributive justice, but the poet invites us to a vision of paradox and suffering.

The combats immediately preceding the Adrestos scene tell the same story. The Trojan slain are sympathetic—where we learn anything about them—and there are no villains among them. Akamas falls to Aias (5), and we hear only that he was "powerful and huge." Next comes Axylos, slain by Diomedes. He was a friend to strangers and welcomed them all to his house by the road.[4] But none of his guest-friends protect him in the end. Is this an oblique reflection of Paris' wrong to Menelaos? Agamemnon, dissuading his brother from mercy, refers to Paris' abuse of hospitality (56):

> Did you receive excellent treatment in your home
> from the Trojans?

But here now is a welcomer of guests on the Trojan side. We remember that in book 13 Menelaos complains to Zeus the guest-god of wrongs done to him in his house, only to see Paris slay an Achaean in revenge for the death of one who had been his own guest. Trojans now fall thick and fast (29), nothing but names, until Adrestos' horses entangle themselves and their master is caught. After his punishment, and while Hector retires to the city, Diomedes and Glaukos hold their celebrated encounter. Then comes "Hector in Troy." This is the context in which the Adrestos incident is set: scenes of pathos and sorrow, courage and despair, chivalry and inwardness— the impending fate of a city and its people, where Agamemnon's rabid zeal stands out hard and ugly.

The troublesome 1½ lines occur twice in close to identical circumstances (books 6 and 7). Agamemnon dissuades Menelaos from an intended course of action (both times a thing to Menelaos' credit), and his success is registered and approved: *aisima pareipon*. This gives us the clue. The lines are a formular reflex, stimulated by associations of situation and character. There are, of course, plenty of small formular mistakes in the *Iliad* and the *Odyssey*. Most of them are easy to understand and accept (or ignore) because they do not go to the heart of things.[5] Bronze is "pitiless" even when used to chop wood (*Odyssey* 14.418); horses are "swift" even when they are slow (*Iliad* 23.304, 310); and a ship's rudder can be misplaced (*Odyssey* 9.482–3; cf. 539–40). But here in *Iliad* 6 something more serious occurs. A rift has opened between Homer's learned verse technique and his creative imagination. The deeper and more unorthodox his perception, the greater the strain on his language—true of any writer, but even more acute for him because his diction was designed to reproduce the stereotype, not the unique idea. It was also easier for him to follow his own vision in the ordering of episodes and scenes, or in the juxtaposition and sequence of events, however standardized even these were in their own right. Dictional formulas, and the habits they brought with them, were less capable of new turns.

Of course Homer's language is not set in concrete, and its usage betrays no pervasive split personality. But the genius of a singer probably revealed itself more in the way he composed narrative than in his use of formular diction. A more profound view of things must have caused fractures between the more systematized components of his style and the rest. I believe something like that happened in the Adrestos scene. (Even in book 7, the 1½ lines acquire an ironical color, but not enough to make them disruptive.) Homer is drawing a dark portrait of Agamemnon from the poem's opening lines. In book 6 he assembles a shimmering constellation: a suppliancy to stand in correlation with others; Agamemnon's misdirected fervor and moral confusion; scenes before and after that set his behavior in perspective. This was an original and audacious conception, expressed indirectly through placement and implication. But the tug of formular habit led the poet to say something at odds with his own thoughts, something flat and conventional that swallows up the things it purports to explain. We should look beyond this to the whole, however, because the meaning is there. In scenes like this, Homer pushed traditional epic to its limits and beyond. The struggle for a new idiom had to begin.

Iliad 12

Book 12 describes how the Trojans first penetrate the Achaean defenses. All the fighting swirls around trench and wall. This unity of place is matched by the symmetry of the narrative: three waves of Trojan assault sweep against the Greek fortifications. They are set in correspondence and led, respectively, by Asios, Sarpedon and Glaukos, and finally Hector. Correlated with that is the running opposition of Hector and Poulydamas. Events start with Hector brought up short at the trench and end with his complete success as he smashes down the gates. This progress from impasse to breakthrough is registered carefully in steps.

Lines 1–35 are an introduction. They set the stage by describing the fate of the Greek defenses years later, placing the impending battle *sub specie aeternitatis*. The wall will remain only until the war is over, a reminder of the impermanence of Hector's success, a qualification of his victory and diminution of the Achaeans' accomplishments. As the fighting burns to a narrow focus, and as the outcome of the war seems to hang in the balance and Hector approaches his zenith, we are invited to observe from the vantage point of long time and overriding perspective. None of this means what it seems, for all belongs to a divine plan invisible to those living it out.[1] Apollo, Poseidon, and Zeus will see to the ruin of the wall, the very gods who guide the action through books 12, 13, 14, 15, and beyond.

The first assault

Combat begins at line 35 and completes its first movement at 196. This comprises Trojan charge, halt at the trench, Poulydamas' advice and Hector's agreement, Trojan regrouping, Asios' disregard of Poulydamas, his attack and repulse by the Lapiths. Hector advances: "He fought as he did before, like a fierce blast of wind" (40). This connects backward precisely to 11.297, resuming the situation before the interlude in Nestor's tent: "And he fell upon the fray like a fierce blast of wind." A second and more elaborate simile now compares his thrust against the Greek line to a lion or boar pitted against hunters and dogs, the men in close array and the animal refusing to retreat.[2] The subject is sustained in what follows: when Polypoites and Leonteus counterattack at 145, they are like boars resisting the onset of men and hounds; Sarpedon, leading the second charge against the rampart, is like a lion going against a sheepfold in the face of shepherds and dogs (290).[3] Here the Trojan onslaught is arrested by the trench, an awesome impediment described in detail (52–9).

Poulydamas warns against the use of chariots: they could block an escape if the Greeks regain the offensive. Hector agrees, and the Trojans align themselves for an infantry thrust, five batallions with three leaders apiece (88–104).[4] Asios now leads the first strike on the wall. The episode falls basically into two parts, although the division is not strongly marked. Asios "ignorantly" (113) attacks by chariot, provoking a solemn prediction from the poet that his expectations will end in death at the hands of Idomeneus. His followers pour across in the same way, also "ignorantly" (127) and expecting quick success. Neither the leader nor his men find what they expect. Asios:

> But he did not find
> the doors closed to bar the entrance, nor the heavy bolt,
> but men held them flung wide open.

His men:

> Fools! For at the gate they found two heroes,
> stalwart sons of the Lapith spearmen.

Polypoites and Leonteus stand at the gates, opening a path for their comrades and warding off the foe. They are like trees deeply rooted. A short list of Asios' followers (139) gives way to another simile for the Lapiths: they now become boars facing down a pack of dogs and huntsmen. A brief general description (151–6) issues into a simile of stones flying like snowflakes (156).

Thus far the first half of this movement. It is dominated by similes and generalizing description without any single combats. It is a picturesque introduction to the single encounters to come in the second part (162–94).[5]

Asios slaps his hips in disgust and berates Zeus, that "lover of deceit," but to no avail. Thirteen lines of man-to-man combat tell how the Lapiths reverse the tide (182–94). With that, the first Trojan onslaught is dissipated. In outline, it looks like this:

A. Hector's charge, description of the trench.

B. Advice from Poulydamas, Hector's reaction, Trojan regrouping and catalogue.

C. Asios versus the Lapiths:

    1. general description, snow simile.

    2. Asios' complaint to Zeus, single combats, the Lapiths stem the Trojan charge.

The second assault

The second sortie against the fortifications is led by Sarpedon and Glaukos and ends in a deadlock. This sequence is a general replica of the first, with ethical comment and dramatic amplification as its specific effects. To reduce it to outline (195–436):

A. The Trojan charge halts at the trench; the eagle-snake omen.

B. Advice from Poulydamas, Hector's angry reaction, Trojan charge.

C. Sarpedon and Glaukos versus the Aiantes:

    1. Aiantes on the wall, snow simile, the Lycians attack.

    2. Menestheus summons the Aiantes, single combats, stand-off fight, similes.

In the general economy of the narrative, I take the *omen* to be the counterpart of lines 50 and following, where the first wave of attack breaks at the trench. Both times the Trojans are stopped short at the brink (50, 199). The description of the obstacle, with its abrupt drop and pointed stakes in the first instance, is replaced in the second by a sign warning them off. Hector leads the storm, eager to cross (41, 196). The omen escalates the fear inspired by the ditch earlier; it is divine corroboration of human perception. The first time around Poulydamas foresaw a Greek counterattack—hence his argument against chariots. The omen has now confirmed his fear and gives it a clear definition. And so his advice grows more negative and insistent: do not cross over at all, for the sign shows we will return in disordered retreat. Hector flares up in a rage. He accuses Poulydamas of cowardice, dismissing all omens and appealing to patriotism. The difference between his two reactions marks his progress into delusion. That descent will continue in direct proportion to his attainments.

There is also movement on the field. At the first thrust we heard that the Trojans expected to breach the fortifications (106); now (257) they actually assail the rampart and begin to dismantle it. Their progress is exactly registered. The first attack was aimed at the trench; now they are suddenly over it (we never learn how) and assail the wall (compare 137 and 252).[6]

The narrative turns inward. Hector and Poulydamas are set in direct and explicit opposition. Hector's valor and failings, his patriotism ("one omen is best, to fight for one's country") and infatuation, receive their primary articulation in conflict with the wise counselor, here and in book 18. But there are other pairs and other mirrors. The first to ignore Poulydamas was Asios. Hector repeats the mistake, but on a grand and decisive scale. Asios is a reckless fool, without distinction in battle, ineptly railing against Zeus for breaking promises the god never made. Hector lives out his error in elevated blindness. As he presses forward, Zeus looms behind him, enigmatic and relentless. The omen is the god's, and so is the persuasion that compels Hector to discount it (252):

> And Zeus, who loves the thunderbolt,
> flung a blast of wind from the hills of Ida
> that swept the dust against the ships. Now that panicked
> the Achaeans and conferred glory on the Trojans and Hector.

Sarpedon and Glaukos against the Aiantes: the details and configuration of this section are different from Asios' feeble effort but the general parallelism abides: both are attacks on the Greek defenses following a speech by Poulydamas to Hector. The second continues to amplify the first. Sarpedon (and Glaukos too) is superior to Asios, the Aiantes are more important than the Lapiths. The struggle is fiercer and more evenly matched; it is more elaborate and lasts longer.

We recall that Asios and the Lapiths were introduced in two stages: first general description, then single combats. The same order prevails again, but with the combatants in reverse priority: first the Greeks, then the Trojans; first general description, then single fights.

The Aiantes bestride the battlements and exhort to resistance in a preview of Aias' last-ditch stand on the ships at the end of book 15. There follows the famous simile of stones falling like snowflakes (278), the crash and confusion of battle muted in a vision of silent nature. This is the second appearance of the same comparison. The first came at 156 during Asios' charge. As with all equivalents binding the two strikes, there is enlargement the second time around. Still another detail reinforces the parallelism. Both similes immediately precede a speech by the leader of the Trojan assault: Asios, then Sarpedon.

Asios and Sarpedon, leading two frustrated thrusts on the Greek positions, are set in powerful contrapost. Asios plunges ahead with stolid self-assertion: "he did not want to leave his chariot behind." Then he blames Zeus for wrecking his hopes. Sarpedon, Zeus's son, urged into the fight by his father (292) and protected by him there (402), enters with a solemn exordium that stands as one of the *Iliad*'s great pronouncements (322):

> Ah, my friend, if you and I could escape this war
> and stay ageless and deathless forever,
> the two of us . . .

Asios, Sarpedon, Poulydamas, Hector: here is a luminous constellation. The main pairs are Asios-Sarpedon, leaders of allied contingents in unsuccessful attack, and Poulydamas-Hector, counselor and leader at odds. Each figure casts light and shadow in a wide circle. Poulydamas, always right and always ignored by somebody, is the touchstone for Asios. But Asios also gives us a measure for Hector and Sarpedon. They are the greatest on their side, but deeply unlike. The Trojan is charged with emotion and deceived; the Lycian is reflective and grave, living his heroism without illusion, like Odysseus.

Book 11 drew a line of Achaean portraits: Agamemnon, Diomedes, Odysseus, and Aias. Book 12 shows the men they fight. Victory here, like defeat there, wears many faces. The plan and control belong to

Zeus, who ignores the futile Asios, inspires and shields his son Sarpedon, warns Hector away and goads him on to his fate, reserving for him the highest ascent and the most shattering fall. Here is a picture of twilight and sweep: the two great men of heroic and unlike spirit, both soon to die, caught up in the dark workings of Zeus, who will let them perish and grieve for them both. The whole of Hector's portion flashes out in book 12: assistance from above to achievement and ruin, and his pathetic enthusiasm for the plan of Zeus: "Let us rather believe in the plan of great Zeus."

When Asios made the first assault, the Lapiths turned him back. In accordance with the universal escalation of the second movement, Sarpedon's adversaries are summoned in an elaborate series of exchanges (331–77). Menestheus dispatches Thootes to bring the Aiantes; Thootes delivers the message; Telamonian Aias leaves instructions with Oilean Aias and Lykomedes, takes Teucer with him, and crosses to the threatened position. Sarpedon and Glaukos are mounting a serious threat. The fight that follows is worthy of the prelude. Both armies lose heavily as they wear themselves down in a desperate stalemate described by two of the *Iliad*'s most memorable similes: the neighbors arguing over a strip of boundary land and the day laborer at her spinning.

The third assault

With this, the second Trojan sally has spent itself. The climax comes suddenly. Hector, inspired by Zeus and in a frenzy, shatters the gates with a boulder and leaps through the breach, unstoppable by anyone but a god (465). The thrusts and counterthrusts, deadlocks, failures and standstills end with a dramatic flourish and rousing depiction of Hector in his moment of glory:

> Then brilliant Hector leaped through,
> with his face like sudden night. He glistened in the
> dreadful bronze that he wore on his body. And in his hands
> he carried two spears. No one except a god could have stood
> and held him off when he assaulted the gates.

The amplification has continued on a large and small scale both, and precisely registered, as always. Asios made no dent in the Greek resistance; Sarpedon ripped away part of the wall, opening a path for many (397); Hector wrenches the gates from their hinges and lets in the whole army. Or again: Aias, resisting Sarpedon, breaks the head of Epiklees with a rock that a strong man of today could barely lift with both hands (378). Hector demolishes the entrance with a boulder that two excellent men of today could barely hoist onto a wagon (445), and a simile describes the ease with which he wields it. But even here the impermanence of his lot is remembered because it is Zeus who makes it light for him (450). When Hector's might reaches its crest, we are reminded that it depends on the favor of the god.

Book 12 is a tight and precisely conceived composition. Objections to the doubling of Poulydamas' speeches, or to the two snow similes, or to Asios' intrusion into the conflict between Poulydamas and Hector, miss the point.[7] The book is built on parallel episodes. The first two assaults are drawn in close accord, the third abandons their pattern and brings a sudden end. As in books 11 and 6, repetition and reciprocity frame, illuminate, contrast. Form makes content.

NOT ALL THE FIGHTING in the *Iliad* has the rich content of books 11 and 12, but even the less inspired stretches are carefully managed. The technical means to this end remain the same: parallelism, symmetry, and correlation. But they do not always point beyond themselves, remaining instead at a surface level. Several passages from book 13 will illustrate.

Lines 361–454 form a short narrative block of less than a hundred lines. The action consists of an exchange of slayings: Othryoneus, Asios, and Alkathoos fall on the Trojan side (we thus follow Asios to his end), Hypsenor on the Greek side.[1] They are fashioned into a distinct group.

Othryoneus is a presumptuous and incompetent upstart who guaranteed to rout the Achaeans in return for the hand of Cassandra. He struts (371) onto the field and immediately suffers the regular fate of the *Iliad*'s great promisers. Idomeneus sends him on his way with mockery: why not contract instead with Agamemnon to marry his loveliest daughter as reward for taking Troy?[2] Asios falls next (384), also to Idomeneus. Deiphobos tries to retaliate but misfires and kills Hypsenor instead. Still he is reasonably satisfied and answers Idomeneus with an acerbic joke of his own: Asios will have the consolation of an escort on his way to Hades (414). Idomeneus' counterstroke is the slaying of Alkathoos, an excellent man and son-in-law of Anchises; his wife surpasses all her peers in womanly excellence. Some more chest beating over the victim closes out the incident and this series of killings.

The basic shape and themes of the passage emerge firm and clear: an exchange of slayings seasoned with derisive bluster, with the Trojans of course getting the worst of it. Othryoneus and Alkathoos, at the beginning and end, stand in contrast with the marriage anecdote as vehicle. The first is a foolhardy bungler, the second a man of worth. The first seeks connection with the house of Priam, the second has married into the family of Anchises.[3] The two rival lines supply a quiet but sustained motif in the sequel.

Asios dies in appropriate association with Othryoneus. His death here was prepared for and predicted when he disregarded Pouly-damas' advice in the last book (12.110) and insisted on driving his chariot over the trench and against the wall. All this receives under-stated and ironic emphasis here at his fall: he topples like a high tree and lies stretched out before his vehicle (392):

> So he lay there, sprawled in front of his horses and chariot,
> screaming.

In book 12 a series of Trojans were aligned in contrast: Hector, Poulydamas, Asios, and Sarpedon. That same technique is used here again, but on a small scale and without the same penetration. Struc-ture remains close to the surface; the narrative is organized but not transparent. In fact, this entire section of book 13 is held together mainly by small details strung in associative repetition. Some examples:

1. A meticulous log is kept of Asios' followers. Iamenos, Orestes, Adamas, Thoas, and Oinomaos join his charge at 12.139. The first two fall at 12.193, the others after him in book 13: Oinomaos at 506, Thoon at 545, Adamas at 567 (these last three in reverse order of their listing in book 12!). The beginning and end of Asios' dysaristeia span two books but remain amazingly consistent in detail.

2. Asios falls like a tree (389). That subject will recur shortly in a simile describing the death of Alkathoos (437).

3. Idomeneus and Antilochos are closely associated through line 565 as each anticipates, repeats, or reflects what the other does. For example, both are forced into retreat by a throng of Trojans (509, 550) after slaying one enemy (506, 545). They are attacked unsuccessfully by a single Trojan in the process (516, 560), while Meriones counter-attacks against each of the assailants, wounding Deiphobos (528) and killing Adamas (567). Here in this first sequence, Idomeneus fells Orthryoneus with a blow to the stomach (371):

> and the bronze corslet he wore
> did not hold, and the spear stuck in the middle of his belly.

The 1½ lines are repeated when Antilochos kills Asios' charioteer (397).

4. The charioteer freezes in panic (394), anticipating on a small scale the fate of Alkathoos, who is rendered immobile as a stele or a tree by Poseidon (434).

5. Deiphobos strikes at Idomeneus but misses and kills Hypsenor instead (402). This is the first in a series of unsuccessful spear casts by the Trojans (502, 516, 560, 646). The two at 402 and 516 are especially close: Deiphobos aims at Idomeneus, misses, and kills another in his place.

6. There is constant interest in the noises of weapons and armor: the rasping of Deiphobos' spear against the rim of Idomeneus' shield (409);[4] the dry thud of a missile breaking Alkathoos' body armor (414); the hollow ring of a falling helmet (530); the cracking of splintered bones (616). We also note in passing the interest in quivering spears, whether agitated by the pierced heart of Alkathoos (442, an eccentric phantasma)[5] or shaking in the ground (504).

The compositional principles of book 13.361–454 are thus clear and familiar: symmetrical arrangements, contrast of the slain with implied comment, repeated details binding the sequence as a unit and connecting it with what follows.

The next section is a transitional piece bridging combats (455–501). Deiphobos retires to find help with Aeneas. The tactic is familiar on the Homeric battlefield.[6] What interests us here is the symmetrical face-off between Idomeneus and Aeneas that follows (470–501):

    A.   Idomeneus stands firm; simile of a boar at bay.

    B.   He calls his friends to his aid; short catalogue of their names.

        C.   Speech of Idomeneus: help me against Aeneas; he has the strength of youth, I am too old to face him alone.

    D.   Aeneas summons his friends; short catalogue of their names.

    E.   The Trojans charge; simile of Aeneas leading his men.

A–B and D–E stand in chiastic sequence and in heraldic opposition. The similes at the start and finish also establish antithesis with the violence of the boar hunt set against the closing pastorale. The two men are placed in summarizing polarity before they engage and again just after (499):

> Two men, more valiant in war than the rest,
> Aeneas and Idomeneus, equals of Ares,
> were straining to tear each other's flesh with the pitiless bronze.

The Greeks maintain the upper hand, with Idomeneus and Antilochos enjoying success and then suffering a repulse in two parallel movements. There is no strict mirroring between them, but a general correspondence with pervasive coincidence of detail. The following outline shows the connections. (Equivalent numbers represent similar actions; italics show repeated items; small capitals indicate comparable but diversified details.)

A. (502–39). 1. *Aeneas* AIMS AT IDOMENEUS BUT MISSES.

2. IDOMENEUS *kills* Oinomaos (*son of Asios*) BUT CANNOT STRIP HIS ARMOR. *He retreats* SLOWLY (his age telling), *pressed in from all sides.*

3. DEIPHOBOS, still enraged, *casts at* THE RETREATING IDOMENEUS AND KILLS ASKALAPHOS INSTEAD.

4. DEIPHOBOS seizes the dead man's helmet; *Meriones* WOUNDS HIM IN THE ARM; DEIPHOBOS *withdraws to his lines; Meriones leaps forward and pulls out his spear* FROM DEIPHOBOS' ARM.

B. (540–75). 1. *Aeneas* KILLS APHAREUS.

2. ANTILOCHOS *kills* Thoas (*son of Asios*) and STRIPS HIS ARMOR. *He retreats* MENACINGLY, *the Trojans pursue him in numbers.*

3. ADAMAS (*son of Asios*) *casts at* ANTILOCHOS, BUT HIS SPEAR BREAKS IN THE SHIELD.

4. ADAMAS *retreats to his ranks; Meriones* KILLS HIM, *then advances and pulls out his spear* FROM THE CORPSE.

Readers can easily discover for themselves still finer relations between the two sequences and with the narrative at large. Two warriors, the aging Idomeneus and the youthful Antilochos, attack and retreat, with Aeneas and Meriones providing the main accompaniment.[7] The order and symmetry are impressive, but no content of significance emerges. The poet is satisfied with the simple exercise of youth and age in similar predicaments and with the play of likes and half-likes in the attendant circumstances.

A final word on Asios. The poet has kept careful track of his sons and followers. Asios himself dies in fitting association with Othryoneus. His sons perish in the two parallel sequences above at the hands of Idomeneus, Antilochos, and Meriones. There is almost a bookkeeper's orderliness about it.[8]

This pairing of consecutive incidents belongs to the poet's manner. The fighting in book 4 supplies another example on the small scale. At 4.517 Peiros (1) strikes Diores with a rock. Then (2) he runs up and spears him in the belly. (3) The victim's entrails pour onto the ground and darkness covers his eyes. Now the slayer perishes in much the same way: (1) Thoas hits him with his spear, (2) advances, draws out the weapon and strikes Peiros in the belly with his sword, but (3) is prevented from stripping the armor by the dead man's companions. Each slaying is accomplished in two stages, each involves a stomach wound, the slayer in the first is killed in the second, each man is leader of a contingent, and they are united in the summation (536):

> And so they were sprawled in the dust beside one another,
> one a leader of the Thracians, the other of the bronze-shirted
> Epeians.

Book 14 at 442 is even more stately. The two sides exchange slayings and boasts after the killing of Satnios by Oilean Aias (442):

A. 1. Poulydamas, defending the corpse of Satnios, kills Prothoenor, 449.

   2. Sarcastic boast by Poulydamas, 453.

   3. Telamonian Aias is angered, aims at Poulydamas but kills Archelochos instead, 458.

   4. Aias boasts to Poulydamas, 470.

B. 1. The Trojans are angered; Akamas slays Promachos, brother of Prothoenor (above, A.1) as he defends the corpse, 475.

   2. Akamas boasts, 478.

   3. The Argives are angered, especially Peneleos. He strikes at Akamas but misses and kills Ilioneus instead, 486.

   4. Peneleos boasts.

Except for the constant variation in small detail, A and B are mirror images. All the vaunting is in the same vein, and the rest is even more regular than the exchanges in book 13. Yet the fixed order delivers little in the way of content in either. Nor is there any effort in our stretch of book 13 to build long integrated episodes. Instead, shorter units are assembled, each with its own small repeats and surface structures and with a thin line of details running from one incident to the next (sounds of armor, and such). The poet moves circumspectly and step by step, controlling his narrative by reducing it to discrete segments. The product is a distinct taxis but little else.

That changes, however, in the immediate sequel. Menelaos enters the scene and with him come irony and paradox. This new section comprises lines 576–672, with concentration on Menelaos at the start and Paris at the close. Something to keep in mind as we proceed: from the entrance of Idomeneus at 361, book 13 shows some of the ugliest killing in the *Iliad* and a concentration of it without parallel: 372, 392, 398, 441, 506, 542, 545, 567, 615, 650. The section in question contains five encounters and ends with a change of scene to Hector elsewhere on the battlefield. All the fighting is in chain-reaction style, as one encounter inspires another. Menelaos is the control figure.

First combat: Helenus slays Deipyros (576–80). The victim's falling helmet echoes 527.

Second combat: Menelaos against Helenus (581–600). Menelaos charges in grief for Deipyros and there is a simultaneous attack, the Greek with his spear and the Trojan with his bow. The spearman wins. The arrow bounces off Menelaos' shield, but Helenus is wounded in the hand and led off the field by Agenor. Strong parallelism binds this to the wounding of Deiphobos (also a son of Priam) just before: the location of the wound (529, 598; cf. 783) and help of a friend in escaping behind the lines (533, 598). A Trojan's quick retreat becomes a refrain throughout the section: 566, 596, 648. Every one of Menelaos' duels here features the enemy's failure to pierce his armor: 586, 607, 647 (cf. 562).

Third combat: Menelaos against Peisandros (601–42). This is another simultaneous attack, with Menelaos winning again. Parallelism and variation persist. The first round is a draw, but in the second Menelaos strikes a blow to his enemy's forehead, smashing it in and knocking out both his eyes. Repeated details and grisly effects continue unabated. The most important part of the incident is Menelaos' speech over the corpse.

Fourth combat: Menelaos against Harpalion (643–59). Harpalion attacks with a blow to Menelaos' shield but fails to pierce it, just like the two before him. He tries to retreat to the safety of his ranks but is shot and killed by Meriones with an arrow to the groin. His father and other Paphlagonians bear him off the field in grief. All this is now familiar: the failure to penetrate Menelaos' armor; the Trojan's attempt to withdraw; Meriones entering the fight at the second stage (cf. 531, 567); the painful death and attention paid to the aftermath (cf. 533, 598).[9]

Fifth combat: Paris against Euchenor (660–72). The chain reaction continues. Paris is angered at the death of Harpalion, his friend and guest. He exacts vengeance by shooting Euchenor, son of the seer Polyidos. That closes out this section of fighting.

The shape of the section stands out firmly: three combats of Menelaos framed at the start and ending with slayings by Trojan brothers, Helenus and Paris, with numerous internal connectors holding them together. Dark and complex issues emerge toward the end. Menelaos delivers a speech over the fallen Peisandros that widens into an indictment of all the Trojans. Because of its importance I quote it in full, in Lattimore's translation (620–39):

> So, I think, shall you leave the ships of the fast-mounted Danaans,
> you haughty Trojans, never to be glutted with the grim war noises,
> nor go short of all that other shame and defilement
> wherewith you defiled me, wretched dogs, and your hearts knew no
>   fear
> at all of the hard anger of Zeus loud-thundering,
> the guest's god, who some day will utterly sack your steep city.
> You who in vanity went away taking with you my wedded
> wife, and many possessions, when she had received you in kindness.
> And now once more you rage among our seafaring vessels
> to throw deadly fire on them and kill the fighting Achaeans.
> But you will be held somewhere, though you be so headlong for battle.
> Father Zeus, they say your wisdom surpasses all others',
> of men and gods, and yet from you all this is accomplished
> the way you give these outrageous people your grace, these Trojans
> whose fighting strength is a thing of blind fury, nor can they ever
> be glutted full of the close encounters of deadly warfare.
> Since there is satiety in all things, in sleep and love-making,

in the loveliness of singing and the innocent dance. In all these
things a man will strive sooner to win satisfaction
than in war; but in this the Trojans cannot be glutted.

This turgid homily has attracted much attention, especially the second
part, where the inept listing of things men tire of has been taken as
a sure interpolation.[10] A useful interpretation has been offered by
Christoph Michel, of which the most important points are these. The
battle is *supposed* to be going against the Greeks, with Hector carrying
everything before him; but in fact the Trojans are losing more men.
Menelaos' speech helps to disguise the fact. What holds the harangue
together is Menelaos' bewilderment. "It is past comprehension that
the Trojans, instead of making reparations, are pressing the fight with
intent to destroy the Achaeans; it is past comprehension that Zeus,
the guest-god, supports the criminals as he does; and it utterly surpasses comprehension that there are actually people like this, who
never get their fill of fighting. After all, even pleasant things bring
satiety!"[11]

This is sound analysis. The speech wells from a sense of moral
outrage and follows an especially difficult and violent combat that
has left Menelaos exasperated. Still it remains a fatuous tantrum from
start to finish, feeble in conception and long-winded. As Leaf re-
marked long ago: "To be unwearied in battle is not a reproach, nor
is success in battle a sign of hybris."

Consider the next event. Menelaos has scarcely finished when he
is attacked by Harpalion—as if to illustrate his complaint. But despite
his intimidating name, this young man is anything but a war criminal
gleefully abetting the cause of injustice. He came to Troy to fight by
the side of his father, makes an ineffectual spear cast, then dies an
excruciating death at the hands of Meriones, who is probably the
grimmest butcher in the *Iliad*. Harpalion is a piteous figure and we
sympathize with his grief-stricken father. There is a disharmony between Menelaos' sanctimonious moralizing and the killings perpe-
trated by himself and others on the Greek side, between the riddle
of Zeus's workings he tries to ponder and the ludicrous inadequacy
of his efforts.

Then comes the final blow. Harpalion's body is scarcely removed
when Paris appears, chief object and incorporation of Menelaos'
charges, symbol and emblem. He shoots and kills Euchenor, a man

bearing strange resemblances to Achilles.[12] He too had a choice: to die at home of disease or to perish in the fight at the ships. His father, like Thetis, told his son what lay in store. Like his counterpart, he chose death in battle, and again Paris is the agent of fate's decree.

This is a suggestive cluster of parallels. We saw something similar in book 11 where Achilles' fate is transferred to Diomedes on a small scale. Now we have a different set of details, again recalling a central story through a refracting prism: Menelaos and Paris, injured party and perpetrator, with somebody like Achilles dying in consequence of their enmity. Menelaos rails against the injustice of things. Immediately a sympathetic Trojan dies hideously at his hands. Menelaos appeals to Zeus the protector of guest-friends. Paris, in maddening verification of the complaint, slays a minor Achilles, but this to avenge the death of one who was his own guest-friend.[13] Where, indeed, is justice, and what is the will of Zeus? The god provides no tidy balance sheet of crime and punishment of the sort the man yearns for. Menelaos gropes toward real issues, but the enigma resists his superficial and moralizing view. He remains on the surface, fumbling his way in turbid, self-righteous speculation. He is as problematical a part of Zeus's inscrutable design as Paris himself.

— II

THE NIBELUNGENLIED

Introduction

> What all non-artists call form is perceived by the artist as content, as "the thing itself." That is the price of being an artist.
> —Friedrich Nietzsche

THERE IS GENERAL AGREEMENT that the *Nibelungenlied* (henceforth NL) is a form-conscious work. But there is disagreement concerning both the definition of form and its content. Most analysis has seized upon the two fundamental and most visible units of composition, the aventiure and the strophe, and set itself the task of demonstrating that these fall into groups held in close numerical correspondence. "Form," or "symmetry," thus means quantitative proportions. The most ambitious effort at the level of the aventiure came from Hans Eggers, whose attention was directed mainly to the Arthurian romances.[1] He assembled an amazing array of figures showing elaborate arithmetical divisions underlying one after the other of these poems, with Hartmann's *Der arme Heinrich* emerging as perhaps the most staggering statistical tour de force of them all. Eggers' exposition gains weight from the medieval fascination with shape and balancing generally, and especially with number symbolism, a fascination grounded at least partly in the notion of a harmonious universe with everything in place and arranged for the best: *omnia in mensura et numero et pondere posuisti.* Many of these groupings express the golden ratio. Interestingly, Eggers' study appeared right at the time when classical literature was being subjected to intense analysis along the same lines.[2] Neither effort has inspired much reaction. They remain unrefuted but at a standstill, fascinating but without aftereffect.

As far as the NL is concerned, the reasons for this are not far to seek. For one thing, Eggers' division into 18–3–18 aventiuren hardly goes beyond the poem's obvious division into halves. For another, and this pertains to all such efforts, the demarcations between aventiuren vary in the transmission and the borders of many remain disputed. That problem compounds itself when all the aventiuren are assigned niches in schematic arrangements. Third, some schemata fall victim to their own excessive refinement. In the interest of a master pattern, the interpreter identifies aventiuren by certain subjects or events that, taken together, render a dazzling symmetry, but often these contents do not in fact dominate the aventiuren they are made to represent.[3] Finally, the overly refined networks resemble figures dancing in a void because it cannot be shown how they influence our reception of the text. The heady generalizations in which structural analyses of the whole NL tend to traffic thus remain tendentious and curiously abstract.[4]

More usefulness and persuasion attach to the division of single aventiuren into corresponding sets of strophes. The most notable exponent of this school is Friedrich Maurer.[5] Not all his examples convince, but he has succeeded in demonstrating that many aventi-uren fall into balanced sections of three.[6] Number 16, for example, breaks into (1) the hunt, (2) the prank with the bear, and (3) the murder. These are related in sets of 28, 26, and 28 strophes respec-tively, with two strophes of introduction and two more at the end. Or, again, aventiure 19 shows strophe clusters of 15–12–15, telling of (1) Kriemhilt's sorrow and reconciliation with Gunther, (2) the trans-port of the treasure to Wormez, and (3) the new affronts to Kriemhilt and her mourning. Aventiure 4 (*wie er mit den Sahsen streit*) has five parts of 28, 27, 28, 22, and 21. Although Maurer overestimates the artistic value of such proportionalism, he never loses sight of two important things: first, these ratios do not exist for their own sakes but work on the audience in the act of reception; second, exact cor-respondence is neither universal nor necessary.[7]

Peter Wiehl took a third approach, namely to insist that both the aventiure and the strophe must enter equally into structural calcu-lations.[8] He points out that the aventiuren by themselves are uncertain quantities because of their disputed boundaries, and because they are of unequal length and singly of disparate content. They are not, there-fore, reciprocally equivalent unities. So, calling for a system that com-bines megalithic blocks of aventiuren with the fine masonry of numerically equivalent strophe clusters, he draws up designs whereby the narrative falls into answering sections that contain the same num-ber of aventiuren and strophes both.

And yet, despite their sophistication and healthy reserve, both Maurer's and Wiehl's final results suffer from the same congenital immobility that undermines Eggers' designs. No matter that their perfection is often suspicious by itself—the medieval reverence for such things forces us to keep an open mind: "Works of poetry from the Stauffian period lay primary emphasis on artistic design. Architectonics represent a mode of poetic expression. As a result, the precise content of this poetry cannot be discerned apart from the artistic devices that create form."[9] The difficulty comes, to repeat, in explaining how complex arithmetic translates into effect on the audience or reader. Even Maurer's divisions carry only a modest aesthetic content, and, as for the rest, they seem to float outside the story as a distant accompaniment, influencing our reception in ways so delicate as to resist useful definition.

The critical debate can easily become totally abstract and thus out of control, however. Nor would it be prudent to deny that elaborate harmonies could be built into medieval poetry without concern for their visibility and palpable influence. I shall, however, take a different approach. First, numbers and proportionalism will figure scarcely at all, and never for their own sakes. Second, I shall narrow the focus from whole aventiuren to discrete episodes inside them. Third, I shall examine how the story is organized in its progress step by step, in whatever divisions it naturally presents itself and without regard for how these relate to the aventiure's frame or to the number of strophes involved.[10] I shall concentrate on those techniques used to organize short stretches of narrative, such as single episodes, speeches, conversations, and descriptions. In short, I shall try to advance beyond static numerical correspondence to a dynamic concept of narrative design. Study needs to begin at this level, in my view, because here there is no separating form and content, and the pertinence of a shaping strategy is most obvious. It is also here that comparison with Homer and other epics is most direct and useful. Emphasis will remain, in fact, on the same phenomena as in Homer: form, symmetry, and organization as these are cast in the formal and repetitive modes of epic style. I leave the question in abeyance whether the poet thought in terms of pleasing shapes to be lifted from their context and enjoyed by the mind's eye.[11] In practice I shall continue to treat textual "shape" only as a cipher, a translation, as it were, into a visual medium of emphases in the poetry and of its natural rhythms. Bodo Mergell has already provided a model of dynamic form criticism with his analysis of character development in Kriemhilt and Hagen from the first half to the second, and of the progression and reversals leading to their final confrontation.[12] I shall work to a similar end, but with single scenes and on a reduced scale.

My analysis of the NL is organized differently from that of the *Iliad* in one main respect. There I treated whole books or longer sections of them. Here I define certain tropes and draw examples from wherever they occur. There are practical reasons for the two procedures having to do with the nature of the respective works. But my method remains the same for both to the extent that I deal always with self-contained sections. It is not my intention to show how different parts of either epic are associated by common structures or themes, something already done by Nagel for the NL.[13] My purpose is to demonstrate something else, that the NL, like the Homeric epics, reveals plan and artifice at the base levels of narration. Oversight and control manifest themselves as much at the elementary stages of storytelling as in overriding structures.

This analysis is based on version B. The reasons for this will be obvious to those familiar with the transmission and the modern consensus on the relationship between the three lines. But I quote the text and strophe numbers from de Boor's edition because it is so accessible and familiar. It is, of course, a composite text but based overwhelmingly on B, and this makes my procedure both possible and justifiable. De Boor's deviations from B are always noted and dealt with wherever they impinge on my treatment of specific passages. I have also maintained a running comparison with version C, and I append a brief résumé of C's text, where that is called for, at the end of my treatment of each passage from B. All references to version A are based on the diplomatic edition of Michael Batts.

Symmetry

THE PRINCIPLE of formal scene drawing assumes many forms in the NL. One of the most important is the orderly disposition of straightforward repeats. The resemblance to Homeric style leaps to the eye. To begin with a simple example, Sivrit overcomes the giant and the dwarf who guard his treasure in two parallel encounters. First the giant arms himself, charges, and inflicts heavy damage on Sivrit's shield. The master begins to fear for his life but is pleased with his servant's performance. He finally overcomes and binds him— all this from 489.1 to 492.3. Now everything repeats itself with the dwarf: arming (494.2–3), charge (494.4), wrecking of Sivrit's shield (495–496.1; observe the progress over the giant), Sivrit's fear for his life (495.4), good will toward his servant (496.3), capture and binding (499). Noise and clamor accompany these highjinks with a spirited discord (the Nibelungen sleep peacefully through it all), from Sivrit's banging on the door (486.3) to the clangor of weapons (492.1, 493.1) and the dwarf's yelling (497.3, 498.1).

Typically for the NL, the second round amplifies the first in some small details such as the damage done to Sivrit's shield, and especially with the humor of beard pulling and the play on *zühte* (manners, up-bringing) and *zuht* (discipline, chastisement; 496.4, 497.4). Whether for fun or in earnest, this poet likes to set things in closely aligned pairs. The effect here is to deliver an episode with a formal shape and riotous spirit, at once perilous and harmless, ceremonious and playful, methodical and rowdy. Active tension of the sort between form and content belongs to the NL's most persuasive and successful efforts.

Sivrit's arrival as messenger in Wormez

At strophe 543, Sivrit arrives at Wormez to announce Gunther's impending arrival with Prünhilt. Giselher and Gernot meet him and assume the worst at not finding their brother in his company. But Sivrit announces good news and assures them all is well. That done, he receives permission to enter the presence of Uote and Kriemhilt.

Giselher prepares the way with a summary report of his own to the ladies. It is terse but unalarming (549.3–550.1):

> uns ist komen Sîfrit,   der helt ûz Niderlant;
> in hât mîn bruoder Gunther   her ze Rîne gesant.
>
> Er bringet uns diu maere,   wie ez umb den künic stê.
>
> Sivrit has arrived,   the warrior from the Netherlands.
> My brother Gunther sent him   to us here on the Rhine.
>
> He brings us the report   of how the king has fared.

Yet Sivrit meets the same pessimism in the ladies' quarters as outside the palace. He needs to repeat the happy word from earlier, that Gunther is headed for home with his bride. The conversation with the men thus repeats itself with the women:

> I   543:   Giselher and Gernot meet Sivrit.
>
>   544:   Welcome, you must be bringing bad news.
>
>   545:   No, Gunther is on his way.
>
> II   551:   Uote and Kriemhilt receive Sivrit.
>
>   552:   Welcome, Gunther is surely lost.
>
>   553:   No, the news is good.

Language reinforces the mirroring:

> I   544 (Giselher to Sivrit):
>
> Sît willekomen, Sîfrit!   ir sult mich wizzen lân,
> wâ ir mînen bruoder   den künic habt verlân.
> von Prünhilde sterke   den wæn' wir hân verlorn.
>
> Welcome to you, Sivrit!   Please let me know
> where you left   my brother the king.
> I reckon the might of Prünhilt   has taken him from us.

522 (Kriemhilt to Sivrit):

Sît willekomen, her Sîfrit,   ritter lobelîch,
wâ ist mîn bruoder Gunther,   der edel künic rîch?
von Prünhilde krefte   den wæn' wir hân verlorn.

Welcome to you, Sivrit,   praiseworthy knight,
where is my brother Gunther,   the noble mighty king?
I reckon we have lost him   because of Prünhilt's might.

II   545 (Sivrit to Giselher):

den liez ich wol gesunden;   er hât mich iu gesant,
daz ich sîn bote wære   mit mæren her in iuwer lant.

I left him quite unhurt;   he sent me here to you.
with news into your land   to be his messenger.

553 (Sivrit to Kriemhilt):

ich liez in wol gesunden,   daz tuon ich iu bekant.
si habent mich iu beiden   mit den mæren her gesant.

I left him quite unhurt;   that I announce to you.
They sent me with the news   to the two of you.

III   545 (Sivrit to Giselher):

          iu unt den mâgen sîn
enbiutet sînen dienest   der hergeselle mîn.

          To you and to his kinsmen
my comrade-in-arms   sends his compliments.

554 (Sivrit to Kriemhilt):

Iu enbiutet holden dienest   er unt diu wîne sîn
mit vriuntlîcher liebe.

He and his beloved   send you gracious compliments,
with familial affection.

IV   545 (Sivrit to Giselher):

Die angest lât belîben.

Put away your fear.

554 (Sivrit to Kriemhilt):

nu lâzet iuwer weinen.

Put aside your weeping.

Sivrit's reception thus proceeds in two stages that reflect each other in order and detail, with the second amplifying the first and climaxing in the exchange of gallantries by the two lovers beginning at 556. The delivery of this news becomes a dramatic interlude, articulated in stages and ascending to a climax in the courtly intimacy of Sivrit and Kriemhilt. The care expended on this scene reflects its importance. As an event of weight, it is given emotional content and dressed in the forms of protocol. Here begins the union between Sivrit and Kriemhilt, the consequence of Gunther's successful and dishonest courtship. The bantering warmth of 556 and the ensuing strophes is set unforgivingly against the distance and chill that separate Gunther and his bride. The two pairs are set in quiet polarity, each casting shadows over the other.

> Version C drops some of these correspondences and adds others of its own. B's *mit mæren* (545.4, 553.4) is kept at C 551.4, but omitted at C559. But C establishes new parallel greetings at 551.1 (*Ir edeln recken beiden*) and 559.2 (*ir edeln juncfrowen*). C also loses the repeated *Sît willekomen (her) Sîfrit* of B544.1 and 552.1 by changing the first to *willechomen, ritter edele* (C 550.1). These are small changes, and the two scenes remain strongly reciprocal in C.

Gunther's return to Wormez with Prünhilt

It belongs to the manner of the NL that important occasions are marked by the solemnity of ordered repeats. Gunther's return is a thing of pomp and circumstance. He brings home a glorious but fallacious victory with his sister and Sivrit already caught in its treacherous wake. The scene at 537 where he dispatches Sivrit to Wormez is a master example of epic style: formal instructions in marked, repetitive cadences. The pattern of the first three strophes is (1) message to a single person, (2) message to a group. The last strophe is directed entirely to Kriemhilt.

537, 1–2: Tell Queen Uote of our high spirits over our mission.
     3–4: Tell my brothers what I have accomplished, and tell my friends, too.

538, 1–2: Best greetings to my sister from Prünhilt.
     3–4: Also to my servants and vassals—how happily I have accomplished all that I strove for!

539, 1–2: Instruct Ortwin to prepare seating for the celebration.
    3–4: And let my kinfolk know about it, too. I intend to celebrate a great festival with Prünhilt.

540, 1–4: Tell Kriemhilt she should welcome my betrothed with full honors (*mit vlîze*). I shall be ever grateful.

The taxis leaps to the eye and requires no further comment—except that only Kriemhilt's name is mentioned twice, and the last strophe belongs to her alone.

Two tendencies converge here. The messenger is Sivrit, who was persuaded to serve only at the prospect of Kriemhilt's gratitude (535). For that he will do anything. His reception by her (549) will more than answer his hopes and is itself an elegant exercise of *courtoisie*. In short, the emphasis on Kriemhilt is pointed: it belongs to the ensnarement of Sivrit in the toils of *minne* and to the disastrous coordination of the two marriages.

Both Gunther's messages to Kriemhilt focus on his bride: first in passing along her compliments, then in the request for a fitting reception. There is no surprise in that, but unobtrusively, almost without notice, a fatal constellation is being set in place. When Prünhilt greets her sister-in-law years later, just before their break, the quality of the two receptions becomes a subject of discussion (783, 787). A shadow crosses Gunther's joy here, unnoticed by him. But the displacement in his union with Prünhilt is already evident (cf. 528) and in ominous contrast with the joy of the other pair. Gunther's success is a lie. The processional of his return makes a glorious show, but behind it the catastrophe is already taking shape. It is characteristic of the NL that its formally structured scenes acquire perspective and depth, where irony and foreboding lie beneath the surface.

> C makes changes and simplifies. The refinement and consistency of B's order disappears (that happens frequently), and with that comes a certain blurring. The loss of B's sharp articulation diminishes the formality of the instructions and reduces the emphasis on Kriemhilt (surprising for C). In outline:

543, 1–2: Tell my mother and sister how happy we are.
    3–4: Tell my brothers and friends of my success.

544, 1–2: Compliments from Prünhilt to Kriemhilt and my mother.
    3–4: Also to all my servants and vassals—how happily I have accomplished all that I strove for.

545, 1–4: Tell my brothers and friends to take note and spread the word: I shall hold a great festival with Prünhilt.

546, 1–4: Ask Kriemhilt to welcome my betrothed with all honors. I shall be ever grateful.

We will see many examples where C's abandonment of the more archaic epic manner leads to the loss of some of its best effects.

Sivrit's growth to maturity

Symmetrical alternation governs the summary in strophes 21–26 of (A) Sivrit's youth and (B) his growing appeal to women:

21: his prowess and adventures

22: his deeds and beauty, his attractiveness to women

23: his careful training and native excellence

24: he matures, is noticed and favored by many a lady and maiden

25: early education and training

26: he attains to man's estate and turns his attention to courting

We note in passing the steady look into the future with the repeated *sît* in strophes 21–23.[1] Chronology is also interrupted and replaced by a pattern of alternation. Strophes 21–22 look forward to early maturity. Number 23 reverts to boyhood, 24 leaps ahead again to young manhood, 25 turns back once more to youth, and 26 hurries us forward still another time to the hero's adult years. Linear time is abandoned for a formal and abstract structure.[2]

C breaks this pattern but creates a new one of its own. An extra strophe (C 21) speaks of countless wondrous accomplishments (this probably looking forward to Hagen's later account of the same),[3] while B 24 is removed. C's pattern is this:

A. 20: Sivrit's mighty and deeds

21: his countless mighty exploits

22: the marvels of his early years, women's favor to him

B. 23: his excellent upbringing, natural talents, later glory

24: his careful training for later power

25: first maturity and courtships

Instead of B's alternation, C composes two movements, each culminating in Sivrit's prowess in the realm of *minne*. Once again the natural temporal sequence is flouted as youth and first maturity stand in reverse order. C's changes seem to aim for clarity and firm groupings.

The strophic form lends itself naturally to symmetrical alternation.[4] Although Homer does not, of course, have that at his disposal the principle is not unknown to him. In book 24 of the *Odyssey* some spirits of the dead converse in the underworld:[5]

I. Achilles speaks, 24–34 (11 verses).

II. Agamemnon speaks, 36–97 (62 verses).

III. Agamemnon speaks, 106–19 (14 verses).

IV. Amphimedon speaks, 121–90, (70 verses).

V. Agamemnon speaks, 192–202, (11 verses).

I introduces the story of Agamemnon's death, V brings it to a conclusion with comparison to the happier lot of Odysseus. I–II together describe Agamemnon's shameful demise, III–IV the return of Odysseus. The ordering principles are of the most simple sort: short speech–long speech, with longs and shorts falling into pairs setting the returns of Agamemnon and Odysseus in contrast.

Prünhilt's arming

To return to the NL: symmetries of the kind cited above are unpretentious and convey only a modest effect. But they reflect the persistent orderliness of the poet's style and they are never otiose. They emphasize, indicate direction, establish tone. We find them also in the service of more important structures. A case in point is the arming of Prünhilt at 428.

First she orders her breastplate and shield to be brought out, then a battle shirt (*wâfenhemd*) that she puts on (428.3–429). Threats and taunts from her men follow against Dancwart and Hagen (430), while

Sivrit steals off for the *tarnkappe* (431–432). Now the ground is prepared and Prünhilt strides out in all her glory (434). Thus the following
ring composition:

1. Prünhilt begins to arm, orders breastplate and shield, dons her bat-
   tleshirt, 428–29 (2 strophes).
2. *Gelf* directed against Hagen and Dancwart, 430 (1 strophe).
3. Sivrit and the *tarnkappe*, 431–32 (2 strophes).
4. Preparation of the circle, 433 (1 strophe).
5. Prünhilt steps forward, her shield is delivered, 434–35 (2 strophes).

Several things stand out. One is the proleptic ring. She orders her
shield at 428.4, but it appears only at 435. Indeed, her brief arming
at 428–29 is only a prelude to the elaborated version of the same after
her reappearance at 434. These proleptic rings are characteristic of the
NL and will be dealt with in a separate chapter. Also note the alternation of one- and two-strophe units: two for Prünhilt at the start
and close of the ring; one each for the *gelf* and preparation of the
circle, with two for Sivrit in between. The patterning makes for gravity; the numbers mark obvious and appropriate emphases.

The last section of the ring (434–35) now becomes the first member
in a closely aligned series:

1. Prünhilt's shield, 435–37.
   Hagen cries out in amazement, 438.

2. Prünhilt's *wâfenroc* and spear, 439–41.3.
   Gunther is aghast, Hagen and Dancwart tremble and object, their
   weapons are returned to them, 441.4–48.

3. Prünhilt's casting stone, 449–50.1
   Hagen cries out in fear and amazement, 450.3–4.

The stringent order impresses. There is even balancing on the large
scale as the Burgonden's fear in the middle section (441–48) is spun
into an episode, while in the first and last there are only interjections
of fright (438, 450). These alternate: Hagen; Gunther-Hagen-Dancwart;
Hagen. And every outburst from the Burgonden mentions the devil
(438.4, 442.2, 450.4). The implements of the contest receive descend-

ing allotments of lines: twelve for the shield (435–37), eight for the spear (440–41) and five for the stone (449–50.1).[6]

The three elements of the contest are thus displayed in a great frontal procession: shield, spear, and stone. But there is more. Each is described singly in a trio of identically shaped presentations:

1. Prünhilt's men bring the shield, 435.1–2.
   2. Description of the shield, 435.3–37.3.
3. Four chamberlains can scarcely carry it, 437.4.
   4. Hagen cries out in fear, 438.
1. The spear is carried out, 440.1–2.
   2. Description of the spear, 440.3–41.2.
3. Three men can hardly carry it, 441.3
   4. Gunther and the rest are terrified, 441.4.
1. The stone is brought out, 449.2.
   2. Description of the stone, 449.3.
3. Twelve heroes can hardly carry it, 449.4.
   4. Hagen cries out in fear, 450.3.

Only one small variation insinuates itself into the fixed pattern: at 450.1 a single verse intervenes between the report of how many men were needed to carry the stone and the notice of fear from the Burgundian side. The whole is a tight composition, related by type to the stylized but precisely modulated arming scenes in the *Iliad*.[7]

As for the effect of this composition, at least three observations are in order. First, these repeats seem somehow archaic in their steady, unhurried tread. We sense the solemn and patient intonations of an old-fashioned style. Second, there is no mistaking the constant play of variation. It needs to be emphasized that structures like these look constraining and rigid only when abstracted from context and reduced to an outline. In our actual reception, certainly as hearers and even as readers, the structure is not obtrusive—this because of shifting detail, the texture of the diction, and the pull of events. The form operates in secret beneath the surface. It is the skeleton of the narrative and visible only upon dissection. And third, that structure brings home the peril that Gunther has entered into. As one battery after another rolls into place, Gunther and the rest can only sweat and look for a way out. The stages of Prünhilt's arming combine into a fearsome processional: cumulative, hammerlike, inexorable, intimidating. Her preparations have a massive assemblage and ponderous menace that take the Burgonden's breath away. What a contrast and relief it is, then, what an almost burlesque change of pace, when Sivrit suddenly reenters, made invisible now by his magic robe, to take Gunther's hand and assume control.

> Versions A and C show little significant variation. A leaves out strophes 439, 442 and 445, bringing both loss and gain. The sequence is tightened without 439 (we pass directly from shield to spear without the dispensable *wâfenroc*), but the triple repetition of the devil goes with 442. The absence of 445 means little either way. C expands by two strophes (C 452 after 442 and C 458 after 447). Both reflect some of C's pervasive tendencies. C 452 paints Gunther's fright and Hagen's near-panic in florid color (*vor leide het Hagene/vil nâch verwandelt den sin*). In C 458 Prünhilt heaps scorn on the Burgonden: it makes no difference to her whether they are armed or not. Gunther and Hagen, two of C's favorite targets, thus cut even poorer figures in his version than in the others. But the firm narrative shape abides.

The discovery of Sivrit's corpse

Decisive events unfold systematically in the NL, even those of mass confusion. The discovery of the dead Sivrit is a good example. The news and reaction to it spread in concentric waves. We begin with Kriemhilt's dispatch of a messenger to spread the report. In the following outline, italics indicate repeated detail, small capitals the maintenance of a fixed order.

1014: Kriemhilt to the messenger: AROUSE SIVRIT'S MEN, THEN TELL SIGMUNT. Perhaps he will want to help me *grieve for Sivrit.*

1015: ANNOUNCEMENT TO SIVRIT'S MEN; *they refuse to believe until they hear the cries of sorrow.*

1021.4–1022: SIVRIT'S MEN ARRIVE; *their grief.*

1023–24: SIGMUNT ARRIVES; *his and Kriemhilt's grief.*

1025: *The wuof resounds throughout the city.*

> Interlude: Sigmunt's and Kriemhilt's men want to take vengeance. Kriemhilt dissuades them.

1036–37: *The citizens hear the wuof and rush to the scene; general mourning.*

Nothing could be simpler than the repetitions shaping this scene: the fixed alternation of Sivrit's men and Sigmunt; their refusal to believe until the cries reach their ears; their arrival at Sivrit's side; finally the wailing heard again, this time by the citizens of the town who also rush to mourn. Yet the effect is considerable. News of the catastrophe gains momentum. It expands impressively from Kriemhilt's private discovery to lamentation by the entire populace. That enlargement occurs in precise stages held in order.

The value of this unprepossessing structure can be measured by some small changes introduced by C. It recasts strophe 1015 (C 1027) so as to remove the detail that Sivrit's men refused to believe until they heard the cries. This is, of course, a refrain in the passage and a shaping device. It also singles out Kriemhilt in contrast to Sigmunt and Sivrit's men both: she knew instantly who the dead man was, even before seeing him (1008). C replaces its excision with a more intense reaction by the men to the news:

> mit disen leiden mæren   wachter manigen man.
> die sprungen âne sinne   vil balde von ir betten dan.

> With these woeful tidings   he wakened many a man.
> And they, out of their senses,   leaped from their beds forthwith.

That small gain exacts a heavy price. (1) The more gradual and dramatic ascent to the *wuof* at Sivrit's side is lost. (2) The repetition of disbelief vanishes, and the refrain is especially effective in a scene of mourning. (3) The intensification of this same detail in the report to Sigmunt is sacrificed. That is, in version B (and A) the skepticism of Sivrit's men is related in one line, but Sigmunt's is elaborated into a conversation covering four strophes. Also the arrival of Sivrit's men at his side is dispatched in 1¼ strophes (1021.4–22), while Sigmunt's covers three strophes, including an exchange between him and Kriemhilt and his embrace of the corpse. In other words, Sivrit's men precede Sigmunt at every step, both in his bed and at the bier, but the lion's share of reaction is given to him. The result is a series of intensifications as effective as they are regular. C throws this crescendo away. It is a finely conceived composition, however unassuming its appearance, where a small change does such damage.

Something of this firm line drawing remains in the sequel. Kriemhilt encounters, in almost heraldic contrast, enemies and friends outside the cathedral on the next day: first Gunther and Hagen, with sharp exchanges of accusation and denial (1040–46); then Gernot and Giselher, who sincerely pity her (1047–49). And finally, as the ceremonies end and burial approaches, the crowds melt away and the focus narrows again to Kriemhilt alone with her grief (1069):

> si huop sîn schœne houbet   mit ir vil wîzen hant;
> dô kustes' alsô tôten   den edeln ritter guot.
> diu ir vil liehten ougen   vor leide weineten bluot.
>
> She lifted up his handsome head,   with her hand so very white;
> She kissed him all so dead,   the noble valiant knight.
> Her eyes so very bright   in grief wept tears of blood.

This reaches back to the moment when she discovered the horror outside her door (1011):

> si huop sîn schœne houbet   mit ir vil wîzen hant.
> swie rôt ez was von bluote,   si het in schiere erkant.
>
> She lifted up his handsome head   with her hand so very white.
> As red as it was from blood,   she knew him instantly.

No mere reminiscence this, and far from a conceit. A cycle has completed itself: from discovery by the queen outside her chambers, to an entire city in mourning, and now back to the widow by herself, holding her husband's lifeless head—a rhythm belonging to things as they are, infinitely persuasive and moving.

Rüedeger's entrance into combat

At strophe 2175 of the 37th aventiure Rüedeger serves notice to the Burgonden that he will engage them. He has arrived at this decision through the impasse of contradictory obligations: duty to Etzel on the one hand, on the other his ties to Gunther and the rest, grown out of *gâbe unt geleit* (gifts and escort) and the betrothal of his daughter to Giselher. His feudal commitments to Etzel carry the day, as they must. It belongs to the integrity of the NL that its ethical dilemmas are profoundly conceived. Every important conflict has its roots in social imperatives interacting with human character. Rüedeger is the supreme example of this. In the exchange with Kriemhilt and Etzel starting at 2145, he struggled to a decision. The great sequence starting at 2175 explores the paradox of it, gives it perspective and tragic definition—and an ethical solution in the gift of his shield to Hagen.[8] Much of the power of this episode derives from the fact that Rüedeger's decision is made before he confronts the Burgonden; hence its elevation and hard finality.

Rüedeger speaks with each of the Burgundian chiefs in descending order of rank: Gunther, Gernot, Giselher, Hagen, and Volker. Special ties were made to each at Bechelaren. Now they pass in review, each opening an inner wound. The first three talks share an order of alternating one-strophe exchanges but with each of the beseiged given a single longer address of two strophes or more: Gunther, 2177–81; Gernot, 2182–87; Giselher, 2188–92. This is an excellent example of the blocklike architectonics of the NL and of the isolating strophic form put to the use of dramatic dialogue.

The exchange with Hagen, following immediately, has a shape of its own:

> Hagen calls out, 2193–95 (3 strophes).
>
> Rüedeger replies, 2196 (1 strophe).
>
> > Effect of the gesture on bystanders and Hagen, 2197–98 (2 strophes).
>
> Hagen speaks, 2199–2201 (3 strophes).
>
> Rüedeger nods in reply, general grief, 2202 (1 strophe).

Only one variation mitigates the severe regularity: at 2200.4 Hagen is interrupted by a one-line reply from Rüedeger. Hagen's speeches themselves show an identical division between the first and second strophes, as he makes a fresh start each time:

> "Ich stên in grôzen sorgen,"   sprach aber Hagene. (2194)
>
> "I am in great anxiety,"   Hagen went on.

> "Sô wê mir dirre mære,"   sprach aber Hagene. (2200)
>
> "Alas for news like this,"   Hagen went on.

Fresh introductions in the midst of speeches indicate gravity and emphasis. They are common, but here they also serve as a shaping device. Observe, too, the refrain of 2193 (*Belîbet eine wîle,/ vil edel Rüedegêr*), 2199 (*Nu lôn' iu got von himele,/ vil edel Rüedegêr*), and 2201 (*Nu lôn' ich iu der gâbe,/ vil edel Rüedegêr*); also 2195 (*sô den du hast vor hende,/ vil edel Rüedegêr*).

Even Volker, in a brief coda, maintains the high tone with his courtly service to Gotelint: he still wears the golden arm rings she gave him in Bechelaren. The irony is touching and mordant at once, as the fiddler's loyalty to his lady adds to her husband's burden.

This is, then, the outer structure of the great scene. It is symmetrical, simple, frontal, repetitive: a grave ostinato, serving as vehicle for the disclosure of issues and the exploration of inner states.[9] But strophe 2200 raises questions:

> "Sô wê mir dirre mære,"   sprach aber Hagene.
> "wir heten ander swære   sô vil ze tragene:
> sul wir mit friunden strîten,   daz sî got gekleit."
> dô sprach der marcgrâve: "daz ist mir inneclîchen leit."

> "Alas for news like this,"   Hagen went on.
> "We have such heavy troubles   to carry as it is.
> If we must fight our friends,   I protest that to God!"
> To that the margrave said: "That grieves me deep within."

The lines help to make symmetry, but they are abrasive in context. C omits them, and de Boor comments: "The more recent strophe (which is absent in C) disrupts the mood and context." Achim Masser has adduced two impressive arguments that 2200 is in fact out of place.[10] (1) Hagen's *Sô wê mir dirre mære* (alas for news like this) has no meaning here. What "news" does he refer to? (2) The four lines fit perfectly after strophe 2175, that is, as an alternative to 2176. Masser would have it that here and elsewhere alternate versions (strophes) are preserved side by side in the NL. They are residue and evidence, he thinks, of the fluctuating tradition. The strongest argument in this case is the fuzzy connection of 2200 with the rest of Hagen's speech. Or did the poet reach here for a free-floating variant to help build a formal order and accept some logical incongruence in the bargain? (I leave the question in abeyance for the moment; it will be taken up again below under ring composition.)

C makes changes—not enough to deface the scene's shape but enough to weaken some of its finer correspondences. (1) We already saw that strophe 2200 is omitted entirely, weakening the affinity to Hagen's first speech. (2) Hagen's remaining *sprach aber* is placed in the third strophe of the first speech instead of the second (C 2254). (3) The refrain *vil edel Rüedegêr* is loosened by omission at 2201 (C 2259). The changes are not easy to explain, although it is no surprise that they have to do with Hagen. Numbers (2) and (3) are probably no more than random variations. In strophe 2200 he might have wanted to expunge Hagen's pious *daz sî got gekleit*, but note that he lets 2199 (C 2257) stand. He also changed 2201.1 (*Nu lôn' iu got der gâbe*) to *Nu lôn' ich iu der gâbe* (also read by A). De Boor accepts it.

Ordered and repetitive composition of this sort is also frequent in Homer. The examples from *Iliad* 12 and 13 were mostly large structures, but we saw some smaller forms in *Iliad* 13 and scattered examples from other books of both the *Iliad* and the *Odyssey*. Here are two more cases from the *Odyssey* that are close in manner and scope to those from the NL.

In book 3 Nestor describes for Telemachos the Greeks' departure from Troy (130). One can imagine some of the problems facing the poet. There were many names and different fates. He would not have wanted merely to compile a list: "X did this, Y went there." This is not a major challenge, but failure to meet it would lead to a dull stretch of text. His solution is simple and elegant. Nestor bases everything on his personal experience and relates the departure as follows. After the fall of Troy, the Achaeans hold an assembly where the army falls into two opposing camps: (1) those following Menelaos who want to sail immediately, and (2) those siding with Agamemnon who remain to complete the sacrifices. The division of the army is emphatic and hostile. The force leaving with Menelaos sails to the island of Tenedos and there splits in half: some, under Odysseus, return to Agamemnon; the rest, with Menelaos, Nestor, and Diomedes, continue on their way. These last now divide again, as Diomedes and Nestor sail ahead in one squadron; Menelaos embarks a little later and overtakes them at Lesbos. Here they consider two possible routes home and choose one after a sign from the gods. Nestor and Diomedes remain as a pair and cross safely to home. Of the others, Nestor can report only from hearsay. The procedure is methodical and tidy, and of obvious convenience to the teller. Selection and distribution reduce a jumble of events to orderly stages with direction and even a modest story line.

In book 5 of the *Odyssey* the poet sets himself the task of describing Odysseus' fight for life against an angry sea. This scene of desperation and violence is reduced to a systematic order:[11]

1. Odysseus holds a monologue, 297–312.
2. A wave shatters his raft, 313–23.
3. He hangs onto the timbers, 324–32.
4. The goddess Ino comes to his rescue, 333–55.

Now this entire movement is repeated

1. Odysseus holds a second monologue (introduced with the same verse as the first), 356–64.
2. A wave shatters what is left of his raft, 365–70.
3. He floats on the timbers, 370–75.
4. The goddess Athena quiets the waves, 382.

Following all this Odysseus hold two more monologues, at 408–23 and 465–73. In both of them he weighs two alternatives, each of them bad. "If I swim too close to shore, I might be crushed in the surf; if I remain in deep water, I might be swept out to sea and fall prey to a monster." The second: "If I spend the night by the river, I might freeze to death; if I enter the thicket, I might be attacked by a wild animal." Between these two deliberations Odysseus is saved twice by Athena, as each time she puts a saving idea into his head. He *would* have been battered on the cliffs, but she inspires him to hang onto a rock until the wave flows by (425–29). But he is wrenched from his hold by the ebb of that same wave and again *would* have perished had she not given him the idea of swimming parallel to the beach until he finds smooth water. There are innumerable examples of such symmetrical composition in the *Iliad* and the *Odyssey* both.

Some final words on numbers in the NL. To repeat: arithmetical progressions reinforce emotional and rhetorical emphases inherent in the narrative. They are neither decorative nor abstract. They signal the very pulse of the story line. Consider Rüedeger's first audience with Kriemhilt. Their talk covers only twelve strophes and ends with nothing resolved. Kriemhilt adjourns the interview until the next morning with the promise of a decision.

In outline:

1. Kriemhilt opens by bidding Rüedeger speak his mind. (1 strophe)
2. He presents his case: Etzel wants to marry her. (2 strophes)
3. Kriemhilt demurs: her grief is too great, she could never give her love to another man. (1 strophe)
4. Rüedeger presses his argument: a new marriage would be the best cure for sorrow. Then he describes the immense power she would acquire. (4 strophes)
5. Kriemhilt remains unconvinced: the loss of Sivrit has filled her with too much pain. (1 strophe)
6. Now the other members of the delegation try to persuade her: she will be happy, and her servants will accompany her. (2 strophes)
7. Kriemhilt dismisses them without a commitment. (1 strophe)

The pattern is obvious and simple. Rüedeger pleads twice, then his delegation takes a turn. Their exhortations follow a curve of two strophes, then four (in the center), and then back to two. The numbers are neither indifferent nor accidental. They express a natural rhythm, the thrust and counter-thrust of persuasion and refusal. They mark the rise to the intensity of Rüedeger's central speech and the descent to separation. Nor is it by chance that in his central, four-strophe plea Rüedeger dwells on the power at stake. That is what will win her over and lead to the final catastrophe. Kriemhilt, on the other side, sits unmoved against the waves of entreaty, delivering an unchanging series of lapidary one-strophe rebuffs. The scene also needs to be visualized: Rüedeger and his train in their finery; Kriemhilt's attendants no less so; Kriemhilt herself in widow's black, with the plan of vengeance already taking shape in her mind. Appropriate intonation and delivery by the reciter will have conveyed the contrasts and pace of this splendid exchange to a listening audience. And all this is achieved with monolithic strophe groups.

Like most effective devices, it is used more than once. Earlier, in the 18th aventiure, Kriemhilt stood fast against the efforts of Sigmunt and his men to lead her back to Xanten. The same curve is used at half scale (1–2–1). Sigmunt appeals to her in one strophe (1084), then in two (1086–87), and finally his men again in one (1089). As in the first example, Kriemhilt holds herself to the clockwork of one-strophe refusals (1085, 1088, 1090). This is set in antithesis to the scene just before (1077–1083) where her family persuades her to stay. That was a scene of agitation and heat, with plenty of give and take and with speeches beginning and ending in fractions of strophes (e.g. 1077.4, 1078.3, 1079.3). With Sigmunt, there is nothing of the sort. All speech runover between strophes stops. They act instead as isolating blocks. Kriemhilt's farewell to her father-in-law is formal and cool, not a debate at all. The scene with her family showed a decision being made; here it is announced. The verse technique expresses that, and again skillful delivery will have emphasized the difference. The strophe thus reveals itself as a subtle and flexible instrument for the creation of scene dynamics.[12]

Questions to Hagen at the crossing of the Danube

At strophe 1577 Gernot demands to know why Hagen threw the priest overboard, but he has to wait until early in the next aventiure for a reply (1587). We look further and discover a whole series of unanswered questions reaching back to where Hagen delivers the raft to Gunther. The king notices blood and draws the obvious conclusion (1567), but for reasons that remain unexplained Hagen denies having killed anybody (1568):

> Gunther asks: "Where is the ferryman? Did you kill him?" Hagen denies it, 1567–68.
>
> Hagen throws the priest into the river. Gernot asks why. No reply, 1575–77.
>
> Hagen destroys the raft. Dancwart asks why. A partial answer: to prevent cowards from retreating, 1581–83.
>
> Hagen explains his act against the priest, 1587–89.
>
> Hagen tells how he slew the ferryman, 1591–92.

The chiasmus stands inside a still larger frame. The water witches described Else and Gelfrat to Hagen before he encountered the ferryman (1545), but there is no more word about the two Bavarian kings until 1592, where Hagen warns against them. Thus: Else and Gelfrat, the ferryman, the priest, and the destruction of the raft come in that order. Hagen explains them in reverse sequence *and all in the next aventiure.*

To put it this way makes the composition seem tighter than it really is, because the introduction and many details of the crossing are left out. But the outline shows the poet's attention to detail and his control of understated shape over a considerable distance.

What use does the structure serve? The fact that it spans two aventiuren gives the answer. The 25th is filled with disquiet and a sense of mystery: the bishop's warning (1508), Uote's dream (1509), Rumolt's alarm (1517); then the river in spate and the water witches, their deception of Hagen even after he seems to have them in his power, the disturbing name of the one (Siglint) and the growing certainty of ruin; then the menacing ferryman; finally crossing to the point of no return. The river is obstacle, angle-point, warning and symbolic boundary.[13] Only Hagen knows what the crossing means. His silence in the face of questions from Gunther and Gernot, and his incomplete reply to Dancwart, belong to all this.[14]

With aventiure 26 a new phase begins: practical measures, guidance, defense, and survival. The time for omens and foreboding is past. So Hagen explains, and they get on with their trek. The long structure arching the two aventiuren serves this strategy.[15]

Version C dilutes the effect by appending an exchange at the end between Hagen and the chaplain (C 1621–24) which closes with Gunther promising to make amends if they return alive. Squabbling and recriminations by the priest damage the scene's mystery and elevation, and this is more harmful than the blurring of its shape. Hoffmann (121) attributes C's additions to its zeal to denigrate Hagen. I am not persuaded of that here because, however badly the priest's complaints dimish the tone, Hagen's reply remains grand and implacable (C 1622):

> Des antwort im Hagen: "nu lât die red wesen.
> mir ist leit ûf mîne triuwe,   daz ir sît genesen
> hie vor mînen handen,   daz wizzet âne spot."

> Hagen replied to him: "Forget that talk of yours.
> I am sorry, by my faith,   that you escaped unhurt
> here from my hands,   I tell you that for sure."

C's addendum is ruinous because it extends the priest's role beyond its proper definition. Once he has survived the cast into the river, his doings become irrelevant. The prophecy of the water witches is confirmed, and Hagen proceeds to destroy the raft with them in mind.

Certainty of death lends his act a luminous depth: "non me oracula certum,/ sed mors certa facit." This is no tactical maneuver (although first explained as such), but affirmation of destiny.

A comparison with Lamprecht's *Alexander* (2642) shows what the chaplain adds to the scene as long as he is held to his pertinent function. Alexander leads his men across the Euphrates, then destroys the bridge they built and explains why (2669–78):

> daz tet ih alliz umbe daz,
> ob man uns jagete,
> daz wir neheinen trôst ne habeten
> heim zô unseme lande,
> sô gedâhte wir wol zen handen
> unde fuhten alse helede.
>
> wandiz ne wirt niemer gesehen,
> daz wir hinnen geflîhen.
> all hie wil ih ê sterben
> oder sige irwerben.

> I did that for just this reason:
> Should we be pursued,
> that we might have no hope
> of return to our homeland,
> and so would remember our might
> and fight like warriors.
>
> No one, in fact, will ever see
> us flee from here.
> It is my intent rather to die in this place
> or win victory.

The NL turns a strategem into high character portrayal, an incentive to fight into acceptance of death. C's additions do not wipe that out altogether, but they undermine it with their tedious concern for the aftermath of Hagen's test.[16]

Correlation

ONE OF HOMER'S favorite devices is to associate things by means of formal repetition. Parallelism draws likes together and enriches the content of both. We saw that principle at work in books 11 and 12 of the *Iliad*, and also in book 6 where Schadewaldt calls it "contrapost." It is this kind of composition in the NL that I shall examine under the heading "correlation." My analysis will augment Nagel's exposition of "architectonic tendencies" and the chapter on "architectonics" in his more recent book.[1] For him, "parallels" and "arches" are the main devices under this rubric. Comparing, for example, the wooings of Kriemhilt and Prünhilt, and the two fatal invitations to festivals, he asserts that these and many other parallel events are set in deliberate correspondence and causal nexus. Indeed, the two halves of the poem comprise a mirrored diptych:

> There is in the first place a striking parallelism of events in the two halves of the poem, a sequence of five identical stages: 1. courtship with successful results, 2. intermission, with apparent stabilization and consolidation of relationships, also separation of the antagonists, 3. invitation, 4. festival, 5. catastrophe. As this outline shows on the large scale, paired correspondences are based on antithesis. Indeed, contrast reveals itself as a fundamental architectural principle of the poem.[2]

Nagel also assembles an interesting group of motif-doublets scattered through the poem, many of which correspond antithetically.

Friedrich Neumann has objected to this approach on the grounds that it imposes an artificial construction on the poem. He sees in Nagel's system something woven together from separate strands that in the NL itself have no live connection with each other. Thus, even though Nagel's patterns derive from real ingredients of the text, Neu-

mann denies that they stand in genuine interdependence. He charges
that Nagel offers a contrived assemblage, something culled by a process foreign to our actual experience of the poetry and also something
suspiciously modern:"Even in the case of Nagel's many-sided study
I think one can discover that it transforms the Nibelungenlied into a
conglomerate soaring free of the written text, whereby it begins to
resemble modern poetry".[3] The disagreement is thus over critical
method, and it goes so deep that most people will pick sides at the
start and remain there for the duration. Advances by either school
will be recognized by the other only to the extent that these can be
assimilated into its own system. Still some mediation might be possible if we stay with single episodes and short passages (as in the
preceding chapters), where the relation between form and meaning
is most direct. If techniques of design can be demonstrated over the
short range, this might serve as a useful base from which to ponder
their wider application.

The journey to Isenstein

To begin with a simple example, the NL likes to connect arrivals and
departures with related particulars. Thus certain details map the journey to Isenstein. As the expedition leaves Wormez, horses are led out
and women watch from the windows (376.3–377.1):

> ir ross hiez man in ziehen;   si wolden rîten dan.
> dâ wart von scœnen frouwen   vil michel weinen getân.
>
> Dô stuonden in den venstern   diu minneclîchen kint.

> The steeds were ordered led out for them;   they wished to ride from
>   there.
> At that there was great weeping   by the ladies fair.

> And then in the windows   the lovely damsels took their stand.

Under these auspices they sail away down the Rhine. Upon their
approach to Prünhilt's country lands and fortresses become visible,
then figures on the ramparts and many lovely ladies at the windows
(389.2–3):

dô sah der künec stân
oben in den venstern   vil manege sccene meit.

Then the king saw standing
high up in the windows   full many a beautiful maiden.

The detail serves as a pictorial bracket joining the beginning and end of their journey. But now simple "watching" turns into something else. As it shifts to the other side, it becomes a pointer and carries weight. After Sivrit helps Gunther single out his intended from the rest, Prünhilt orders her women to quit their posts and not let themselves be stared at by strangers (394.1–3):

Dô hiez diu küniginne   ûz den venstern gân
ir hêrlîche mägede.   sin' solden dâ niht stân
den vremden an ze sehene.

Then the queen gave orders   to her splendid retinue
to go back from the windows.   They should not tarry there
for strangers to stare at.

This command sets the stage for what comes next: the watchers become the watched. Having left to adorn themselves, the ladies return as silent and earnest watchers in their own right. Sivrit leads a horse onto land (the act of a vassal), and the women see it (396.3):

daz sâhen durch diu venster   diu wætlîchen wîp.

The glorious women   saw that through the windows.

He holds the beast steady for Gunther to mount, and that is taken in as well (398.4):

daz sâhen durch diu venster   die vrouwen schœn' unde hêr.

The fair, exalted ladies   saw that through the windows.

When they ride to the castle in splendor, Prünhilt sees that, too (401.4):

daz sach allez Prünhilt,   diu vil hêrlîche meit.

Prünhilt saw all of that,   the very splendid maiden.

This insistent scrutiny puts a seal of accomplishment on the deception. The men act it out, the women "see" and take it for fact. The deceit takes, and the acts of observation, restrained and understated, become a solemn refrain marking the beginning of evils. Similar details at departure and arrival are used with economy and weight, as the tearful sentiment of the first mutates into the tragic finality of the second.

Notice that this bracket spans two aventiuren. A concurrent litany of questions and answers also joins them. Gunther asks and Sivrit replies:[4]

1. Women at the windows, the boat sails away, 377.1–3.
2. Gunther asks: "Who will guide the ship?" 377.4.
3. Sivrit replies: he will take charge, 378.1–3.

   The journey, 378.4–381.

1. Arrival at Isenstein, 382.
2. Gunther sees towers and lands and asks: Whose are they?" 383.
3. Sivrit replies: "This is Prünhilt's country." 384.

   Sivrit explains the ruse, 385–388.

1. They sail in close and see women at the windows, 389.
2. Gunther asks: "Who are they?" 390.
3. Sivrit helps him single out the queen, 391.

The refrain steers us from Wormez to the first view of Prünhilt's country, then to a view in close as figures become visible on the ramparts: a fine optical effect. As usual, the repetitions serve a purpose. The string of questions confirms Sivrit as leader and Gunther as follower, and a singularly passive one at that.*This is placed right before the exchange of roles.* One can scarcely imagine a wooer of Prünhilt less competent to the task than Gunther or a more convoluted and treacherous relation than Sivrit enters upon with the two women.

Arrival in Etzelnburg

Women at the windows marking the passage from friends and security to a hostile place: the trope repeats itself as the Burgonden leave Bechelaren and approach their destination.[5] The departure is at once emotional and foreboding as the leaders pass in review: Gunther receives armor, Gernot the sword that will slay the giver, Hagen the shield that Rüedeger will later replace, Dancwart clothing, and Volker the arm rings. These gifts consummate the idyll at Bechelaren and look forward to the catastrophe at the end.

> Dô wurden allenthalben   diu venster ûf getân.
>
> Windows were opened   then on every side.

Departure is taken with observance at the windows and the weeping of women. Under these familiar auspices the guests set out on the last stage of their journey while the poet hints darkly at sorrows to come. Waiting for them is Kriemhilt (1716.1):

> Kriemhilt diu vrouwe   in ein venster stuont.
>
> Kriemhilt the queen   stood at a window.

The contrapost is abrupt and powerful. And there is more. After the heartfelt generosity of Rüedeger, establishing as it does the character of the man and creating the ethical dilemma still awaiting him, Kriemhilt ponders gifts of her own and of another kind (1717):

> swer nemen welle golt,
> der gedenke mîner leide,   und wil im immer wesen holt.
>
> Whoever wants to take my gold,
> let him remember my grief,   and I shall favor him forever.

C removes the detail of Kriemhilt at the window, thereby erasing the effect. Strophe 1717 (C 1756) is totally recast and another (C 1757) added. Her menace is now directed against one person alone (Hagen), and the motive of revenge predominates. The changes are characteristic of C. They belong to the "systematic softenings of his Kriemhilt portrait."[6] This is an excellent example of C's indifference to dramatic effect in favor of its own preoccupations.

Sivrit's challenge at Wormez

Sivrit's challenge to Gunther makes for difficult interpretation. The abruptness of it catches us off guard, its vague withdrawal no less. We are also surprised by the Burgonden's passivity after Sigmunt's

predictions about them.[7] The scene thus lacks motivation and verisimilitude. Different approaches are taken. The audience's acquain-
tance with such things will have reduced the surprise, for decisions
of war and peace through duels was an ancient Germanic tradition.[8]
Sudden challenges from strangers at court are also familiar from the
Arthurian romances[9]. Heusler's observations are fundamental:

> We will be less surprised . . . at such sudden changes in behavior if
> we keep in mind that medieval storytellers compose differently from
> Ibsen. They do not start with a firm notion of a person's character
> and derive everything that is said and done, as consistently as pos-
> sible, from that. For them the primary thing is the ACTION, the large
> and small strands of the story. They try to distribute these among
> appropriate actors, who are in turn either traditional or invented for
> the occasion. The role mints the character.[10]

Nagel has more recently taken a different approach and argued for
an unbroken development from the scenes in Xanten to the challenge
at Wormez, and this in Sivrit's personality as well as the power question.[11] But despite the ingenuity with which Nagel presses his case,
I remain convinced that the search for consistent motivation in the
NL is doomed to failure and is indeed at odds with the nature of its
composition. Wachinger has assembled evidence and arguments for
this that are, I think, final.[12] Mergell, using still another method,
removes the conflict of persons to another plane. He finds that Sivrit's
very presence in Wormez—not to mention his challenge—brings to
light a fundamental conflict between two worlds. Sivrit wants, and
represents, the direct correlation between strength and status (one
thinks of Sarpedon's excursus on performance and privilege in *Iliad*
12). Set against him is a rule grown hereditary, where the dependence
of position on competence has grown dim.[13] This is attractive interpretation because it bypasses overclose reconstruction of Sivrit's own
thoughts and lends him a figurative dimension. The dislocation in
his position in the Burgundian court becomes a major theme, sustained through the Saxon war, the courtship of Prünhilt, and indeed
his very murder. It lies at the heart of the catastrophe and flashes out
in even smaller encounters.

   It is also useful to consider the scene's movement and context. It
explodes at the start and then descends to mutual accommodation in
three stages. (1) Gunther makes polite inquiry into the reasons for the

visit, and Sivrit lets fly with his challenge (106). One strophe records the Burgonden's amazement and a second Gunther's flaccid reply (111, 112). Sivrit repeats and enlarges: let the winner rule both their kingdoms. Here Gernot intervenes (115): they are rightful lords and will enter upon no such wager.[14] The hardest clash comes right here between the two kings. These ten strophes contain Sivrit's longest and most belligerent speeches. Gernot is silent until the end, but then he begins to assert himself. (2) Next in line is Ortwin, unintimidated but dismissed with contempt (116–18). To his credit, he remains uncowed (119), but Gernot brings him to silence with a plea for reconciliation. (3) Hagen now makes a feeble entrance, wishing none of this had ever happened (121). That stirs Sivrit to another outburst (122), but here Gernot assumes control. He forbids more contention (123), calls for peace (124), holds the Burgonden to silence one last time (125.4), calms the challenger down and bids him formal welcome (126). With that the crisis is past. All three clashes feature Gernot as peacemaker, hence a natural curve from Gunther through Ortwin and Hagen, as Sivrit's aggression slowly diminishes and Gernot's efforts become more insistent and successful. By strophe 123 he has become the dominant figure and stands out as the hero on the Burgundian side.

We discover, then, a finely spun sequence with a distinct pace and shifting momentum. It also stands in correlation with events at the start of the next aventiure. When envoys arrive from Denmark and Saxony carrying a message of war, the council that follows is staged as a companion piece to Sivrit's challenge just before. We note the following: (1) Gunther meets this declaration with no more courage than he did the last (147); (2) as before, voices are raised both in resistance (150) and caution (151); (3) Sivrit carries the day with his advice to stand firm and with his offer to take charge.

Little of this will seem remarkable at first glance. Indeed we seem to have before us no more than a typical scene. But observe how both caution and despite acquire a different value. In the first scene hard resistance comes only from Ortwin, a reckless youth who presumes above his station and beyond his strength. He is dismissed with derision. Hagen's hand wringing only makes matters worse. Gernot, urging caution and accommodation, emerges as the only one standing between the Burgonden and annihilation.

But the new challenge calls for a different response. Now it is Gernot who states his defiance in a ringing pronouncement (150):

"Daz wer et wir mit swerten,"   sô sprach Gêrnôt.
"da sterbent wan die veigen: die lâzen ligen tôt.
dar umb ich niht vergezzen   mac der êren mîn.
die unsern vîande   suln uns willekomen sîn."

"Yea, let us resist that with steel,"   thus spake Gernot.
"Only those so fated die;   let them lie dead.
I cannot forget my honor   because of all of that.
Let our enemies   consider themselves welcome."

Hagen, urging caution (151), comes off as badly as before, while Sivrit shows the same temper as Gernot.

Here, then, is an ingenious and instructive interplay on the themes of challenge and reconciliation, reason and bravado, resistance and compromise. In the first, Gernot's diplomacy is the voice of wisdom, while Ortwin is given over to mindless anger. But in the second, Hagen's temporizing is out of place. Gernot and Sivrit show the proper response. Expression and details correspond. Compare Ortwin at 117 and Sivrit at 160:

Ob ir und iuwer bruoder   hetet niht die wer,
und ob er danne fuorte   ein ganzez küneges her,
ich trûte wol erstrîten,   daz der küene man
diz starkez übermüeten   von wâren schulden müesse lân.

If you and your brothers   had no defensive force,
and even if he brought   a whole king's army with him,
I'm sure that I could force it,   that this bold man
would have to drop, and for good reason,   his mighty insolence.

Swenne iuwer starken vîende   z'ir helfe möhten hân
drîzec tûsent degene,   sô wold' ich si bestân,
und het ich niwan tûsent.

If your powerful enemies   should have on their side
thirty thousand fighters,   I would face them still,
and had I only a thousand.

The first is sound and fury, the second a boast we take seriously. Sivrit's own assurance never wavers:

118   ich bin ein künec rîche,   sô bistu küneges man.
jane dörften mich dîn zwelve   mit strîte nimmer bestân.

I am a mighty king,   as you are a king's vassal.
Listen, twelve like you   could never stand up to me in combat.

161 Sô heizet mir gewinnen   tûsent iuwer man,
   sît daz ich der mînen   bî mir niht enhân
   niwan zwelf recken;   sô wer ich iuwer lant.[15]

   So order mustered a thousand   of your men for my command,
   since I have no more   than twelve bold adventurers
   of my own with me here;   thus I shall defend your lands.

Except for Gernot, the Burgonden cut poor figures (Giselher is con-
spicuously absent). Future alignments are already in place as Gunther,
Hagen, and Ortwin, the later conspirators, stand together. Gunther
is as nonplussed at the second challenge as at the first. But the one
who threatened to strip him of everything now guarantees his throne
(174):

   belîbet bî den vrouwen,   und traget hôhen muot.
   ich trouwe iu wol behüeten   beidiu êre unde guot.

   Stay with the royal ladies,   and hold your spirits high.
   I'm sure that I'll defend,   both your honor and possessions.

Variation, reversal, contrast: the two episodes trace Sivrit's rise to
ascendency and examine challenge and response in changing circumstances. They also demonstrate the awesome power of *minne*, for it
is this that has changed Sivrit from dethroner to court champion. The
two scenes do indeed portray character, but only in block letters: force
and weakness, courage and timidity, discretion and bluster. The dominant perspective remains Sivrit's fall into the bondage of *minne*, with
motivation concentrated into that single line. Hence his declaration
of war on the Burgonden; also his stay and defense of them. The
correlation of the two scenes is built on that.

   This single motivation remains in the sequel and continues to violate
consistency. When the army disbands after the Saxon war, Sivrit re-
quests permission (!) to return home (258). This is surprising. What
of Kriemhilt? Why leave now? In fact he does remain only because
of her (260):

   Durch der scœnen willen   gedâht er noch bestân.

   Because of the lovely maiden   he turned his thoughts to staying.

In short, his desire to leave the palace occurs only to be overcome by
his reason for staying. And the same happens again at the close of

the next aventiure. When the festival ends, Sivrit plans to depart with
the rest (320), even though his fondest hopes have just been realized
with daily attendance of the princess. But it is the fatal power of *minne*
that interests the poet, not believable grounds for Sivrit's intent. He
is again persuaded to abide, and to his own ruin (324):

> Durch ir unmâzen scœne   der herre dâ beleip.
>
> Because of her extravagant beauty   the lord remained there.

These two attempted departures by Sivrit at the end of aventiuren 4
and 5 are classic examples of the NL's emphasis on theme and characterization by scene at the expense of consistency and linear
motivation.

Rüedeger and Wolfhart

Beginning with aventiure 35, the Burgonden are assaulted in waves:
Irinc (35), the fire (36), Rüedeger (37), Wolfhart (38), and finally Dietrich (39). Each attack starts with exchanges between assailants and
the beseiged. Together they comprise an obvious series. Rüedeger
and Wolfhart are drawn together and set in antithesis.

Aventiure 38, where Wolfhart falls, describes the annihilation of
Dietrich's men, with its beginning and end marked by announcement
of disaster and by lamentation. At the start, Dietrich hears cries of
grief from the palace. Helpfrich is dispatched and reports back that
Rüedeger is slain. But that message is too bad to be believed, and so
Hildebrant is sent to find out for sure. Wolfhart persuades him to arm
himself, and the rest do the same:

> Dô garte sich der wîse   durch des tumben rât.
>
> Then the veteran armed himself   at the advice of one unseasoned.

All but Hildebrant perish in the melée. At the close, Dietrich receives
word a second time: Rüedeger has fallen indeed, and all his own men
too. The aventiure is thus framed by bad news and outcry. Wolfhart
is the chief casualty on the one side, Giselher on the other.

Rüedeger engaged the Burgonden under the compulsion of social
and ethical imperatives, with respect—even love—for his adversaries,

and in despair. Wolfhart belongs to a different world. With him the fight returns to the level of insult and taunt as heated tempers overturn the negotiations for Rüedeger's corpse. His brief and disastrous step into the limelight has been carefully prepared. When he volunteered to investigate the wailing at the start of the 38th aventiure Dietrich refused, with good reason (2240):

> Dô sprach der herre Dietrich: "swa man zornes sich versiht,
> ob ungefüegiu vrâge   danne dâ geschiht,
> daz betrüebet lîhte   recken ir muot.
> jane wil ich niht, Wolfhart,   daz ir die vrâge gein in tuot.[16]

> Then master Dietrich answered: "Where one expects to encounter anger,
> because of unruly questions   it then happens
> that warriors' tempers   quickly turn grim.
> Wolfhart, I absolutely do not want you   to put the question to them."

But the next time around Wolfhart's folly carries the day. He had entered on a discordant note at his first appearance (1993, also there in opposition to Volker and in association with Dietrich), where he almost upset his master's efforts to remove Kriemhilt and the others from the hall:

> "Wie vlêhet ir sô schiere?"   sprach dô Wolfhart.
> "ja hât der videlære   die tür nie sô verspart,
> wir entsliezen si sô wîte,   daz wir dar für gân."

> "Why are you so quick to beg?"   spake Wolfhart then.
> "There is no way the fiddler   has barred the door so fast
> that we cannot open it wide enough   for us to go out through it."

Compare his last outburst at 2265:

> "Wie lange suln wir vlêgen?"   sprach Wolfhart der degen.

> "How long shall we plead?"   spake Wolfhart the warrior.

Why so much care expended on a character of essentially no consequence? He is prepared and elevated for one appearance in contrapost with Rüedeger. Their aristeiai run parallel. Each inflicts heavy losses on the Burgonden, thereby provoking a counterattack from his final opponent (Gernot, 2216; Giselher, 2293: these are of course a pair as well). Each kills that final enemy and dies himself in the process, and in similar order of battle: one man receives the death blow, then slays the other before giving up his spirit (2219, 2296). And their deaths make the final join as Wolfhart perishes trying to recover Rüedeger's corpse.

Two poles of heroic temper: each stands close to Dietrich, and together they draw him into the fray, climax, and end of the story (2326):

> Dô sprach von Tronege Hagene: "ich sehe dort her gân
> den herren Dietrîchen,   der wil uns bestân."

> Then spake Hagen of Tronege   "I see coming here
> Lord Dietrich;   it is his intent to face us."

This reaches back to the onset under Wolfhart (2253):

> Dô sprach der videlære: "Ich sihe dort her gân
> sô rehte vîentlîche   die Dietrîches man,
> gewâfent under helme: sie wellent uns bestân."

> Then spake the fiddler: "I see coming here
> in right hostile manner   Dietrich's men,
> armed and with their helmets on;   it is their intent to face us."

From here another link connects to Rüedeger's march on the hall (2170):

> Dô sah man Rüedegêren   under helme gân.
> ez truogen swert diu scharpfen   die Rüedegêres man,
> dar zuo vor ir handen   die liehten schilde breit.
> daz sach der videlære: ez was im grœzlîche leit.

> Then they saw Rüedeger   coming with his helmet on.
> They carried sharpened swords,   those men of Rüedeger,
> and also in their hands   their shields bright and wide.
> The fiddler saw it: great was his regret.

Parallel sequences, similar details, antipodal personalities. The poet sets them side by side, to our intense disquiet, as different types of the heroic personality and fate, one old and Germanic, the other modern and Christian. Rüedeger is swept by emotional and ethical

crosscurrents, lives out a high dilemma, and dies in redemptive conflict—"endures," as Wapnewski puts it, "a germanic destiny but as a
Christian character."[17] Wolfhart, the one-dimensional warrior fired
only by defiance and pride, closes his eyes in peace. He has lived the
old code to the full and takes its reward (2302):

> Unde ob mich mîne mâge   nach tôde wellen klagen,
> den næhsten und den besten   den sult ir von mir sagen,
> daz si nâch mir niht weinen;   daz ist âne nôt.
> vor eines küneges handen   lige ich hie hêrlîchen tôt.

> And if my kinsmen want   to lament me for my death,
> to the closest and the best,   tell them this from me,
> that they should not weep for me;   for that there is no need.
> Slain at the hands of a king   I lie here dead in glory.

der hürnîne Sîvrit

Sivrit's invulnerability sits uneasily in the NL. It is never mentioned
until the end of the 14th aventiure (875), and then so indirectly ("the
story") that exact knowledge of it by the audience must be assumed.
Hagen's discovery of the defective place brings deep and ineradicable
discrepancies with it. Kriemhilt is persuaded to sew a marker over
the spot on his battle dress. But Sivrit is murdered during the hunt
when he is wearing a different set of clothes (described in detail
starting at 951). As de Boor puts it (on strophe 915): "The little silk
cross is thus sewn on a garment that is not even present at the decisive
moment."[18]

The poet thus paid a high price for the motif. What did he get in
return? First of all, the bogus war (the excuse for sewing on the
marker) draws the end of Sivrit's career at Wormez together with the
beginning and lays bare the injustice done to him. This new invasion
is just like the first when he repelled the Saxons and Danes. Even
the enemies are the same. In fact, the entire course of events is repeated: Sivrit finds Gunther deep in care(883; compare 153; there is
something intolerably humiliating in Gunther's mimicry of his own
incompetence); questions him and learns the cause (883; compare 156);
offers to take charge of defense (884; compare 157). None of this is
to be dismissed as formular detritus. The ironies are too strong and
pertinent.

But the true value of the *lintrachen* story is realized in the depiction of Kriemhilt's mistake. This brings a new dimension to her fatal role in Sivrit's life. It is a doubling of the error she made with Prünhilt, and this time with the best of intentions. Two correlated scenes show it happen, the consecutive interviews with Hagen and Sivrit, set respectively at the end of the 15th aventiure and the start of the 16th.

The first (891) is one of the poem's finest psychological studies, but its subtlety has been strangely overlooked. Heusler (73) described Kriemhilt's confidence in Hagen as "unsuspecting," and de Boor follows suit with his belief in her "blind trust" in the man: "For him [the poet] kinship ties are a decisive factor in life. The same is true for his character Kriemhild. This is the source of Kriemhild's blind trust in Hagen before Siegfried's murder."[19] Kinship ties do indeed carry the day for Kriemhilt, but only over half-understood suspicion and against a nagging doubt somewhere in the deeper levels of her mind. Something—never articulated, never faced—makes her distrustful. That is why she reminds Hagen of Sivrit's services to her family (892), apologizes for the injury to Prünhilt (893), and describes the punishment meted out by her husband (894—a shocking glance behind the courtly facade). She comes back repeatedly to the subjects of kinship and *triuwe*:

898 Si sprach: "du bist mîn mâc,   sô bin ich der dîn.
ich bevilhe dir mit triuwen   den holden wine mîn."

She spake: "you are my kinsman,   likewise I am yours.
I commend my loving dearest   in loyal trust to you."[20]

901 Ich melde iz ûf genâde,   vil lieber vriunt, dir,
daz du dîne triuwe   behaltest ane mir.
dâ man dâ mac verhouwen   den mînen lieben man,
daz lâz ich dich hœren;   deist ûf genâde getân.

With trust in your good will,   I'll reveal it to you, dear friend,
that you may keep your faith   in respect to me.
I will now let you hear   where one can strike a mortal blow
against my beloved husband: this is done with trust in your good will.

ûf genâde: "with reliance on your good will." The double emphasis betrays unease. She is, in fact, throwing herself on Hagen's mercy, hoping that appeals to family and ethics will carry the day. Here is no innocent confidence in blood ties, but misgivings and premonition, overcome for now with hope and an effort of the will but reasserting themselves in her last talk with Sivrit.[21] It is that instinctive distrust here which explains her dread of a simple hunt there (her dream wells from the same premonition), and also why she will know instantly who is lying dead outside her door and also who murdered him. Here is a splendid encounter: Kriemhilt wrestling with guilt and disquiet, on the defensive, struggling to suppress the inner voices of alarm, finally throwing herself on the mercy of her worst enemy. Against her stands Hagen, cunning and implacable.

This emotional turbulence is held in check by the scene's stated tempo. It divides into two movements, the first (892–97) setting the stage and leading to Hagen's question: how can Sivrit be protected? In the second, Kriemhilt reveals the secret (898–905). In both, a series of one-strophe exchanges is introduced by a longer appeal from the queen:

I. Kriemhilt, 892–894 (3 strophes)
   Hagen, 895 (1 strophe)
   Kriemhilt, 896 (1 strophe)
   Hagen, 897 (1 strophe)

II. Kriemhilt, 898–902 (3 strophes)
   Hagen, 903 (1 strophe
   Kriemhilt, 904 (1 strophe)
   Hagen, 905 (1 strophe)

Kriemhilt's speech at the start of II has a distinct shape of its own:

898, appeal to trust, request for help

899, first part of the *lintrachen* story

900–01, her fears, appeal to trust

902, end of the *lintrachen* story, revelation of the spot

As usual, form has meaning. The secret comes out slowly and only at the last, bolstered by two sets of appeals that it not be used against Sivrit.

The leave taking of husband and wife at the start of the next aventiure (918) is set as a companion piece. Again Kriemhilt struggles with inner conflict and fear, her anxiety in contrast to Sivrit's impervious optimism. She fears for him but dares not tell what Hagen has already learned (920.1). She relates her dream but fails to convince him of secret grudges because a guilty conscience keeps the strongest reason unspoken. The dark connection with Hagen drives a wedge between husband and wife. Secrets betrayed and withheld in the two encounters comprise Kriemhilt's error.[22]

All this paints a compelling portrait of the wife delivering her husband into the hands of his enemies. It also establishes a tense contrapost between the two meetings: Hagen and Sivrit, with Kriemhilt at the center. The motif of invulnerability is built into the story at this high level.

Scene correlation in the NL is complex and understated. It is comparable to Homer's and represents an advanced development of the technique. Other evidence of the late stage of this art is the pairing across aventiuren. Observance at the windows and the litany of questions and answers binds aventiuren 6 and 7; the two challenges to Gunther are distributed over 3 and 4; Kriemhilt's encounters with Hagen and Sivrit come near the end of 15 and start of 16; Rüedeger and Wolfhart dominate 37 and 38. Some comparisons with Lamprecht and Veldeke, and then several more with *Kudrun* and Wolfram, will confirm this perspective.

Lamprecht sets Alexander's expedition against Paradise in the form of a lesson with two rigidly corresponding halves. He has conquered the world and all nations serve him, but these accomplishments grow mean in his sight. Why should heaven not also pay him tribute? (6605–21)

    A.   Alexander asks his advisers: should he make an assault on Paradise? (6622–30).

        1. The old and wise say no, 6631–39.
        2. The young and foolish say yes, 6640–66.

      He follows the unwise advice. With much toil and misery to themselves, they march across country, sail up the Euphrates, and arrive at Paradise. An old man at the gate warns Alexander against his presumption and gives him a magic stone.

    B.   Alexander asks his advisers again: what should he do?

        1. The old and wise say go home, 6959–65.
        2. The young and foolish say continue the attack, 6966–86.

      He follows the advice of the wise and sails away.

Smaller correspondences reinforce the reciprocity. Each time (A1, B1) the advice of the wise is related indirectly while the foolish are given direct speech. Each time the foolish receive exactly three times the lines of the wise: 27 to 9 in the first instance, 21 to 7 in the second. The first council is introduced with a description of Alexander's arrogance (6613):

> des ne dûhte ime allis niht genûc.
> sîn hôhmût in dar zû trûc,
> daz er sih hîz wîsen
> gegen den paradîse.

> That seemed to him by no means enough.
> His insolence took him so far,
> that he sought directions
> for an assault on Paradise.

The second follows the gatekeeper's sobering advice on the subject of human frailty (6919):

> und ob er welle genesen,
> sô sal er ôtmûte wesen
> . . .
> ein man ist als ein ander
> beide fleisc unde bein.

> And if he wanted to avoid evil,
> then he should have a humble spirit.
> . . .
> One man is like another,
> both flesh and bone.

The point is driven home with fixed oppositions: old-young, wise-foolish, good advice and bad, pride and humility. Structures of the sort are rare for Lamprecht. This one is rectilinear, frontal, and didactic.

Veldeke builds associations more frequently, but usually with the same conspicuous pairing and on a large scale. Thus Pallas and Camilla are held up for comparison: both perishing in early youth, one lamented by Turnus, the other by Aeneas (8021,9321), with full description of the corpses' transfer to their homelands, burials, and monuments (8105, 9369). Strong verbal ties will reveal themselves easily upon examination. Or, again, Aeneas and Lavinia fall in love in two answering scenes: Lavinia, struck by Venus' arrow (10,031), holds a long monologue on the subject of her passion (10,064) and can neither eat nor sleep for the pangs of *minne* (10,451). Aeneas is also pierced by love's arrow, this time from the bow of Amor (10,982); he, too, can neither eat nor sleep (10,996) and ponders his condition in a long speech to himself (11,117). Veldeke is more alive to the possibilities of the device than Lamprecht, but he is still far removed from the plasticity and fine shading of the NL. Still the comparison is useful to show the younger poem's sophistication in its handling of traditional motifs and narrative formulas. It also shows—and I shall return to the point—that the devices in question are not the exclusive property of heroic epic.

The *Kudrun* epic allows still closer and more useful comparison. This work, dating most likely from the fourth decade of the thirteenth century (about forty years after the NL),[23] traces its descent from a line closer to the NL's own, even though lying farther removed from Germanic sources and spirit. Although it was certainly not orally composed, it is heavily formular and deals in repetition, stereotyped action patterns, and elaborate parallelisms. Its conventional style has been thoroughly analyzed by Hinrich Siefkin. *Kudrun* swarms with schemata like "Dispatch and Reception of Envoys," "Reception in the Women's Quarters," "The Court Festival," "The Hero's Growth to Maturity." One main pattern underlies all the rest: "The Courting Expedition." Conventional details predominate: the maiden is of extraordinary beauty; she is of equal birth to the king who tries to win her; she lives far away, often across the sea; the king decides he will have her as his bride or no other.[24] It is to be expected that the girl's father will refuse the suit. This will be followed by abduction, pursuit, and fighting, with varied consequences. Much of this is familiar from the NL, but thematic similarities between the two works remain almost entirely on the surface. The *Kudrun* epic is inferior to its great predecessor in its ability to infuse convention with life.[25]

The main courtship story is Kudrun's own. She is abducted to Normandy by Hartmuot, then made to perform menial tasks for refusing to marry him. Among these is washing laundry on the beach. She and a faithful maid labor at this for six and a half years. Then one day an angel appears to them at the shore in the form of a bird, bringing news of impending rescue. The audience proceeds in two stages of three questions apiece.[26] Questions and answers occupy one strophe each. The two sets of queries are separated by a short intermezzo, in which the angel wants to be on his way but then consents to give more information. In outline:

A. 1. Is Hilde alive? (1171)
        Hilden dîne muoter   hân ich gesunt gesehen. As for your mother Hilde,
        I saw her in good health. She is sending an army. (1172)

    2. Are Ortwin and Herwic alive? (1173)
        die sint wol gesunt. They are in good health. They are on their way
        over the sea. (1174)

    3. Are Irolt and Morunc coming here? (1175)
        die hân ich gesehen. I have seen them. If they arrive there will be a
        great fight. (1176)

B. 1. Will Horant come here? (1180)
        Dir kumt von Tenemarke   Hôrant der neve dîn. Horant your nephew
        is coming to you from Denmark. (1181)

    2. Is Wate coming? And Fruote? (1182)
        dir kumt in ditze lant   Wate von den Stürmen. Wate from Stürmen is
        coming to this country. Fruote is coming too. (1183)

    3. When shall I see messengers from Hilde? (1184)
        dir gêt vreude zuo. Joy is coming to you. You will see them early
        tomorrow. (1185)

Smaller correspondences fill in the rounded shape still more. Kudrun's questions start and end with Hilde. Promise of happy news stands at the beginning and close (1169.2 and 1185.1). A1 and B1 show a question about one person, A2–3 and B2–3 about two. Compare 1171.1 and 1178.3, 1167.4 and 1179.4, and also A2 and B2:

> die sah ich in den ünden   ûf des meres muoder.
> die ellenhaften degene   zugen vil gelîche an einem ruoder.
>
> I saw them on the waves   on the surface of the sea.
> the mighty warriors   were pulling together on a single oar.

> der hât in sîner hant
> ein starkez stierruoder   in einem kiel bî Fruoten.
>
> He has in his hand
> a strong steering oar   in a ship with Fruote.

This is the style under discussion in the *Iliad* and the NL from the start. The symmetry is as rigorous and sustained as any. But it does

not point beyond itself: there is no internal movement, no emotional
or dramatic rhythm. The list of questions and answers leads only to
a complete report as Kudrun learns about everybody who concerns
her most. This gives the exchange a static regularity that blunts the
edge of the moment's natural joy. The same manner betrays itself in
the series of persons (Ortrun, Hildeburc, Hartmuot) presented to
Hilde at 1579 in reconciliation or reunion and again in Kudrun's marriage arrangements, one after the other, at 1617 (Ortwin–Ortrun, Hartmuot–Hildeburc). The NL and *Kudrun* use the same tools; execution
separates them.

Many incidents in *Kudrun* run parallel. Sometimes this means nothing, but sometimes there is correlation. This can occur in short com-
pass, for example in the paired combats between Hartmuot and Ortwin
at 1403 or Ludewic and Herwic at 1430. Personal ties and oppositions
make these into appropriate matchups. Other reciprocities are drawn
at long distance, such as the associated wooings of Hetel and Hartmuot, with pursuit by the maiden's father ending in combat. Much
of this is sheer formula, but associations still emerge. Hagen's pursuit
of Hetel and Hetel's chase after Hartmuot years later for the sake of
his own daughter share a heavy accumulation of similar details and
language, but end differently.[27] Hagen is reconciled with the abductors
but Hetel falls attacking them.[28] The concurrence of the two stories
continues even in the similar narration of nonequivalent parts. Thus
Hetel's arrangements for his courtship of Hilde (260) are coordinated
with Hilde's plans later to rescue Kudrun (941, 1072).[29] Here is a long-
range parallelism spanning the epic. But whether over short or long
range, structures and correspondences in *Kudrun* remain by and large
at the level of formula, minimally differentiated and without the re-
sponsiveness and content of those in the great epics. Mirroring is
often no more than the by-product of type scenes, in itself both accidental and inevitable. It lacks the spirit that gives life.

Kudrun's use of free-standing detail rises no higher. For example,
at strophe 559 of the 8th aventiure Hagen says goodbye to his daughter, never to see Hetel's kingdom again:

>er und sîn gesinde   gesâhen nimmer mêr
>daz lant ze Hegelingen;   si kômen in ze verre.

>He and his followers   never saw again
>the land of Hegeling;   they moved too far away from them.

The fact itself is indifferent and the explanation of it downright pedestrian (they moved too far away). With his daughter happily married, Hagen can settle into a peaceful old age undisturbed by hard
travel. The "scourge of all kings" lives, we presume, comfortably ever
after.[30]

The figure repeats itself near the end of the 31st aventiure (1690)
when the newlywed couples depart from Hilde's country:

> ir sumelîcher scheiden   alsô dâ geschach,
> daz si dar nâch vil selten   gesâhen einander mêre.
>
> The parting that took place   was such a one for all
> that never afterwards   did they see each other again.

The pain is slight, and Kudrun softens it even more by promising to
send news of herself three times a year (1699). These separations
occur with trials overcome and sorrows behind, and just after marriage. They will all live happily ever after, whether they see each other
again or not.

The NL shares the motif and gives it content. Prünhilt, won fraud-
ulently by Gunther, also leaves her country, never to return (526):

> In tugentlîchen zühten   si rûmte ir eigen lant.
> si kust' ir vriunt die nâhen,   die si bî ir vant.
> mit guotem urloube   si kômen ûf den sê.
> zuo ir vater lande   kom diu vrouwe nimmer mê.
>
> She left with refined decorum   the land that was her own.
> She kissed her closest kinsmen   that she found by her side.
> Taking friendly leave   they gained the open sea.
> The queen never again   returned to her fatherland.

The ambience is threatening, and circumstances hint at coming trouble. Prünhilt's marriage rests on a lie that she seems already to suspect
(cf. 528). Her union with Gunther is wrong, crisis and disaster lie
ahead. All this makes her failure to return a thing of bitterness and
sorrow.[31] The heavy march of consecutive one-verse sentences adds
a final melancholy touch. The archaic verse technique is employed
with perfect timing.

It is of course the case that the *Kudrun* poet had no sense for the
grim mechanics into disaster that we call tragic consequence. In fact,

he rejected it outright and delivered an edifying exemplum of hatred and enmity overcome.[32] But since his optimisim tends to the simplistic, emotions become trivialized and sentimental. Thus Kudrun and her maids take leave of Hilde with tears and laughter, turning around repeatedly as they depart (1700):

> mit lachen und mit weinen   si und ir magedîn
> verwendiclîche giengen   ûz . . . Matelâne.
> ir sorge hête nu ende.   man gesach nie niht sô wol getânes.
>
> With laughter and with tears   she and her lady servants
> left . . . Matelan   looking back repeatedly.
> Their cares now had an end.   Such loveliness was never seen.

"Their cares were ended." That sets the tone, and tears only heighten the ladies' charm. We compare Andromache taking leave of Hector, she too smiling through her tears (6.484) and turning back again and again when they separate (6.496). The gesture is concentrated on one figure, not dissipated over many. For Andromache, as for Prünhilt, the worst is yet to come.

Examples like this reveal the dense texture of Homer and the NL, and their sure touch. One more will confirm the point. *Kudrun* mentions in passing (1661) how men compared the beauty of ladies and argued over their merits. The debate remains polite and harmless, a touch of courtly decor.[33]

> dô si zesamene kômen,   von helden wart gestriten
> umb ir aller schœne,   welhiu diu beste mære.
> man lobete ir aller tugende.   hie mite sô gestuonden disiu mære.
>
> When they came together   there was debate among the warriors
> about all the women's beauty,   which of them was best.
> They praised the looks of all of them.   With that the conversation
>   stopped.

"They praised all the women's beauty and it was left at that." The NL also relates a comparison of the sort. It is made (with little more obvious emphasis than in *Kudrun*) when Kriemhilt and Prünhilt meet for the first time (593):

> Die vrouwen spehen kunden   unt minneclîchen lîp,
> die lobeten durch ir schœne   daz Guntheres wîp.

dô sprachen dâ die wîsen,   die hetenz baz gesehen,
man möhte Kriemhilden   wol vor Prünhilden jehen.

Those who could judge ladies   and women's loveliness,
they praised Gunther's wife   because of her beauty.
But then the experts said,   for they had looked more closely,
that one could well pick Kriemhilt   over Prünhilt.

Kudrun paints the scene on a flat surface: the NL sets it in deep
perspective. The judgment of the connoisseurs quietly confirms a
rivalry already established and identifies the fatal dislocation that will
wreck the two unions: Sivrit the servant of *minne,* Prünhilt deprived
of her natural partner. The tableau carries the pall of unhappy days
ahead, and the judgment of the observers confirms the young queen's
secret humiliation.

Kudrun is stylistically backward. Wolfram had already taken these
ancient devices and given them a new lease on life with his own
idiosyncratic manner. The following examples will illustrate the point
and suggest new dimensions in Wolfram's relation to heroic epic.

In book 4 of *Parzival* the young hero wins the hand of Kondwiramurs by defending her city against a truculent suitor. Events unfold
in two movements held to a close parallelism with consistent enlargement at the second stage. Parzival does combat twice: first with
Kingrun, seneschal of the beseiging lord; then with Klamide, the
king himself. The encounters follow the same track and share binding details; they show the same finish and aftermath; they are preceded by scenes of Parzival and Kondwiramurs lying together in
growing intimacy.

1. Both fights start (conventionally) with a joust preceded by a
long charge and followed by sword play (197.4, Kingrun; 211.13,
Klamide) . Both men are unhorsed in the first (the saddle girths
break and the mounts are knocked back on their haunches, 197.6).
Neither unseats the other in the second. They fight from the saddle
until both animals are spent, then they dismount and continue with
swords (211.20). Thus firm parallelism of horses and riders in both
duels; a longer fight from horseback in the second.

2. Parzival strikes such blows that both opponents imagine that
catapults are raining missiles on them (197.20, 212.6). The figure is
expanded into a conversation in the second instance.

3. We hear in a line where Kingrun's horse came from (196.28).
With Klamide, this is expanded into an anecdote: the steed's name,

origin, donor, and the infantry Klamide received at the same time (210.5).

4. Both defeated enemies emphasize the glory Parzival has won, Klamide at greater length (198.8, 213.4).

5. The aftermaths are designed as a piece.

A. *Kingrun*

Parzival: Make your submission to Gurnemanz.
Kingrun: No, better death than that. I slew his son.
Parzival: Then submit yourself to my lady.
Kingrun: That would be the end of me, for I have done much hurt to the people of Pelrapeire.
Parzival: Then go to Arthur in Britain and announce your submission to a lady there who suffered unjustly because of me.
Kingrun: Agreed.

B. *Klamide*

Parzival: Make your submission to Gurnemanz.
Klamide: Oh no, I slew his son with the help of my seneschal. Make me do anything but that.
Parzival: Then go to Arthur in Britain and give your submission to a lady who was beaten for my sake.[34]
Klamide: Agreed.

Both defeated knights do as instructed and separately. Klamide's arrival at Arthur's court is told at length, Kingrun's much more briefly, and Keie figures prominently in both but more so in the second (206.5, 216.3).

6. Before Parzival faces Kingrun, he and Kondwiramurs spend their first innocent night together (193.15). Their marriage rewards his victory, and they lie together again - chastely still for several nights until she finally becomes his wife (201.18). Now enter Klamide to start the second round of fighting.

The parallelisms stand out and still more details could be added to the list. The narrative has something of the fixed marching pace of heroic epic, but that is loosened by Wolfram's idiosyncracy and temperament: editorial comments, personal asides, thrusts at his audience, intertwining of the two duels and follow-ups, and the pervasive irony. All the repeats are set in an ascending curve: the lovers' nights together, the combats, the scenes with Arthur, Keie's discomfiture, Parzival's rising star in the city in the eyes of friend and foe alike. We see the old epic manner undergoing still another mutation in Arthurian romance: stylization and block repetition as vehicles of a complex and intensely personal utterance.

Comparison with Chrétien is revealing. He has the two combats of course (2175, 2653), the increasing intimacy of the lovers, and the enemies' trips to Arthur. But the French writer does not build the sharp reciprocities of Wolfram: for example, Enguigeron and Clamadeu travel to Arthur together (2748) and the conditions of Clamadeu's release are related indirectly (2682, probably to *avoid* excessive repetition. There are also fewer repeated details (no imagined interference from catapults). Wolfram thus reverts to what is basically a more archaic manner, one closer to heroic epic.

Other episodes in *Parzival* show the same manner, a framework of rigidly parallel sequences interwoven and buoyed by Wolfram's high spirits and ironic distance. Consider the attacks on Parzival by Segremors and Keie when he falls into a trance outside Arthur's camp (284.30, 290.3). The two assaults run an almost identical course: permission requested and received from Arthur to engage the stranger, opening challenge, Parzival's oblivion, his horse turned away from the blood drops on the snow by the other knight's maneuvers, awakening, the opponent's charge and repulse, with Arthur's man landing flat in the snow (much more damage to Keie) and Parzival falling back into his spell by gazing at the marks again. Tight correspondences of this sort and the stylized and visionary quality of Parzival's enchantment suggest a scene that is stiff-legged and abstract. But the opposite is true. Events are boistrous and wayward, on the verge of chaos and bufoonery, then alternating with serious reflection and mockery: the ignorant bawling of Kunneware's page (perhaps even an indecent play on her name? 284.12), Segremors' pulling the covers off Arthur and Ginover as they sleep, Segremors' and Keie's humiliating falls, Keie's wrangling with Gawan, Wolfram's own disquisitions on *minne* and on Keie and his thrusts at Walther, the vein of humorous incongruence running through from start to finish. Are Wolfram's scenes of this sort related to those in the NL (such as Sivrit's battle with the giant and the dwarf, Kriemhilt's betrayal of Sivrit) where formal structure constrains a rowdy or emotional content? That is, did Wolfram learn the technique from progressive exponents of the heroic epic? Perhaps his relation to the NL needs to be redefined in larger terms.[35] There are many other such pairings in *Parzival*, most notably the combats of Gawan-Parzival and Parzival-Gramoflanz in books 13 and 14. But there the interconnections reach such a staggering complexity as to resist summation here.

Ring Composition

RING COMPOSITION is a device of such variety and wide distribution that no single definition will usefully comprehend its many uses. I shall concern myself only with a certain type that is used to introduce and start things off. These figures consist basically of three parts: (1) the introduction and beginning of an action; (2) a narrative or descriptive digression on the subject of number (1); (3) a return to the first item and its complete development. Ring composition of this sort is extremely common in Homer, and I draw my first illustrations from the *Iliad*.[1] To repeat: I am confining my definition and examples to this single type. That implies no restriction on a wider definition of the figure (such as verbal ties between beginnings and ends), but only on the examples I treat.

In book 9 of the *Iliad* three friends (Phoinix, Odysseus, Aias) try to persuade Achilles to be reconciled with Agamemnon and return to the fighting. As part of this effort, Phoinix tells the story of Meleager, another warrior who withdrew from combat in anger. Intransigence there led to evil consequences both for Meleager and for his city. In the course of his story Phoinix describes how Artemis sent a wild boar to devastate the vineyard of Oineus (533). He begins with the goddess' action and her reasons for it. This is item 1, the first part of the ring. Then he breaks off to tell how Oineus offended her in the first place—part 2, the central digression. Finally, he returns to the boar and tells about that to the end (part 3). Observe how the story actually begins in item 1: the main point is set out briefly but in all its essentials (533–35):

> And golden-throned Artemis sent an evil upon them.
> She was angered because Oineus sacrificed no first fruits
> of his vineyard to her.

Next (part 2) comes the explanation of how Oineus made his mistake (535–37)

> The other gods received hecatombs to feast on,
> but he neglected one of them, the daughter of mighty Zeus.
> He either forgot or was careless. But his blindness brought him disaster.

Finally the main story resumes (part 3). Artemis visits them with a destructive beast (538):

> She, the goddess, dispenser of arrows, sent upon them in anger
> a wild boar, fierce and with flashing tusks.

The tale is now told to the end: how Meleager organized a band to hunt the animal and the consequences flowing from that. Verbal connections also hold the ring together. The phrasing at point 3 reaches back to 1. Thus, *ōrse* ("sent," "inflicted," 539) repeats the same verb from 533; *cholōsamenē* ("in anger") of 538 resumes *chōsamenē* ("angered") of 534.

Why single out so unremarkable a figure? One reason is its sheer frequency in Homer, which by itself makes it worthy of notice. More important, it is functional. It condenses the narrative and imposes a subordinating order. Things are not strung out in straight sequence, as for instance: "Oineus angered Artemis, so she sent a boar against him." Instead: "Artemis sent destruction upon Oineus. It was because he had angered her. And so she sent an evil upon him, it was a boar," and so on. The story is summarized at the start. The middle section is a flashback setting the stage for the full development. The narrative is not linear or purely successive, but is structured by reducing the flow of events to an arbitrary configuration.

Perhaps this seems like a ponderous conclusion to draw from a simple device, but Oineus and Artemis are used only to illustrate the basic anatomy of the figure. The death of Simoeisios at *Iliad* 4.473 is a more ambitious example. This young fighter enters in order to be slain by Telamonian Aias and then to disappear forever:

1. Aias struck (*ebal'*, 473) Simoeisios. (1 line)

    2. Account of the young man's life, his birth and rearing, 474–79. (6 lines)

3. Resumption and conclusion: full description of how Aias struck (*bale*, 480) and slew him, 480–89. (10 lines)

Again, a verbal connector ("struck") binds the first and third sections. The killing is first related flatly in a single line. Then the middle section fills in details of the victim's life, lending dimension and pathos. It is against this background that the full details of his death are set out in part 3. Large numbers of the *Iliad*'s slayings are related in this manner, and Homer stands alone in the ancient tradition in his extensive use of it.

A closer look at Simoeisios reveals a fine integration of the middle section.[2] It tells how his mother bore him by the banks of the river Simoeis when she had once gone with her parents to see their flocks. Hence the boy's name, Simoeisios. That idyll is painted with a few strokes and set off poignantly against the shortness of the young man's life and its harsh end. After he falls, in part 3, a simile compares him to a poplar tree growing in a water meadow that is cut down to be made into chariot railings—again the piercing irony of pastoral origins and violent death. That tree (we are still in the simile) then "lies drying out by the banks of a river," another sorrowful reminder of the circumstances of the warrior's birth. The link between the middle part of the ring and the other two is alive and resonant.

What ring composition accomplishes as a narrative strategy is this: (1) It sets the ingredients of the story (present action and background) into the most efficient possible order, thus amplifying all the natural effects of contrast and association. (2) It tempers run-on parataxis. It imposes order at even the simplest level and tightens the narrative. Hypotaxis, then, at the bottom line. The effect of this over long stretches is considerable, especially in the battle scenes with their welter of events. Most rings in the fighting are less ambitious than the one constructed for Simoeisios. The form remains constant, enlarged or curtailed at will. The slaying of Phaistos by Idomeneus in book 5 shows a ring reduced to its essentials:

1. Idomeneus slew Phaistos,

    2. son of Lydian Boros, who came from fertile Tarne.

3. Idomeneus, the famous spearman, struck him with his mighty spear in the right shoulder as he was about to mount his chariot. Phaistos fell back and hateful darkness overcame him.

With these examples in mind we turn to the NL. Ring composition is much less frequent there than in Homer and in general less important. Still it is used with purpose and skill and with some interesting similarities to the Homeric manner.

Report on the Saxon war

In aventiure 4 (227) a messenger delivers his report to Kriemhilt on the Saxon war. Interestingly, his speech starts in the fourth verse of 226 and ends in the third of 240. The report calls attention to itself by its length: fourteen strophes make it the second longest in the NL. The messenger arranges it as follows:

1. Sivrit's deeds, 227–30 (4 strophes)
    2. Accomplishments of the Burgonden, 231–35 (5 strophes)
3. The feats of Sivrit, 236–40 (5 strophes)

The emphasis is obvious and appropriate. It is her suitor who interests Kriemhilt most, even though he is not the one she asks about directly. But there is a still finer relation between the first and third parts. The information about Sivrit in (1) remains general: many men slain, sword strokes and flowing blood, wives widowed and grieving (this last a typical detail, but pointed here to Kriemhilt). With the return to Sivrit in (3) the news becomes detailed and specific: the kings taken hostage, five hundred or more wounded prisoners, eighty stretchers with the critically hurt, and all on their way to the Rhine bringing glory to Gunther and his land. In other words, the second installment on Sivrit enlarges on the first in specificity and grandeur. The Burgonden are relegated to the middle and subordinated from the start (228):

> Swaz die recken alle   in strîte hânt getân,
> Dancwart und Hagene   und ander 'sküneges man,
> swaz si striten nâch êren,   daz ist gar ein wint
> unz eine an Sîvriden.

> What all the tough campaigners   accomplished in the strife,
> Dancwart and Hagen,   and the rest of the king's men,
> however they strove for honor,   that is paltry indeed
> compared with Sivrit by himself.

As in Homer, verbal connectors join the first section to the third: "ze ernste und ze strîte" (227)—"strît den aller hœhsten" (236); "dâ wohrte michel wunder/ des küenen Sîvrides hant" (227)—"den tet vil willeclîche/ diu Sîvrides hant" (236).

This shaping lends the passage immediacy and movement, from mighty but unspecified deeds to names, numbers, hostages and captives on their way and soon to arrive. There is a rising curve into a climax. The ring is no more a dead figure than in Homer. Even at this basic stage of storytelling, the narrative is shaped according to compositional strategies. Events do not pour forth in an undifferentiated flow; there is artifice at the ground level.

The dismissal of Liudegast and Liudeger

Gunther's festival and its aftermath close out the 5th aventiure. Having celebrated with much honor to himself (309), the king announces his intention of giving gifts to his guests before they depart (310):

> Er sprach: "ir guoten recken,   ê daz ir sceidet hin,
> sô nemt ir mîne gâbe: alsô stêt mîn sin,
> daz ichz immer diene,   versmâht iu niht mîn guot,
> daz wil ich mit iu teilen,   des hân ich willigen muot."

> He spoke: "You brave campaigners,   before you leave from here
> accept my gifts: my mind is so inclined
> that I will be ever grateful.   If you do not scorn my wealth,
> I wish to share it with you;   that I am eager to do.

But that has to be shelved for a while because another question intervenes, namely the release of Liudegast and Liudeger (311.3):

> wir gern stæter suone;   des ist uns recken nôt.

> We desire an abiding settlement;   we fighters need it badly.

This means, of course, that they are offering ransom; we learn the amount at 314.[3] Gunther consults Sivrit (with the apparent intention of accepting their offer), but is advised against it: he should simply send them on their way with no more than their word not to invade again. Gunther makes this humane and grandiose gesture, dismissing

his erstwhile foes with a show of complete indifference to their gold
(316.3):

> ir goldes gerte niemen,   daz si dâ buten ê.
>
> Nobody wanted their gold   that they had offered there.

Now the ring closes as he turns his attention back to the guests and
enriches them lavishly (317):

> Manege scilde volle   man dar scatzes truoc.
> er teiltes âne wâge   den vriwenden sîn genuoc,
> bî fünf hundert marken,   und etslîchen baz.
>
> Many a shield filled   with treasure was carried in.
> With a free and lavish hand   he shared it with his friends,
> as much as five hundred marks,   and even more than that.

Although this is a minor scene and in some respects highly conventional (leave taking and gift giving after festivals belong to standard
ceremony), the ring is quietly impressive, for it emphasizes an un-
derground content. Gunther, in a customary pose, hopes his guests
will not scorn his wealth. Then he proceeds to treat the kings' offer
of ransom as though it were beneath contempt. That, of course, puts
an even better front on his own largesse and emphasizes his supe-
riority.[4] But, as usual, a paltry reality lies behind Gunther's gestures.
It is Sivrit who persuades him not to accept anything from Liudegast
and Liudeger. And we learn at the end (317.4) that it was Gernot who
advised him to enrich his guests so freely. We have not forgotten that
it was these very two who pushed Gunther into resisting the declaration of war in the first place. No doubt, then, where the true credit
lies. This is cool mockery, and it looks forward to the next aventiuren
where Sivrit will guide Gunther against Prünhilt. Their relationship
shows imbalance even now, and this is brought into relief by the
shape of the story.

Sivrit's last words

In strophes 994–97 the dying Sivrit commends Kriemhilt to the mercy
of her kin:

1. Sivrit replies to Hagen (994.1–3): what makes his death most bitter is Kriemhilt's fate (994.4).

    2. The pity of his son, now to bear disgrace (995).

3. He commends Kriemhilt to their mercy and good will (996–97).

As always, the shape carries emphasis. Sivrit's last words circle around his wife and her family, and that will be the central issue for the rest of the story. These final thoughts thus point to the future and articulate the continuity between the poem's two halves. There is also the usual movement and intensification. Kriemhilt receives only a one-line mention at 994.4, but she dominates two strophes the second time around. Verbal connections reach back to earlier scenes:

> und lât sie des geniezen,   daz si iuwer swester sî. (997.1)
>
> Since she is your sister,   let her benefit from that.

This recalls Kriemhilt's last conversation with Hagen and her appeals to kinship there (898.1):

> du bist mîn mâc,   sô bin ich der dîn.
>
> You are my kinsman,   likewise I am yours.

Words are recalled from even earlier in that scene (893.1–3):

> Vil lieber vriunt Hagene,   gedenket ane daz,
> daz ich iu gerne diene   und noch nie wart gehaz.
> des lâzet mich geniezen   an mînem lieben man.
>
> My very dear friend Hagen,   keep in mind that I
> am your willing servant   and have never borne you ill will.
> Let me benefit from that   in respect to my dear husband.

These links backwards are concentrated in the third part of the ring.

C erases this structure entirely in favor of two of its pervasive tendencies: denigration of Hagen and emphasis on the Burgonden's guilt.[5] It adds C 1005 between 995 and 996 (denunciation of the betrayal) and C 1008 after 997, again with accusation of perfidy plus the grisly detail "er rampf sich bitterlîche." The same tendencies influence still other details of C's version of the scene.[6] But with the ring goes the effective concentration of the hero's last words on his wife and son.[7]

Kriemhilt's return to Wormez

Kriemhilt's reception with Sivrit in Wormez in aventiure 13 (785) is staged with a finely conceived ring. Prünhilt and her train adorn themselves with appropriate splendor and ride out to meet the guests, accompanied by a retinue of knights (785–786.3). As the women come together (phase 1) we hear of joyous hospitality: here is a welcome that exceeds Kriemhilt's to Prünhilt long ago. Onlookers feel their spirits rise at the first sight of Sivrit's queen (787):

> Mit wie getânen vreuden   man die geste enpfie!
> si dûhte, daz vrou Kriemhilt   vroun Prünhilde nie
> sô rehte wol enpfienge   in Burgonden lant.
> die si ê nie gesâhen,   den wart vil hôher muot erkant.

> With what great joy   the guests were received!
> People thought that Princess   Kriemhilt had not
> received Queen Prünhilt so well   into the Burgonden's land.
> Those who never saw Kriemhilt before   learned about inspiration of
> the heart.

But now the scene shifts to the men (phase 2). Sivrit and Sigmunt get a high-spirited greeting from Gunther and his brothers with warm expressions of friendship and exuberent riding that raises a cloud of dust. Then, back to the two queens (phase 3), who complete the ceremony (792) and round out the structure. This is the ring: the queens, the kings, the queens.

The men's reunion sets a background of hearty good cheer, and they *are* only background because our attention is already fastened on the two women. Storm clouds have been gathering long since. Prünhilt's resentments have been made clear enough, and so have her not-so-friendly reasons for issuing the invitation in the first place (724). The question of Sivrit's status gives her no rest. She wonders why Kriemhilt holds her head so high and seems to refer to the same thing in her oblique question to Gere at 771 (different from Uote's sincere concern just after, 772).[8] The meeting of the two queens is elaborate and correct but frosty (793):

> Dô giengen zuo ein ander   diu minneclîchen wîp.
> des was in grôzen vreuden   vil maniges ritters lîp,
> daz ir beider grüezen   sô schône wart getân.

Then the lovely women   went toward each other.
Many a knight   was filled with joy
that their greeting to each other   was carried out so courteously.

The genial welcome by the men is amplified by two direct speeches
full of warmth (789, 790). No exchange is recorded between the two
women. Attention moves quickly to their honor guards and attendants (793–794). There is no open hostility here and certainly no
rebuff. But the contrast between the two sets of greetings, underlined
as it is by the ring composition, casts a pall over the proceedings and
hints darkly at coming estrangement. Comparison with other such
receptions confirms this impression.

Despite the assertion at 787, the welcome that Prünhilt first received
at Wormez was distinctly more friendly. She was kissed by her mother-
and daughter-in-law over and over (589.4):

vrou Uote unt ir tohter   die kusten dicke ir süezen munt.

Queen Uote and her daughter   kissed her sweet lips again and again.

The greetings lasted long, many another pair of red lips had a firm
kiss planted on it, and note was taken of how long the ladies and
their corteges stood together and chatted (591.1–3):

Ê daz ir gruoz ergienge,   daz was ein langiu stunt.
jâ wart dâ geküsset   manic rôsenvarwer munt.
noch stuonden bî ein ander   die küniges tohter rîch.

Before their greeting ended,   a long time passed.
Many indeed were the rosy lips   that there received a kiss.
The royal princesses   were still standing together.

Uote, the queen mother, is absent on this second occasion, perhaps
a matter of protocol because Prünhilt is now the ranking queen.[9] But
her presence would also loosen the unspoken confrontation and mitigate the chill.

Gotelint's reception of Kriemhilt in Bechelaren also combines formal
ceremony with a show of feeling. Correct procedure is maintained:
Gotelint dismounts first, Kriemhilt responds by doing the same.[10]
Now comes the welcoming kiss and best wishes from both sides
(1312). Finally their maids exchange greetings, following the regular

order. The tone is distinctly warmer and more encouraging that at Kriemhilt's return to Wormez. The parties embrace and converse.

Taken together, the three scenes reveal a normal procedure. Variation indicates different states of mind behind the outward forms. The scene at Wormez thus becomes the vehicle for one of the poet's favorite contrasts: a show of courtly manners on the surface, turbulent emotions below and looming disaster. The ring composition serves that end. Another tension also flickers now and again from the start of the festival. The quarrel between the queens will have belonged to the core of the story in all versions and doubtless underwent much variation in placement and manner. The NL's audience waited for it and wondered: when will it come and what will spark it? Several situations arise where it could break out but does not, and this uneasy reception at the start is one of them. The technique has a close relative in book 17 of the *Odyssey* where Odysseus, disguised as a beggar, is brought to the brink of recognition by his wife and maidservant. The audience knew he had to reveal himself eventually and there seem to have been versions where he revealed himself sooner than Homer allows. Will this happen now? The poet takes us to the edge, then draws back and reunites the wife and husband much later and in a different way.

Before leaving the subject of ring composition, I should repeat that I have confined myself to a single kind. All these rings feature an action barely begun or stated in brief, then broken off and finally resumed—prolepsis in the first part and suspension in the second, with a natural continuum of action or theme between the opening and close. They stand at the beginning of things or the introduction of persons. It is a dynamic figure, holding the narrative in tension between start and fulfillment.

These rings are to be distinguished from others, possibly related, of a less elastic type. Compare, for example, two balladlike repetitions from *Ortnit*. The first is at strophes 81–84, where Lamparte's mother gives him the magic ring with instructions for its use:

1. Daz vingerlîn ist rîche,   und dunct dich nihtes wert.
   du suochest âventiure;   sît des dîn herze gert,
   wil du in die wilde rîten,   sô lâz ez von dir niht.
   du vindest âventiure,   von dem steine daz geschiht.

The little ring is mighty,   though you think it nothing worth.
You seek adventure;   since your heart desires that,
if you wish to ride into the forest,   never let it from your side.
You will find adventure,   it is the stone that causes that.

    2. Description of the ring's power, directions to the linden tree. (82–84.3)

3. *solt du âventiure vinden,   daz muos aldâ geschehen.*
   If you are to find adventure,   it will have to happen there. (84.4)

The second is at strophes 94–96. Lamparte finds (he thinks) a child sleeping under the linden tree and falls into a plaintive monologue:

1. *"ouwê wâ ist dîn muoter?"*   sprach künic Ortnit.
   "Alas, where is your mother?"   spoke King Ortnit.

    2. You wear fine raiment, I dare not startle you, would that you were my son, there would be no honor for me to carry you off.

3. *ouwê wâ ist dîn muoter,   vil liebez kindelîn?*
   Alas, where is your mother,   my dear little child?

In both examples we have to do only with a *refrain*. And it is essentially static, for neither action nor description is moved forward by it. It effects emphasis but no movement, and only an inert cohesion. Compare Veldeke's account of the duel between Aeneas and Turnus (12. 175):

1. The men prepare for battle and ride out; formal conditions and arrangements. (12, 175–12, 207)

    2. Lavinia's monologue. (12, 208–12, 301)

3. The duel. (12, 302)

This is natural and familiar. The start of the duel is "delayed" by the account of Lavinia, but it is not started before her entrance nor does she interrupt it. This is, in fact, one of the most familiar of all storytelling devices. A useful effect is achieved here by staging the fight, when it actually occurs, against the backdrop of her feelings. This order of narrative also creates a modest suspense. To this extent the middle section functions like those of the close-knit rings, but there is no trace here of their tensile coherence.

The same applies to Kriemhilt's introduction in the NL. This is also a ring of sorts, stately and purposeful. Strophes 2 and 3 bring her on in a conventional and general description. Nine more strophes introduce her brothers and their court (4–12), and then Kriemhilt returns for the last seven to close out the first aventiure. There is the usual enlargement the second time around from stereotyped attributes to her peculiar character (aversion to *minne*) and approaching fate. It is also the case that strophe 19's dark look into the future is more effective coming after the picture of her brothers in all their glory and prowess in battle. There is no doubt, I think, that a ring like this is related to those I have have treated, but it is more purely descriptive and less active. It is a large-scale structure, not a smaller shaping device. It does not emerge as a free-standing entity held together by its own inner balance of forces.

A similar example can be drawn from *Kudrun*. Hartmuot and Ortwin close in combat at 1403–09. But before that issue is decided the scene shifts for seven strophes to other fights on both sides: Wate, Herwic, Fruote, Morunc, Irolt, and Ludewic (1410–16). All these new combattants are named in a catalogue that acts as a backdrop to the main duel. That contest is now resumed and Hartmuot wins (1417–18). This looks a little like a ring and should perhaps be treated as one, but it does not allow a clean separation from the narrative at large. The third section (the wounding of Ortwin) widens into another attack on Hartmuot from Horant (who is also wounded) and then into the rescue of them both. Hartmuot disappears from the action again (with his place taken by Ludewic, spanning two aventiuren, 1430–48), and he returns only upon learning of his father's death. In other words, the combat of Hartmuot and Ortwin lacks the clear boundaries and sharp definition that mark the rings in Homer and the NL. It comes close to dissolving simply into alternating appearances of Hartmuot. And the events between the start and finish of the duel between Hartmuot and Ortwin lack the immediate pertinence to their enclosure that marks the sharply profiled rings.

Wolfram also uses ring composition with some frequency—another of the many features he shares with (learned from?) heroic epic. An example from *Parzival* shows how useful the device is in distributing background information over several stages. It also illustrates, on the small scale, Wolfram's habit of weaving family connections between events remote in space and time.

Parzival lets his horse go where it chooses and so rides toward the abode of Trevrizent (452.5). The hermit is now introduced with a description of his austere sanctity (452.15–30) and the announcement that he will tell about the grail. This is the first part of the ring. Here Wolfram intervenes in his own person on the subject of literary squabbles and the activities of Kîôt, his alleged source and authority for the tale. This leads still farther afield to the history of Flegetanis, the heathen, who read the secret of the grail in the stars and wrote it down in his own tongue. Kiot (with a wisdom born only of faith, 453.15) found these documents and passed them on. They told also of a Herzeloide and one Gahmuret, whose child is now on his way to Trevrizent. So ends the middle part. Reenter Parzival, who arrives at the hermit's abode to begin the long scene of instruction and correction (455.22).

Thus the first information about Trevrizent sets the stage: this is the man who will instruct Parzival about the grail and cure his spiritual malady. The digression explains how the grail became known among men and how Wolfram himself guarantees the authenticity of his version. By the time Parzival and Trevrizent meet we are already equipped with considerable information. The story also seems to have been progressing (if slowly) all the while. As in Homer, then, and the NL, information and background are fed in without the sense of stalled forward movement.

Again in standard fashion, repeated details tie the first and last parts of the ring. As Parzival heads for Fontâne la Salvâsche we are reminded that it was here he encountered Orilus (452.14). When he reenters the narrative at 455.22 he recognizes the place for the same reason (455.25):

> er erkande ein stat, swie læge der snê,
> dâ liehte bluomen stuonden ê
> (daz was vor eines gebirges want),
> aldâ sîn manlîchiu hant
> vroun Jeschûten hulde erwarp
> und dâ Orilus zorn verdarp.

> He recognized a place, despite the snow that lay there,
> where bright flowers had stood before
> (that was in front of that mountain's face),
> right where his manly hand
> had won grace for Lady Jeschute
> and where Orilus' wrath had faded away.

Still other details interweave and join, such as the chastity of the persons involved (Trevrizent, 452.15–20; the people of the grail, 454.27, 455.8; and somewhat before, Parzival himself, 451.4).

But observe as well that two rings interlock here—the middle section (Kiot and Flegetanis) is a ring in its own right:

1. Kiot instructed Wolfram to explain about the grail only when the story required it. He found the documents in Toledo, written in a heathen tongue, and his Christian faith enabled him to decipher them without recourse to magic (453.1–22).

    2. The author of this account was a pagan named Flegetanis. His arts and accomplishments are described (453.23–455.1).

3. Kiot searched for this story in Latin tomes and found it among the chronicles of different countries. He learned of the people of the grail, of Titurel, Frimutel, Amfortas, Herzeloide and Gahmuret—and their child (455.2–22).

The middle ring closes with that. Here Parzival reenters and the outer ring closes as well. In outline:

1. Parzival rides towards Trevrizent.
    2. A. Kiot guarantees this information about the grail.
       B. Flegetanis was the Saracen who discovered it among the stars.
    A. Kiot uncovered it in books that told of Parzival's family.
3. Parzival arrives at the hermitage of Trevrizent.

The structure dispenses information in a series of regulated doses; it creates the illusion of narrative movement; and it moves by a dynamics of its own whereby we start with the lone figure of Parzival, move to the wider world of Wolfram and Kiot, still farther to the lore of Flegetanis and his search among the stars, back to Kiot and his Latin chronicles, to a still narrower focus on the people of the grail, then to Parzival's own family, to his parents, and finally to the hero himself— riding as he was a hundred lines before but marked by the threads of ancestry and a fate written in the heavens. The picture of Wolfram that emerges is the same we saw earlier: intriguing resemblances to the style of heroic epic but with a quantum advance in complexity and range.

Prolepsis

BURGHART WACHINGER identified an interesting trope in the NL whereby an event is first sketched with a few sentences and in general terms, then resumed and told in detail. He called these "preliminary summaries."[1] The contents of a section are summarized in advance by a chapter title, as it were. It is an essentially "primitive" technique and natural to the oral style. It is related to the various modes of foreshadowing but does not belong to them entirely. The main difference is that these advance notices summarize events to come inside the very section or episode where they themselves stand, while foreshadowing, strictly defined, pertains to events at a greater distance. As an example Wachinger cites strophes 87 and the following where Hagen tells Gunther and his court the tale of Sivrit and the Nibelungen treasure. It begins with the slaying of Schilbunc and Nibelunc, actually the climax of the story:

> die küenen Nibelunge   sluoc des helden hant,
> Schilbunc und Nibelungen,   diu rîchen küneges kint.

> The hero's hand slew   the bold Nibelungen,
> Schilbunc and Nibelunc,   the mighty king's sons.

Then comes the account itself: Sivrit rides out to the Nibelungen, he is asked to divide the treasure, a dispute follows, then combat with many slayings, the land of the Nibelungen falls under his sway, and (96.1):

> Dar zuo die rîchen künege   die sluog er bêde tôt.

> What is more, he slew   both the mighty kings.

It appears certain that these scenes with prefixed resumés are related to ring composition. They share the look forward with excursus and resumption. They seem actually to stand closest to the Homeric slaying rings, where a warrior's death is registered without ornament in the first line and then returned to and elaborated at the end. In my examples from the NL the first section of the ring has been not so much a simplified précis of the whole event as it is a start that is then interrupted for a change of subject or scene.

There is a whole group of scenes in the NL (and elsewhere) related to Wachinger's examples, but their first summary is shaped more like an actual account. Sometimes, in fact, the event seems to be over and done with in the introductory section and not awaiting or requiring elaboration in the third member—so much so, in fact, that the return to the first subject appears to cause a fracture in the narrative. I am calling this phenomenon *prolepsis*. For example, in aventiure 26 Eckewart announces to Rüedeger that the Burgonden are near:

1. Eckewart delivers the message: Rüedeger had not heard such good news in a long while. (1641)

    2. Back in Bechelaren Rüedeger sees the messenger coming and greets him at the gates (1642–43)

3. Eckewart tells him the news. Rüedeger is delighted. (1644)

The disjuncture is surprising. Strophe 1641 looks for all the world like an account of something performed and finished:

> und sagete dô Rüedegêre,   als er hete vernomen.
> im was in manigen zîten   niht sô lieber mære komen.

> And then he told Rüedeger   as he had learned himself.
> Such good news had not reached him   in a very long time.

But suddenly (1642) Eckewart is still only on his way. Rüedeger just meets him at 1643 and now is pleased again, this time in full detail, at 1644–48.

C adds to the prolepsis by letting Gotelint receive the message in advance as well (C 1681). One suspects the change stems from C's courtly manner, but it creates a contradiction with 1649 (C 1689): *noch enwistes niht frou Gotelint,/ diu in ir kemenâten saz.* In fact, the next episode (the start of aventiure 27) is Rüedeger's report to his wife about the guests.

I referred earlier to Achim Masser's theory of alternate strophes in the NL. He believes they sit side by side without accommodation. The news to Rüedeger here could be taken as an example of that. Thus 1641.2–3 would represent a condensed rendition of 1642ff. where the same thing is expanded (although the alternative here is represented by only half a strophe). Masser adduces some other striking examples of his own at 1163.[2] These also stand in connection with news to Bechelaren. At 1163 Rüedeger's wife and daughter await his arrival with anticipation:

> Dâ ze Bechelâren   im warte Gotelint.
> diu junge marcgrâvinne,   daz Rüedegêres kint,
> sah ir vater gerne   unt die sîne man.
> dô wart ein liebez bîten   von schœnen kinden getân.

> There in Bechelaren   Gotelint awaited him.
> The young Margravine,   Rüedeger's daughter,
> loved to see her father   and the men of his.
> There was a fond waiting   by lovely young maidens.

But at strophe 1165 (after a quick flashback in 1164 to Rüedeger's exit from Vienna) their delight is repeated and enlarged in the act of welcome. Thus 1163 is the short version; 1165ff. is the long version. On the other hand, this section has all the earmarks of the rings under discussion: brief anticipation, pause, resumption and expansion. But suspicion of unassimilated variants remains because of the contradiction between 1160–1161 and 1170 (Gotelint's different reactions to the news of Etzel's marriage).

Both explanations, Masser's and my own, try to account for breaks in linear narration. The same thing is said more than once and at changing length. The account seems to leap forwards and then back again instead of proceeding in a straight line. Masser's theory has the advantage of offering an explanation for outright contradictions (where these occur) between the different versions. But inconsistencies of the sort are not universal, and then we are better served by the hypothesis of a conventional manner. (1) It explains why the text has its peculiar shape–strophes are not merely inserted into the first best place because the poet was reluctant to discard traditional variants. (2) It associates these cases of extreme prolepsis with the many less radical uses of ring composition. (3) The additional examples to be adduced from the NL and elsewhere, as they accumulate, point more to a narrative device then to the constant clash of variants. Still each case must be decided on its own merits, and we might even have to do with several different phenomena.

To proceed: two rings interlock where envoys are dispatched to Wormez with the invitation to Etzel's festival. First the king gives instructions, then the queen begins to speak with the emissaries in private. This is told in brief, but the two lines for Etzel seem to summarize the entire event:

> ouch wart in von dem künege   diu boteschaft geseit,
> wie si dar laden solden   Gunther und sîne man.
> Kriemhilt diu vrouwe   si sunder sprechen began. (1409)
>
> Dô sprach der künec rîche: "ich sage iu, wie ir tuot . . . (1410)
>
> The embassy was also explained   to them by the king,
> how they should invite   Gunther and his men.
> Kriemhilt the queen   began to speak with them privately.
>
> Then spake the mighty king: "I will tell you how to proceed . . ."

Two lines for the king and one for the queen; then they resume in the same order. Etzel instructs the envoys for over three strophes (1410–13.1); then Kriemhilt summons them to her chambers for her own directions, these even more elaborate than her husband's (1413–1419). The proleptic manner is unmistakable: first a summarizing report, then a second start that is elaborated and carried to the finish.

This example fits nicely into Wachinger's category, but it also allows explanation by Masser's. There are two versions of instruction giving, one short, the other longer; both are allowed to remain. This gains some force from the fact that there are almost certainly different accounts combined here of Etzel's decision to invite the Burgonden—strophe 1400, on the one hand, and strophes 1407–08 on the other.[3] The evidence is considerable: use of *ir* in strophes 1401–06 and *du* in 1407; the abrupt shift of scene from bedroom (1400–06) to throne room (1408); the uncourtly use of troubadors as envoys to Gunther. But the double instruction giving lies just outside this turbulent stretch of text and could be independent of it.

What persuades me, however, that we have to do with a genuine mannerism—in most cases, at least—is that it belongs fundamentally to the style of much other medieval poetry. Ferdinand Fellmann has identified and explained its use in *The Song of Roland*.[4] A few examples will suffice. Oliver dies in laisse 150, lines 2010–20. Roland sees it and weeps (2021–23):[5]

> Morz est li quens, que plus ne se demuret.
> Rollant li ber le pluret, sil duluset,
> Jamais en tere n'orrez plus dolent hume!

> The count is dead, he lingers no more.
> Noble Roland weeps over him and laments over him,
> You shall never see a sadder man on earth!

But the next laisse (151) resumes at the point where Roland first notices that his friend is dead (2024–26):

> Or veit Rollant que mort sun ami,
> Gesir adenz, a la tere sun vis.
> Mult dulcement a regreter le prist:

> Now Roland see that his friend is dead,
> Lying prone, his face toward the earth.
> He began to lament over him very softly.

Roland's lament is performed to the full only the second time around. Lines 2021–23 remain a bare notice, kept in general terms, and of course there is no exact repetition between the two.[6] There are many examples of this in *Roland*. The technique is the same as in the NL; it causes the same temporal discontinuity; it stems from a similar experience of epic time and produces the same effect. We are informed of something in advance, in its totality, and thus prepared for it. Then we start afresh and receive the report in detail. Add to this *Roland*'s habit of repeating the same thing in successive laisses, and our sense of flowing time is disrupted. Events do not glide forward in smooth succession but break down into discrete segments. These take us forward in jerks and starts, as each seems to take a step backward before continuing its advance. Fellmann writes: "The laisses represent self-contained, largely independent entities, each with its distinct content. As a result, progressive narrative time breaks down into separate temporal units and its flow backs up along their sutures."[7]

The consequence of this is not chronological disorder but a whole different sense of time. Events are conceived in their totality and ordered not by temporal relationships but in terms of narrative pace and dramatic rhythm. Fellmann notes an astonishing example in laisses 109–11, where the Saracen king, Marsile, is about to burst upon the battle with his force. So far the French have been holding their own, but Marsile's arrival spells their end. The weight of the event is measured in three consecutive laisses that explore its consequences for the future: Marsile will appear; Roland will die; Ganelon will be tried and executed. These three events are distributed over the three laisses, *but in reverse chronological order.* Laisse 109 looks farthest into the future and describes the fate awaiting Ganelon; 110 describes a terrific storm and darkness over the earth, nature's sign of Roland's impending demise:

> Dient plusor: "Ço est li definement,
> La fin del secle ki nus est en present!"
> Il nel sevent, ne dient veir nïent:
> Ço est li granz dulors por la mort de Rollant.

> Many say: "This is the end of all things,
> The end of the world that we are witnessing!"
> They do not know, they do not talk sense:
> This is the great mourning for the death of Roland.

And then, in laisse 111, as the French search in grief and pity for their relatives, Marsile is suddenly upon them. The order in which things actually happen is turned around, but the effect is a rising curve into Marsile's climactic appearance. Fellman writes: "The single laisse sections stand in both vertical and horizontal relationship to each other. That is decisive for the effect created by the exceedingly artful structure of this laisse group. It leads to the removal of temporal suspense and helps create an epic world suspended in itself."[8] Anticipation, preparation, timelessness: these lie behind the proleptic manner in *Roland* and the NL both. There are many examples elsewhere. Consider the slaying of Adalrot in the *Rolandslied*. Roland strikes first after an exchange of threats (4055):

> er vieng in oben zeder achselen an,
> er zetailte ros unde man.

He struck him high, at the shoulder,
he cut horse and man in half.

With that, the combat should be over. Roland delivers a speech of triumph that could apply to a dead foe or a live one (4057–61):

> di rede scoltu mir gebuzin,
> Machmeten zetrit ich unter minen fuzin
> unt allez daz hie mit im ist.
> daz gebiutet mir der heilige Christ.
> dinen botich gibe ich den himel vogelen.

> I will see that you pay for those words,
> I will trample Mohammed under my feet,
> and everything that is here with him.
> The holy Christ commands me that.
> I will give your corpse to the birds of the sky.

But then he strikes and divides the Saracen and his mount again (4062):

> er ramte sin obene,
> et tailte ros unt satelpogen,
> deiz tot ze der erde bechom.

> He aimed a blow at him high,
> he split the horse in half
> and the saddle down the middle,
> so that it fell dead to the ground.

The second round shows variation and more detail, but the action was already complete in the first instance.

Kudrun supplies an example early in its fourth aventiure. Having returned safely home and been recognized, Hagen leaves the seashore with the rest while many assemble at the castle from all sides at the unexpected news of his return (161). Two strophes (162, 163) now look forward, describing his precocious attendance on the ladies he rescued and his growth to maturity:

> Hagene sîne frouwen   niht unberuochet liez.
> baden ze allen zîten   er si vlîzlîchen hiez.
> den minneclîchen meiden   den diente er vil lîse.
> man gab in rîchiu kleider;   er was in sînen jungen jâren wîse.

Wahsen er begunde   bevollen ze einem man.
dô phlag er mit den helden   swes man ie began,
daz ritter prüeven sollten,   mit werken und mit handen.
sît wart er gewaltic   in sînes vater Sigebandes landen.

Hagen did not leave   his ladies unattended.
He instructed them earnestly   to bathe frequently.
He served the lovely maidens   very courteously.
They were given elegant garments;   he was knowledgeable at a young
    age.

He began to mature   fully into manhood.
Now he joined the warriors   in whatever they undertook
that would make a man a knight,   in deeds and strength of hand.
He later became mighty   in the lands of his father Sigebant.

Hagen seems well on his way to manhood, but the next strophe (164)
suddenly returns to the time just after his rescue. After two weeks
of recovery, the pilgrims from Garadie are dismissed:

Nâch tagen vierzehenen   scheiden man dô lie
die wazzermüeden helde,   die bî in wâren hie.

After fourteen days   the sea-weary warriors
who had been with them there   were allowed to depart.

With that, the account returns to Hagen growing up (165):

Der junge Hagen lernte   daz helden wol gezam . . .

Young Hagen learned   what befitted warriors . . .

This text shows the same indifference to linear chronology as the rest,
and it reminds one especially of NL 21–26, the summary of Sivrit's
growth to manhood. The swing back and forth in time belongs to the
proleptic manner. Anticipation and backtracking break the straight
temporal sequence.

The *Chanson de Roland* provides still another stately example at
Charles's return to Aix (laisses 267–271, verses 3695ff.):

1. Charles rides without interruption *until he arrives at Aix*. Upon entering
    the palace *he summons judges from all corners of the empire* (3695–3703):
    Des ore cumencet le plait de Genelun (*now begins the trial of Ganelon*).

2. *Charles has returned from Spain and come to Aix:* the death of Alda (3705–33).

3. *Charles has returned to Aix,* Ganelon is chained and abused by his guards (3734–41).

4. *Charles summons men from many lands. They assemble at Aix and the trial begins.*

The weight of the occasion is underlined by the litany of Charles's arrival:

> Carles cevalchet e les vals e les munz,
> Entresqu' a Ais no volt prendre surjun. (3695–96)

> Charles rides through valleys and over mountains,
> He does not wish to interrupt his march before reaching Aix.

> Li empereres est repairet d'Espaigne
> E vient a Ais, al meillor sied de France. (3705–06)

> The emperor has returned from Spain,
> He comes to Aix, the capital of France.

> Li emperere est repairet ad Ais. (3734)

> The emperor has returned to Aix.

The report of his homecoming introduces each step of the proceedings: the summoning of judges, the encounter with Alda, the chaining of Ganelon. Items 1 and 4 in the outline describe the same event, the convoking of judges and the start of the inquisition. Number 1 is sheer anticipation, laying out the entire proceeding on a broad canvas. Numbers 2 and 3 (aside from the repeated notice of Charles's arrival) tell what happens at Aix before the trial. Turoldus is a master of formal repetition. Here it is ceremonious and emphatic—a momentous event is about to unroll. A few verses summarize Charles's measures in advance. Then, with the preliminaries behind him, the poet turns to the convening of judges and the actual trial. The look forward in lines 3699–3704 is programmatic and controlled; the notices of Charles's return to Aix are like the ominous beat of a drum. Solemnity and marchlike insistence are the intent and effect of this structure, the sequential inconcinnities fade into irrelevance beside them.[9] The NL does the same thing on a smaller scale. The leaps ahead in time set the stage, emphasize and enrich, prepare us to receive the account in full perspective.

Wolfram also uses the device. A simple example: Segremors rides out to challenge the unknown knight (Parzival) who has taken a stand before Arthur's camp (286.25). The first course of events is set out in brief at the start (287.5):

> sus vuor der unbescheiden helt
> zuo dem der minne was verselt.
> weder er ensluoc dô noch enstach,
> ê er widersagen hin zim sprach.
>
> Thus rode the imprudent warrior
> toward him who was given over to the power of minne.
> He struck him with neither sword nor spear
> before delivering a challenge to him.

After a description of Parzival's trance and a self-ironic aside from Wolfram (287.9–20) Segremors rides up to the stranger and makes his challenge (287.21).[10]

A more complex example: at 192.20 Kondwiramurs slips from her room and goes to Parzival at night. The enemy at the gates allows her no sleep, and so she risks disgrace by stealing to the sleeping stranger to ask his help. She falls on her knees before the bed. Here begins a prolepsis (193.1–14):

> ûf den teppich kniete si vür in.
> si heten beidiu kranken sin,
> er und diu küneginne,
> an bî ligender minne.
> hie wart alsus geworben:
> an vreuden verdorben
> was diu maget, des twanc si scheme.
> ob er si hin an iht nehme?
> leider des enkan er niht.
> âne kunst es doch geschiht,
> mit einem alsô bewanden vride
> daz si diu sünebæren lide
> niht zuo ein ander brahten.
> wênec si des gedâhten.
>
> She knelt down before him on the rug.
> They both were ignorant,
> he and the queen,

of how lovers lie together.
It went like this.
Bereft of joy
was the maid, shame made her so.
Will he take her to him at all?
Sadly, he has no skill at that.
But it happens artlessly,
under conditions of truce,
that they did not bring together
their conciliating limbs.
They did not think of that at all.

The question of lovemaking, brought instantly to the fore by the queen's action, is anticipated and answered before Parzival even awakes and the scene proper begins. This last now happens immediately: Parzival hears her weeping and invites her into the bed; she agrees under the conditions of "truce" (cf. 193.11 and 194.3); they lie together innocently while she explains her troubles and secures his help. This scene structure belongs entirely to Wolfram; Chrétien has no prolepsis at all.

Another example at 456.26 recalls the NL 26.1641 (Eckewart's message to Rüedeger). Parzival dismounts before Trevrizent, announcing his purpose and telling him how he found his way:

er tet im von den liuten kunt,
die in dar wîsten,
wie die sîn râten prîsten.
dô sprach er: "herre, nu gebet mir rât:
ich bin ein man, der sünde hât."

He informed him about the persons
who directed him there,
how they praised his counseling.
Then he said: "Sir, now give me counsel:
I am a man who has sins."

Again, a few lines contain the essentials of the long scene to follow. Trevrizent promises help and asks who directed Parzival to him (457.3–4), information presumably given just before (456.26–8). But this time Parzival supplies a description and Trevrizent much new information.

There is an especially interesting example at 657.2, where Arnive tells Gawan the story of how Klinschor was castrated. The first time around she is tentative and embarrassed (656.30):

in der dienest was er komen,
unz sis mit minnen lônde,
dar um der künec in hônde.
muoz ich iu sîniu tougen sagen,
des sol ich iuwern urloup tragen:
doch sint diu selben mære
mir ze sagene ungebære,
wâ mit er kom in zoubers site.
zeinem kapûne mit einem snite
wart Klinschor gemachet.

He entered her [Iblis'] service,
until she rewarded him with love,
for which the king humiliated him.
If I am to tell you his secret,
I must have your leave:
indeed this very story
is awkward for me to tell—
how it was that he turned to the practice of sorcery.
Klinschor was turned
into a capon with a stroke of the knife.

Gawan laughs long and loud at this (657.10–11), so Arnive proceeds to tell the story again and in lusty detail. In this case, prolepsis serves verisimilitude. Gawan's amusement lets Arnive shed her reserve and retell the story as she likes.

The introduction of Prünhilt

To return to the NL, the manner in question helps to explain the introduction of Prünhilt. The story of Gunther's courtship begins like this:

1. Stories reach the Rhine about lovely maidens; Gunther decides to win one for himself. (325)
   2. Description of the formidable queen (unnamed). (326–28)
3. Gunther decides to contend for the hand of Prünhilt. (329)

The story is pointed in a certain direction right from the start with a summary of Gunther's intent:

der gedâht' im eine erwerben   Gunther der künec guot.

Gunther, the goodly king,   thought to win one for himself. (325)

Background follows with a list of Prünhilt's fearsome attributes. Then events resume their pace and move to completion. But the implications of Gunther's decision have been made clear. Start, background, continuation: here is the familiar manner.

But there are problems. Strophe 325 is different in all three versions (C 327, A 324), and only A sets it at the start of aventiure 6. In B and C it belongs to number 5. Their sixth aventiure begins with *ez was ein küniginne/ gesezzen über sê* (there was a queen, residing across the sea). Two things, then, complicate interpretation: substantial textual differences, especially between versions B and C, and different distribution of strophes at the juncture of aventiuren 5 and 6.

Michael Curschmann has argued that, as things now stand, the Prünhilt story has two beginnings.[11] The first is in strophe 325 (*iteniuwe mære—new reports*), the second in 326 (*ez was ein küniginne—there was a queen*). This second start "marks the beginning of a new story or major episode in highly typical, stereotyped fashion (echoing, by the way, the introduction of Krimhild and Sigfrid in chapters one and two respectively), and what follows immediately . . . is completely in keeping with this style."[12]

As for strophe 325 (*iteniuwe mære*), it "is not only redundant but completely undermines the effect of the following introduction. Indeed all three branches of the manuscript tradition seem to treat it as a kind of foreign body that needs to be neutralized somehow." Curschmann theorizes that strophes 325 and 326 represent two different renderings of the Prünhilt story, with 325 deriving ultimately from a conjectured "Short Lay of Brünhild." He also points out that the meaning of *iteniuwe mære* in C 327 is different from B 325. In C, "the news never heard before" is that Gunther's relatives urge him to take a wife. "This arrangement in C leads into chapter 6 in a way which parallels most closely the standard introduction to such courtship tales."[13]

Curschmann thus takes an approach similar to Masser's: the narrative develops fractures along the lines of abrading versions. I believe, on the contrary, that the text is explained better and more economically on the basis of a standard narrative form. The rift between strophes 325 and 326 belongs to the style itself, that is, it is caused by the proleptic ring. The meaning of *iteniuwe mære* in C also strikes me as artificial and derivative, smacking of forced adjustment to a new context. "News never heard before" adequately describes news about lovely maidens, but it is downright clumsy as applied to advice from Gunther's relatives. Not that B is without its own rough spots. The *dâ* of 325.2 hangs without a referent. Where is the "there" that the maidens live? Questions thus remain, and all three versions betray the seams where the Prünhilt story was stitched in. But I think the manner in which the tailoring occurred is characteristic of the NL at large, and that overly precise conjecture about source versions is unwarranted.

Version C creates a ring of its own. Like B's, it spans two aventiuren:

1. Gunther's men counsel him to take a wife, 327–328.

   2. Description of Prünhilt, 329–330.

3. Gunther hears of her, confers with kin, decides to woo her.

The ring is standard in every way. The first council is related briefly with no formal end and no consequences. The second time around it is expanded into a full-scale debate, with Sivrit dissuading and finally agreeing under the well-known condition. Thus B (along with A) and C introduce Prünhilt somewhat differently, but all employ the same trope.

Accumulation

To THIS POINT I have discussed certain techniques by which the narrative is reduced to fixed shapes of the sort that allow translation into symmetrical outlines. Whatever the figure, the principle remains the same: things are arranged symmetrically and in stages. This style expresses itself in still other but less spectacular ways. Many scenes are built around purposeful repetition but without a fixed architecture. Methodical disposition and controlled emphasis remain. Thus a fundamental manner abides through a variety of realizations.

At strophe 273 of the 5th aventiure, Ortwin (of all people) advises Gunther to present the ladies of the court to the guests, and especially Kriemhilt herself. The reason (274):

> Waz wære mannes wünne,   des vreute sich sîn lîp,
> ex entæte sœne mägede   und hêrlîchiu wîp?

> What would be a man's delight,   in what could he rejoice,
> were it not for beautiful maidens   and glorious ladies?

Led by the queen mother and princess, the women make a glorious procession as servants clear the way (284.1, 287.1–2). Onlookers jostle for position (280.2, 284.2–3), and spirits are raised by the spectacle (283.4). All this is courtly manner and temper at its purest. Meanwhile, Sivrit despairs to himself of Kriemhilt's love, although death itself would be better than separation (285). But it is, in fact, *he* who is handsome as a painting.

Now the second stage: Gunther is advised again (this time by Gernot, 288) to allow Sivrit the honor of greeting Kriemhilt. Now *his* spirits are raised (292.4) while the rest are left to hold secret thoughts (296). Three strophes describe the hero's joy.

Third stage: again servants free a path as Kriemhilt and her mother proceed to mass (299). Again she is gazed at and made the subject of hopes fond and vain (300). Once more Sivrit is invited to attend her (303), and now begins their first conversation (303) followed by twelve days of constant association.

The narrative proceeds in stages marked by the repetition of details: advice to Gunther, permission for the lovers to meet, servants clearing the way, secret hopes of onlookers, spirits raised at the sight of beautiful ladies. There is no close symmetry and not every detail is mentioned at each stage. There is much spectacle and little action. The real events are symbolic and inward. A basic tableau is set out repeatedly while the story ascends to the increasing intimacy of the happy pair.

> The changes introduced by C are minimal but characteristic. Ortwin's sudden entry at 273 is softened with a strophe inserted just before (C 274) in which Gunther asks for advice on how to make his festival praiseworthy. This smoothing tendency is typical of C.[1] It also removes the jostling at 280.2 (C 282.2), while leaving it in at 284.4 (C 286.2–4).

Kriemhilt's wedding with Etzel is described in a related manner. The pilot repetitions are (1) comparison of this marriage with her first to Sivrit, (2) the splendor of the occasion, (3) the extravagant gift giving.

1365: *Wedding at Pentecost; Kriemhilt did not gain the service of so many men through her first husband.*

  1366: The gifts she distributes and the surprise they occasion.

  1367: length of the celebration (17 days); no king's festival was ever greater; all wear new clothes.

1368: *Kriemhilt reckons she never presided over so many men at home. Rich as Sivrit was, Etzel has more men.*

  1369: Nobody ever distributed such presents at his own wedding as they all did in honor of Kriemhilt.

  1370: They make presents of whatever is asked and give the shirts off their backs.

1371: *Kriemhilt remembers Sivrit and her life on the Rhine. She weeps hidden tears.*

1372: the generosity of Dietrich and Rüedeger.

1373: Blœdelin lavishes gifts.

1374: Wärbel and Swemmel are enriched.

Royal splendor and generosity on the heroic scale: this is set out in three different sets of strophes that are introduced each time by Kriemhilt's memories of her first marriage. These climax in secret tears amidst her elevation, as once more the poet develops his favorite paradox of a happy occasion infused with melancholy and premonition. This also points the scene forward because Kriemhilt's memories will take a virulent turn in the next aventiure (1391) where again remembrance of past ills combines with her immense power and wealth under Etzel (1390), this time to crystallize in the great plot. The abrupt entrance of the two *spileman* at 1374 belongs to the same preparation. Bitter memories from days gone by, limitless power now: the refrain drives it home. The dragon's teeth are sown as Kriemhilt ascends the throne.

—III——————
OTHER TEXTS

Chanson de Roland and Rolandslied

A BRIEF EXAMINATION of the *Chanson de Roland* (henceforth *Roland*)
and Pfaffe Konrad's *Rolandslied* (henceforth RL) will provide
a useful control of my observations to this point. We discover much
the same stylistic habitus in these two epics as in Homer and the NL:
heavy use of narrative formulas, block repetition, ordered sequences,
parallelism, and correlation. What I shall present is only a survey, a
collection of illustrative examples, yet even this will suffice to reveal
a common stylistic idiom between the various epic traditions. The
coincidence, once understood, is useful for the interpretation of each
of them singly and carries implications for their origins. The RL is
especially interesting in this respect: it is *not* an oral composition; yet
it shares all the basic compositional techniques examined in Homer
and the NL, without managing to transform them into vehicles of
great poetry.

To begin with *Roland*, the architectonics of this epic are well known.[1]
For example, Turoldus[2] makes parallelism on the large scale in the
double plots of (A) Charles-Marsile-Baligant and (B) Roland-Ganelon,
and contrast in the pervasive opposition of French and Saracens
throughout. Smaller but pointed setoffs are the conferences at the
courts of Marsile and Charles at the start, the preparations for battle
where peers from each side group themselves around a leader, and
the personal oppositions of Roland–Oliver, Roland–Ganelon, and
Charles–Baligant.[3] This is only a small sampling. These same techniques are also reduced in scope to shape single incidents.

1. In a boistrous scene starting at laisse 69, twelve Saracen peers
step out, one by one with name and origin, to lead the attack on the
French. Breathing menace and threats, they swagger in review before
Marsile. The series is shaped by a strong repetitive parallelism. One
after the other, the entries emphasize the Saracen's ferocity and evil

character and expand on his boasts of confounding the French. So, for instance, in laisse 73:

> Uns almaçurs i ad de Moriane,
> N'ad plu felun en la tere d'Espaigne.
> Devant Marsile ad faite sa vantance:
> "En Rencesvals guierai ma cumpaigne,
> .XX. milie ad escuz e a lances.
> Se trois Rollant, de mort li duins fiance,
> Jamais n'ert jor que Carles ne se pleignet."

> There is an Almaçor from Moriane,
> There is no greater villain in the land of Spain.
> He made his boast in front of Marsile:
> "I shall lead my company to Roncevaux,
> Twenty thousand with shields and lances.
> If I find Roland, I give my oath that he shall die,
> A day will not go by that Charles will not lament."

Most others follow the same pattern. Many details and even shifting patterns of assonance weave a continuous and varied strand.[4] The steady march of the repeats constrains the wild surge of the warriors' parade. The scene is rowdy and solemn at once, tumultuous and stately, its turbulence held in check by its measured tread. These Saracen peers will perish in the same order as they march by here to gesture and brag.

2. The first three to die in that later scene are, accordingly, Aelroth (93), Falsaron (94), and Corsalis (Corsablix, 95), slain in heraldic sequence by the three leaders of the French: Roland, Oliver, and Turpin. The combats form an obvious series with repeated components: the Saracen threatens and reviles (*vile Frenchmen* 1191; *today Fair France will lose its honor*, 1223; *we must show great contempt for the men before us here*, 1240); the Frenchman mauls him hideously and mocks his corpse. Finely spun connectors of other sorts build irony and moral emphases.[5]

3. Starting at laisse 40, Marsile and Ganelon begin the negotiations that will lead to the betrayal of the French rear guard.[6] Marsile speaks, Ganelon responds. *The king opens with the same questions and assertions repeated three times in three successive laisses.* I quote extensively to let this litany speak for itself. "Charles is old and gray; I understand he is over two hundred years old":

laisse 40:   Il est mult vielz, si ad sun tens uset,
             Men escïent, dous cenz anz ad passet.

laisse 41:   Carlemagne, ki est canuz e vielz.
             Men escïentre, dous cenz anz ad e mielz.

laisse 42:   Carlemagne, ki est canuz e blancs,
             Mien escïentre, plus ad d .II. C anz.

"He has conquered many lands and taken many blows."

laisse 40:   Par tantes teres ad sun cors demened,
             Tanz colps ad pris sur sun escut bucler,
             Tanz riches reis cunduit a mendisted.

             He has knocked about so many lands,
             He has taken so many blows on his shield,
             He has reduced so many powerful kings to beggary.

laisse 41:   Par tantes teres ad sun cors traveillet,
             Tanz cols ad pris de lances e d'espiet,
             Tanz riches reis cunduiz a mendistiet.

             He has punished his body in so many lands,
             He has taken so many blows from lances and spears,
             He has reduced so many powerful kings to beggary.

laisse 42:   Par tantes teres est alet cunquerant,
             Tanz colps ad pris de bons espiez trenchanz,
             Tanz riches reis morz e vencuz en champ.

             He has conquered his way across so many lands,
             He has taken so many blows from good sharp spears,
             He has slain and vanquished in battle so many powerful
                kings.

"When will he stop waging war?"

laisse 40:   Quant ert il mais recreanz d'osteier?

laisse 41:   Quant ert il mais recreanz d'osteier?

laisse 42:   Quant ier il mais d'osteier recreant?

*As Marsile asks the same question three times, Ganelon gives him the same
answer to each.* "Yes, indeed, Charles is a great man," (530, 545, 558),
"and he fears nobody" (549, 562). Here is the third reply:

"Ço n'iert," dist Guenes, "tant cum vivet Rollant.
N'ad tel vassal d'ici qu'en Orïent.
Mult par est proz Oliver, sis cumpainz.
Li .XII. per, que Carles aimet tant,
Funt les enguardes a .XX. milie de Francs.
Soürs est Carles, ne crent hume vivant."

"Not," said Ganelon, "so long as Roland lives.
There's no knight like him from here to the Orient.
His companion Oliver also has great worth.
The twelve peers, whom Charles loves so well,
Are in the van with twenty thousand Franks.
Charles is secure and fears no man alive."

The exchange is astonishingly repetitive and without an equivalent even in Homer. It may seem stiff and unwieldy at first glance but the opposite is true. As in the introduction of the Saracen peers, the repetitions stand as a frame against a subtle flow of action. The repeated compliments to Charles give the talk a touch of diplomatic realism. Marsile probes obliquely and Ganelon responds in kind. They maneuver for a while at a safe distance, learning where they stand and reaching accommodation in the safety of unction and flattery. Roland and the peers are singled out for destruction in the guise of a compliment: "Charles is safe while Roland lives" (544: *tant cum vivet sis niés*; 557: *tant cum vivet Rollant*). Ganelon insinuates this plan as part of his praise: "The twelve peers, whom Charles loves so well, are in the van with twenty thousand Franks." He says that twice (547–48; 560–61; cf. 574–76) before suggesting the rear guard as their target. By the time Marsile sheds his reserve the treachery has been offered and accepted. This is an inspiringly effective use of block repetition and what we might call strophic correspondence. Here it creates a veil of complaisance and tact that discreetly mantles the descent into villainy.[7]

It was Jean Rychner who first named and described this technique of *laisses similaires* in *Roland*.[8] There are different forms but one fundamental manner: the narrative is articulated by means of repetition and parallelism with the laisse as the building block. Rychner writes: "The total impression is, then, of a poem that is shaped, and indeed shaped on the basis of the laisse. For the author of Roland the laisse was the basic narrative unit, the dramatic unit, the lyric unit. In short, the laisse is the primary building material" (124). Parallel laisses mark out decisive moments, give them definition and weight, make them into mark points and signposts: "It was undeniably the author of *Roland* who made the most of the lyric potential of similar laisse groups. His clusters of similar laisses retard the narrative at its most dramatic and decisive moments. They create checks, as it were, lofty lyric vantage points, before the narrative again resumes its course" (93).

But *Roland*'s coherence at all levels also makes it untypical with respect to its contemporaries.[9] In fact, Rychner divides the *chansons de geste* into two basic types: those with articulated narratives based on the laisse and those without them. Only the first achieve high quality. The unshaped and indifferent flow of the others remains at the level of recitation. "True epic elevation seems to me attainable only by poems of the first type. They alone are capable of the profound transformation of recitation into poetry" (125). What Rychner identifies as the peculiar excellence of *Roland* takes its origin in those features I have singled out in Homer and the NL: narrative design at all levels, symmetrical repetition, controlled emphasis. And each of these epics holds lonely preeminence in its own tradition.

Pfaffe Konrad composed the RL about 1170 (or approximately seventy years after *Roland*). It is not strictly a translation from the French, although he comes close to calling it that, having first rendered his original into the more familiar Latin and thence into German (9080):

> also iz an dem buoche gescribin stat
> in franczischer zungen,
> so han ich iz in die latine bedwungin,
> danne in di tutiske gekeret.

> Just as it stands written in the book,
> in the French tongue,
> I translated it into Latin,
> and then rendered it in German.

It is not known what text of *Roland* he used but certainly not Turoldus', which is profoundly different in detail and spirit. Hans-Erich Keller, who devoted a lengthy study to the question, concludes that no surviving texts of *Roland* can be considered Konrad's source.[10] In fact, less than one fourth of his lines represent verses in other know versions. There were doubtless many more of these than we possess, but Keller's conclusion is that Konrad used a composite text.

Originality on the part of Konrad seems to be excluded from the start by his claim not to have added or removed anything from the original (9084):

> ich nehan der niht an gemeret,
> ich nehan dir niht uber haben.

> I have added nothing to it,
> I have left nothing out of it.

Set against Turoldus this is, of course, wildly untrue. But one wonders if it can be taken at face value in any case. The assertion reminds us of Lord's oral poets who describe their own original efforts as word-for-word renditions of songs heard from others. Not that Konrad was an oral poet—far from it—but his claim to literal fidelity might be no more than a convention picked up along the way. In that case, we would need to reckon with considerable stuff of his own. He will not have undertaken his "translation" without a strong interest in epic and familiarity with it. The clergy was not always immune to its siren call, as we know from the case of Bishop Gunther of Bamberg (died 1065), who not only commissioned the *Ezzolied* but who had a passion for heroic epic. A contemporary chronicler describes him with ironic disapproval: "He is always pouring over Attila, Dietrich von Bern, and other . . . marvelous creatures." For Konrad, his version was a desirable blend of the sacred and profane—or, rather, a full transformation of the second into the first. It represents an appropriation of the one by the other, a calculated effort, whether by Konrad or his source(s). His opening prayer, that it be vouchsafed him to relate the truth, probably stems from his own hand:

> Schephare allir dinge,
> cheiser allir chuoninge,
> wol du oberister ewart,
> lere mich selbe diniu wort;
> duo sende mire zemunde
> din heilege urkunde,
> daz ich die luge vermide,
> die warheit scribe.

Creator of all things,
Lord of all kings,
O thou highest guardian of the law,
Teach me thyself thy words;
Send thou unto my lips
Thy sacred instruction,
That I may avoid falsehood
And write the truth.

That plea has deep roots in both clerical tracts and worldly epic of the middle ages, but it loses point as the prelude to a straight translation. The fact that the French original was filtered through a double translation increases suspicion. Both Latin and German will have imposed their own traditional diction, thereby coloring and skewing the respective versions. Unfortunately, speculation takes us only a short distance. Even if Konrad's originality was greater than he pretends, it remains impossible for us to measure.

I shall, in any case, treat Konrad mainly in comparison with Turoldus. This does not imply the assumption of a direct connection between the two. The purpose is always to illuminate the nature of Konrad's text. In the interest of brevity and simplicity I shall give him credit and blame for everything, but all variation might derive from his source(s), either entirely or in degrees beyond our power to identify.

The RL is not divided into strophes. Instead, Konrad uses a variable short line with an average of six to eight syllables[11] and in indifferently rhymed couplets. The isolating and architectonic powers of the laisse were thus lost to him, but analysis will show that he achieves many of the same effects without it; in fact his text is even more elaborately structured than its French counterpart. The basic manner is thus independent of strophic or single-line form, a fact confirmed by the comparison of the NL and Homer. Rychner's conclusions about the role of the laisse as the fundamental artistic module in *Roland* remain valid, but similar results can be achieved by different means.

The Saracen peers

We begin with the gathering of the Saracen peers. Turoldus' version was described above, with emphasis on its parallelism and repeats. Konrad works with similar elements to the same end. In a bold move, he actually introduces only eight leaders while speaking repeatedly

of twelve (3575, 3813). A numerical rhythm in the passage shows this
is no accident.

The enemy step out one by one, each demanding the privilege of
killing Roland or promising to do so (except for Margariz, who men-
aces Karl) and Marssilie replies to each—a more insistent refrain even
than *Roland*'s. The speeches on both sides decrease in length from
the first through the middle entries, then expand again through the
end: no strict arithmetical progression, but a nice arc that creates a
varied tempo, starting with emphasis and building again to the finish:

1. Alterot, 354–62 (23 lines)
    Marssilie, 3563–95 (32)

2. Falsaron, 3595–3614 (19)
    Marssilie, 3615–24 (10)

3. Cursabile, 3625–40 (16)
    Marssilie, 3641–49 (8)

4. Malprimes, 3651–59 (9)
    Marssilie (indirect speech), 3660–63 (4)

5. Ammirat, 3665–72 (8)
    Marssilie, 3673–81 (8)

6. Targis, 3681–3708 (27)
    Marssilie, 3709–24 (15)

7. Margariz, 3725–58 (28)
    Marssilie (no answer)

8. Cernubiles, 3759–92 (33)
    Marssilie, 3793–3812 (19)

Marssilie's silence in number 7 breaks the pattern but there is a
reason for it. Margariz (7) and Cernubiles (8) appear regularly together
as a pair. The first is handsome and sought after by women; the second
is monstrously strong and ugly and from the devil's own country.
They are put side by side in the Saracen catalogue at 2673–95 with
the same attributes (no equivalent of this in *Roland*), and they are in
sequence again at 5045 where Cernubiles is slain by Roland and Margariz beaten off by Oliver. Here they receive a single reply because
they are considered a team.

What is the total impression? Some shapes from *Roland* remain: the
series, the threats. Others change: Marssilie's replies, the controlled
length of the speeches. Thus symmetry answers symmetry, although

each is different. This is important. Did Konrad translate, compile, or compose? Whichever, the sense of form is unmistakable. The two works resemble each other at this basic level. The techniques are traditional and belong to the genre, whatever the mode of composition.

Still Konrad's effort proves (if we need the demonstration) that orderly composition is no guarantor by itself of good effect or depth. If anything, his ponderous system oppresses, devoid as it is of both color and transparence. Even the description of Cernubiles' hellish country remains bookish and abstract (3770):

> sin lant daz was fraissam,
> daz liut daz ist grimme,
> der sunne der ne gescain dar inne,
> die tuvele puwint dar unwerde;
> iz ist diu verfluochet erde.

> His country, it was dreadful,
> The people, they are fearsome,
> The sun does not shine there,
> Devils dwell there in shameful wise.
> It is the accursed soil.

Roland's penchant for ebullient and grotesque detail finds few echoes in Konrad. Turoldus brings on Aelroth (Konrad's Alterot, Marssilie's nephew) with a lively flourish (860):

> Li niés Marsilie, il est venuz avant
> Sur un mulet od un bastun tuchant.
> Dist a sun uncle belement enriant.

> Marsile's nephew came forward
> On a mule, which he prodded with a stick.
> Laughing heartily, he said to his uncle.

An unforgettable picture: flaring, undignified, alarming, full of brio. Konrad solemnly reduces all that to the pedestrian and unpictorial:

> Alterot der wilde
> furt ein stap in der hant;
> er ilte da er den chuonc vant.

> Alterot the fierce
> Bore a rod in his hand.
> He hastened to where he found the king.

Konrad's limitations are nowhere more visible than in the face of *Roland*'s heathen: those cunning, supple, mirthful, volatile, temperamental, and violent devil's disciples—splendid villains, every one.

Abrasion inside the French ranks is not to Konrad's liking either. The scene where Charles picks the envoy (spy) to Marsile is constructed by Turoldus with the frontal symmetry of parallel laisses.[12] Four men volunteer: Naimes (laisse 17), Roland and Oliver (18), and Turpin (19). Naimes and Turpin receive a single laisse, Roland and Oliver share one in the middle. Charles refuses them all and dual repetitions in his speeches mark the series (note that offer and refusal come each time in one complete laisse):

A. 17.   Seignurs baruns, qui i enveieruns
En Sarraguce, al rei Marsiliuns?

My lord barons, whom shall we send
To Saragossa, to King Marsile?

18.   Seignurs baruns, qui i purruns enveier
Al Sarrazin ki Sarraguce tient?

My lord barons, whom can we send
To the Saracen who rules Saragossa?

B. 17.   Par ceste barbe e par cest men gernun,
Vos n'irez pas van de mei si luign.

By this beard and by this mustache of mine,
You'll never go far from me.

18.   Par ceste barbe que veez blancher,
Li duze per mar i serunt jugez!

By this white beard that you see before you,
The twelve will not be nominated or else!

C. 17.   Alez sedeir, quant nuls vos sumunt!

Go sit down, no one has called upon you!

18.   Ambdui vos en taisez!

Be still the both of you!

19.   Alez sedeir desur cel palie blanc!
N'en parlez mais, se jo nel vos cumant![13]

> Go sit down on that white silk cloth!
> Don't say another word unless I order you to!

The scene is heated. Charles is in a prickly temper and irritated with every one of his volunteers. Roland and Oliver, vying for honor, are set down hard, and Naimes and Turpin (!) scarcely less so.

Konrad reduces the volunteers to three, joins them with a different set of repetitions and typically removes Karl's acerbic commands. In outline:

A. Roland volunteers, 1298–1305.   (8 lines)
   Karl refuses, 1306–9. (4)

B. Oliver volunteers, 1310–19. (10)
   Karl refuses, 1320–31. (12)

C. Turpin volunteers, 1332–53. (12)
   Karl refuses, 1354–63. (10)

Repetition and variation are carefully planned. Roland and Oliver leap forward to speak (*uf spranc*, 1298, 1310); the more dignified Turpin rises (*uf stunt*, 1332). The volunteers please Karl as much as they annoy him in *Roland*.

> swich du neve Ruolant,
> des ne habe ne heinen gedanc;
> ich ne gesende dich dar iarlanc.   (1307)

> Be silent, nephew Roland,
> do not even think of that;
> I will never send you there.

> nu habe michelen danc,
> siz widere an dinen banc.
> du bist mir ze allen eren vil lib;
> ze boten wil ich din nicht. (1322)

> Accept my warmest thanks,
> sit down again on your bench.
> I am pleased to confer every honor upon you,
> but I do not want you as envoy.

> Der Kaiser antwerte ime mit minnen: (1354)

> gewaehne is nicht mere, Turpin,
> also liep mir dine hulde sin (1362)

The emperor answered him with affection:
do not mention it again, Turpin,
dear as your devotion is to me.

In sum, Konrad's scene is as orderly as its French counterpart. The
organizing details are different, the principles remain the same. Konrad censors out the tension between Karl and his men, replacing it
with courteous deference and bleaching away color. Only the one
fundamental and edifying conflict is allowed to persist: Karl and the
peers on one side, Genelun on the other. Later Konrad will trivialize
in similar fashion the conflict between Roland and Oliver over the
blowing of Oliphant.

The first encounters

I described above how the first three Saracens to die in *Roland* are
drawn together in a defined series: insults and threats against the
French; violent demise at the hands of Roland, Oliver and Turpin
respectively; answering mockery from the victor. The episodes are
short, self-contained, and consecutive (laisses 93–95). The other nine
Saracen peers perish in the next nine (shorter) laisses.

Konrad retains the order and correspondences but expands each
encounter with a considerable aftermath of general battle description.
This puts the duels at considerable remove from one another. The
enemy insults and challenges; the Frenchman replies, slays him, delivers another harangue, and leads his men into the fray. These se-
quels to the three clashes vary much in detail as other French leaders
enter them all and minor Saracens are also dispatched. About 150
lines separate the death of Alterot and the appearance of Falsaron,
and almost another 100 intervene before Cursabile challenges Turpin.
Konrad's effort, more than Turoldus', is to draw the armies at large
into the picture and to depict a general melee.[14] This is a modernizing
trait.

1. Alterot—Roland, 4020–68
   sequel, 4069–4216

2. Falsaron—Oliver, 4217–75
   sequel, 4276–4370

3. Cursabile—Turpin, 4371–4420
   sequel, 4421–86

The effect of this is to make Konrad's series less visible than Turoldus' and less immediate. It has less of that paradelike effect and the single entries are not so meticulously adjusted to one another (Turpin, for example, delivers no speech of triumph).[15] The encounters widen into collisions of large masses and extra minor fights. Konrad makes a firm sequence but it is more elaborate and less direct, more contrived and less forceful. Set against Turoldus' version it leaves the impression of imitation, elaboration, refinement. It belongs to the same manner but to a more literate stage. It feels derivative and self-conscious. Konrad's style is generally more fluid than the French, less abrupt, divided less into noticeable beats, striving for smoother contours and even flow. In this respect it is a transitional piece marking the rapprochement of traditional epic to the style of the courtly romance.[16]

Further patterning

I assigned the first three fights conducted by Roland, Oliver, and Turpin to a self-contained series. Both *Roland* and the RL mark them off by their position and content. In both poems, leaders of other enemy contingents now take their turns. *Roland* keeps close track, assigning each of them to a short laisse (96ff.) wherein to perish at the hands of his French counterpart, and even helping the audience to keep count (1308):

> Des .XII. pers li .X. en sunt ocis.
> Ne mes que dous n'en i ad remés vifs.

> Ten of the twelve Saracen peers have been killed,
> Now only two of them remain alive.

Konrad, for his part, delivers a much expanded version with a different formal order. The tendencies observed in the first three pairs abide as single episodes enlarge to embrace the action over the entire field. Konrad also emphasizes the conflict of religions and the Christians' sanctity and passion for martyrdom.

Roland makes a visible break between the duels of the first three peers and the other nine. For these last the laisses are shorter, the encounters simpler, and the correspondences less striking. But Konrad gives the second series its own features no less than the first. He also begins it already in the encounter between Cursabile and Turpin. This duel becomes a transition piece, sharing identifying marks of both series and allowing one to glide into another—an example of Konrad's smoothing tendency described just above but also something that he shares with Homer. The patterning is best illustrated in outline.

A. Cursabile—Turpin (4371)
  1. Cursabile challenges.
  2. Turpin answers and kills him.
  3. More single slayings and general battle; emphasis on the Christians' valor.
  4. 64 of Turpin's men fall.

B. Malprimes—Egeris (4487)
  1. Malprimes enters with 12,000 men.
  2. Egeris counters with 1100 and kills him.
  3. More single slayings, general fighting, emphasis on the Christians' success.
  4. 71 of them fall.

C. Amurafel—Egeriers (4536)
  1. Amurafel and Egeriers face each other over a trench.
  2. Egeriers leaps over and kills him.
  3. Another single slaying, general battle, Christian success.
  4. 87 Christians fall.

D. Amarezur—Samson (4589)
  1. Amarezur enters with 12,000 men, all splendidly armed and mightily proud; he challenges the Christian leader.
  2. Samson replies and kills him.
  3. General fight, the pagans' armor is rent and covered with blood.
  4. 108 Christians fall.

E. Targis—Anseis (4659)
  1. Targis, worshipper of Apollo, enters with 12,000 men.
  2. Anseis fires his men against the unbelievers.
  3. Hard duel with strong contrast of Christian vs. pagan. Targis is slain.
  4. The Christians, fighting for eternal salvation, kill all the Saracens and the devil takes their souls.
  5. 308 Christians fall.

F. Eschermunt—Engelirs (4763)
  1. Eschermunt enters with 12,000 men and challenges the Christian leader.

2. Engelirs answers and kills him after a considerable fight.
3. More single combats, general engagement, all the Saracens die.
4. 108 Christians fall.

G. Estorgant—Hatte (4851)
1. Hatte leads 1100 Frenchmen, pious and brave.
2. Estorgant opposes him with 12,000 followers.
3. Considerable duel, Hatte wins.
4. Other French warriors also wreak havoc, but the enemy resists strongly.
5. 410 Christians die.

At this point the series ends (4949). Three enemy peers remain to die but outside this sequence. The outline sets down only the universals binding all the entries and just some of the variations.[18] Except for entry F, each episode increases the number of Christian slain.[19] We saw arithmetical progression used elsewhere to control tempo. These simple numerical increments help compensate for the articulating powers of the strophe or laisse that Konrad did not have at his disposal.

These examples show how methodically Konrad assembled certain long stretches of his poem. Indeed, all the fighting from the first onset through the seven-part series just described is organized in distinct units set in a grand design. But at 4949 this slackens. The close and long-range patterning gives way to looser blocks. Stalmariz, the tenth Saracen peer to fall (4993), is a transitional figure: his 12,000 men tie him to the string just ended but otherwise he is different from them. Now enter Margariz and Cernubile, paired here as always, followed by a review of the French leaders sweeping all before them. After that begins the slaying of the French peers.

As for this last, *Roland* is more compressed and systematic. Frenchmen are slain in a series of laisse-couplets:

114: Climborin kills Engelier.
115: Oliver avenges him.

116: Valdebrun kills Samson.
117: Roland avenges him.

118: Malquiant kills Anseis.
119: Turpin avenges him.

120: Grandoine kills Gerin and three others.
121: Roland is enraged.
122: Roland takes vengeance.

Konrad proceeds in more leisurely fashion. First he allows three French peers to die and be avenged (5285), then one more at 5851 after much action in between. These Saracen successes are introduced respectively by reports to Marssilie from the field: the first by Grandon (5191), the second by Margariz (5630). The design is unmistakable, but neither Turoldus nor Konrad follows all the French peers to their end with the same formal consistency as their Saracen counterparts, and both mitigate these disasters with vast losses by the enemy.

Scene doubling in the RL

On a smaller scale, Konrad has the interesting mannerism of developing things in two parallel stages. At 2415 Genelun tells Marssilie how to deceive Karl. The speech falls into two halves, the second being essentially (but not entirely) a recapitulation of the first.

I   A. *Do sprach der ungetriuwe man* ("Then the faithless man spoke"), 2515.

  B. Here is my advice (*nu wil ich iu raten*), 2416.

  C. Collect your army with all speed (*vil drate*), 2418.

  D. Send Karl gifts and your son as hostage, 2421.

  E. Be careful not to meet him face to face (*huotet daz er iuch icht gesprechen mege*), 2422.

  F. Once they have your presents, they will be eager to return home, 2424.

  G. Description of Roland and the peers, 2425.

  H. Conclusion: I would rejoice to hear of their fall, 2450.

Now that advice is repeated in all its essentials:

II A. *Do sprach der ungetriuwe man,/der dem tuvil manige sele gewan* ("Then the faithless man spoke,/ who won the devil many a soul"), 2453.

  B. If you want my advice, here is what you should do (*wilt du, herre, rat der zu,/ich sage dir rehte wie du tuo*), 2455.

  C. Collect your army in a hurry (*ile daz du lute gewinnest*), 2457.

  D. Wait until Karl departs. Do not show yourself to him so that nothing will go wrong, 2459:

so huote der cite
so der Kaiser wider uber gereite.
niemmir geoffin dich sin e,
daz dir icht misse ge.

Wait for the time
when the emperor rides away again.
Do not show yourself to him before he does so,
lest you suffer a mishap.

E. I will keep you advised, send out your spies, attack them, 2463.

F. Conclusion: if they are all slain, Karl will never recover.

There is no strict mirroring. The first half enlarges on Roland and the peers (I.G), the second on Karl's impending ruin (II.F). But the central plan, preceded by close to identical introductions (A and B) is laid out twice: marshall your forces quickly, avoid Karl until he leaves for home, then attack. At the simplest level, repetition creates emphasis. That is its use here as Genelun drives home his point. What attracts attention is the repeat of things in order. Another nice effect, one that brings a flush of realism, is Genelun's shift from *ir* to *du*. This actually happens near the end of the first round (2434) and continues through the second. Genelun allows himself increasing intimacy as he warms to the task.

In a related manner, Genelun takes his leave for the journey to Saragossa in two steps: first from Karl, then from his men. Similar details tie them together:

I A. Genelun bows to Karl, 1636.

    B. His speech: the twelve are happy now, but they will pay for it if I escape with my life, 1637.

    C. Genelun takes his leave; description of his mount, the Saracens admire it, 1648.

    D. Seven hundred men follow and grieve, 1661.

II A. Genelun bows to Karl, 1668.

    B. He retires to a meadow and addresses his men: thank you for your loyalty (1672); serve Karl and care for my orphaned son if I die (1688); care for my widow (1710).

    C. Genelun's departure, great mourning by his followers, 1728.

The leave taking builds through the second round. Genelun's second speech is longer and so is the lament at separation. The manner is reminiscent of those passages from the NL where an action is developed through two expanding stages. The same anticipatory interlocking can also be observed: the Saracens, with whom Genelun will ride to Saragossa, enter the picture already at I.C.

I mentioned earlier that in *Roland* Ganelon's exchange with Marsile starting at laisse 40 runs parallel to his talk with Blancandrin during the ride to Saragossa (laisses 28ff.). Konrad increases the similarity between the two, drawing them even closer together and developing the betrayal as it were in two acts. The scenes begin respectively at 1760 and 2224.

Genelun—Blanscandiz

   A. Blanscandiz: Genelun, you are a splendid and impressive person. You French have conquered many peoples. Karl has taken many blows and become old. Why does he not let you stay at home in peace? (1760)

   B. Genelun: Karl and all of us do battle for the Christian faith. God himself commands Karl. Nobody can harm him. He hates evil and would die for our salvation. (1788)

   C. Blanscandiz: Yes, indeed, Karl is a great man and he has wise advisers. But tell me, who is this person Roland? Yesterday I heard him promise Karl to conquer us and make all earthly kingdoms subject to him. (1822)

   D. Genelun: Roland and the twelve are the cause of all our troubles. They want to subdue the whole world. Would that they might come to a bad end. I could lay a plan with you to bring them down. Better for the twelve to die than the rest of us. (1858).

   E. Blanscandiz rejoices. (1898)

Genelun—Marssilie

   A. Marssilie: Genelun, you are a person of firm and excellent character (*stete unde biderbe*). Tell me, who gave Karl authority that he subjects me and the entire world? He has waged war for many years, he is old and must be weary. He should let his men rest and allow me to enjoy what is mine. (2224)

   B. Genelun: Karl is a great man, nobody could describe all his excellence. He would gladly die for God, Who has instructed him to convert the heathen. We are glad to help him. (2241)

C. Marssilie: It is a fine thing for him to serve God and to enlarge His service, but not to take my kingdom by force. (2255)

D. Genelun: That is all Roland's doing, and of the other peers. They want to conquer the world. (2264)

From this point their talk turns to completion of the plot. This graded development is like that from the last example and those from the NL: the second act resumes the first, elaborates, and builds to completion. To review some of the details shared by the two scenes:

1. Flattery to Genelun: 1762, 2224.

2. Karl is old: 1782, 2235.

3. He has waged many wars: 1781, 2234.

4. Why does he not stay at home and let you do the same? 1783, 2236.

5. God himself gives Karl instructions: 1796, 2252.

6. He does not care about things of this world: 1814, 2251.

7. He would gladly die for the faith: 1818, 2250.

8. Roland and the peers want to conquer the world: 1869, 2272.

9. Roland and the peers are causing all the trouble: 1859, 2264.

10. They threaten even Babylon: 1870, 2272.

The familiar relation between *Roland* and the RL emerges again: formal, structured, repetitive style in both, but different specific shapes and different effects. Konrad's effort is to make a diptych of the two interviews: flattery of Genelun; questions about Karl (his wars, his age, his relentless aggression); defense by Genelun; repeated question; Genelun's accusation of Roland and the peers. Everything is close to the surface. The narrative is ordered, clear, thematically consistent, modestly effective.[20]

Turoldus does not tune the two conversations so finely one to the other, and the litany of Blanscandiz' questions is bolder and more striking. But his master's touch shows itself as those solemn repeats create a subtle and shaded exchange. A subtext is established beneath the flow of words before the irrevocable is spoken aloud. Konrad is less obvious, with greater complexity and less content. Turoldus is more archaic and more suggestive, simpler on the surface and deeper.

One final observation on reduplication. The technique is not un-known to Turoldus, and laisses 3 and 4 offer a good example. Blan-candrin tells Marsile how to deal with Charles. Laisse 3: send him gifts, tell him to return to Aix in France; you will be converted there at Michelmas; send him hostages—"far better that they should lose their heads/ than that we should lose our lands and offices/ and be reduced to begging." Laisse 4 now repeats all of this, placing it in the future and sure to happen: the French will return home; Charles will be in his chapel at Aix to celebrate Michelmas; he will have the hos-tages decapitated, "far better that they should lose their heads/ than that we should lose fair Spain, the beautiful,/ or that we should suffer disasters and privations."

It is curious and invites speculation that Konrad uses recapitulation in Genelun's advice to Marssilie on how to deceive Karl, while Tur-oldus uses it to report Blancandrin's promptings on the same subject. But the two scenes occur at different parts of the respective poems. As usual, the effects differ. In *Roland* the device is sophisticated and persuasive. Those positive future tenses on the adviser's lips the second time around make it all seem sure to happen—indeed almost to have happened already. They convey a grand assurance and paint a vivid picture. Konrad delivers emphasis with his repeats but little more.

Beyond the Epic

THIS STUDY EMPHASIZES what the epics share with other literature and not what sets them apart; more specifically and with reference to current debate, not the anatomy of formular systems but their use in refined composition. The number of single techniques is almost infinite, but they arrange themselves in a small number of permanent categories. It will be useful to consider how some ancient and modern texts traffic in specific figures much like those of the epics. Their use is everywhere the same, the shaping and distillation of experience that is the primal effort of all serious narration. More simply, they belong to the art of good storytelling.

The Gospel of Mark

Among the synoptic gospels Mark stands alone in his predilection for ring composition, and he has some interesting examples of the type singled out in Homer and the NL. Perhaps this reflects his relative proximity to oral versions. The best and most finely conceived example is the healing of Jairus' daughter (5.22–43). This is also the only one of Mark's rings that survives in Matthew and Luke, although these show differences. Here is a summary, distributed in the usual three parts:

1. A synagogue leader named Jairus begs Jesus to come to his home and cure his dying daughter. Jesus leaves with him immediately.

2. Along the way he passes a woman who was suffering from hemorrhage. She says to herself: "If I can only touch his clothing I shall be healed." She does so. Power passes from the master and he notices. He discovers the woman and assures her that faith has worked the cure.

3. As they approach Jairus' house, word reaches them that the girl has died. Jesus enters and restores her to her family.

The two incidents are interlaced, not set in straight sequence. The first healing is performed on the way to the second. This is, in fact, the only place in the gospels where two miracles are joined. Although they may actually have occurred that way,[1] or the girl's death in the second may have been caused by the delay of the first,[2] we can also detect their close accommodation to each other. The connections are these: two miraculous healings are both performed under the dominant perspective of faith. The woman is sure she need only touch Jesus' clothing. That effects the cure and Jesus emphasizes the same in his words to her: "Daughter, your faith has saved you." That theme is amplified when they reach Jairus' house: word comes that the child is already dead, they should trouble the teacher no further, the mourners are already at their lamentation. But Jesus says to the father: "Do not be afraid, only have faith." The same point is emphasized in negative contrast when laughter greets Jesus' assertion that the girl is "sleeping." Therefore the connection of the two miracles in time and place reinforces their common salvific message: healing (salvation) is through faith.

These are the main associations, but smaller connectors abound. Jairus' daughter is twelve; the woman had suffered from her condition for the same number of years (5.42, 5.26). There is emphasis on touching and contact (with ceremonial uncleanness resulting). Jairus asks Jesus to lay hands on his daughter; crowds press in on the master from all sides; the woman lays hold of his garment and he feels power pass from him at her touch; he takes the maiden by the hand when commanding her to rise. A close bracket is effected between parts 2 and 3 of the ring by the notice that Jesus "was still speaking" (to the woman, 5.35) when word arrived of the girl's death. Both miracles show a sharp interchange between Jesus and the others. In the first he turns around at the woman's touch and wants to know who did it. His disciples, obviously impatient, ask how he expects to identify a single contact in a pressing throng (5.31). The crowd in Jairus' house laughs at him and he turns them all out (5.40). Both sufferers slip from bad to worse. The child is sick at the start and dead by the time Jesus arrives. The woman had spent all her money on doctors but her condition only declined. Both cures arouse fear and trembling.

As Jesus looks around for whoever touched him the woman approaches in a fright (5.33). The reaction in Jairus' house is even stronger: the people are beside themselves (5.42).

The two miracles thus convey the same lesson and share a similar staging: a crowded street and house; tense verbal exchanges; release from desperate straits causing amazement and dread; the awesome healer and his message of faith.

Matthew's account is severely curtailed (9.18–26) and has none of Mark's thematic integration. In fact, not one of the parallels between the two cures listed above survived the abbreviation. The ring composition stays at the level of a static figure. Luke (8.40–56) also condenses, especially throughout the section in Jairus' house, but he keeps all the main connections, including those listed. Mark's version remains the most detailed and dramatic.

None of Mark's other rings achieves the complex perfection of the double healing, but some of them are good examples of the style in their own right. Judas' betrayal is one. Luke (22.1–6) relates in a straight line the authorities' desire to arrest Jesus and Judas' treason. The high priests and scribes plot together but fear the people; Satan enters Judas; he goes to them and arranges betrayal and payment, to their great delight.

Mark (14.1–11), followed by Matthew (26.1–16), breaks this into two parts by inserting the incident of the woman with the jar of perfume in between:

1. Passover is approaching and the high priests and scribes search for a way to capture Jesus and kill him—but not during the feast for fear of an uproar among the people. (14.1–2)

2. Jesus in Bethany at the house of Simon the Leper (14.3–10): a woman anoints him with costly oil. The apostles object but Jesus defends her: "She has anointed my body for burial in advance." (14.8)

3. Judas goes to those in charge. They rejoice and instruct that money be given to him, and he seeks an opportunity for the betrayal. (14.10–11)

The woman's act stands in counterpoint to the persons and events before and after: loyalty against hostility and faithlessness. Jesus' impending death is prefigured in the anointing and set inside the actions of Judas and the authorities on either side.[3]

Sometimes Mark's rings suffer from a certain obscurity caused by the process, no more to be surely reconstructed, by which the materials coalesced in the early transmission. A good example is Jesus' curse on the fig tree (Mark 11.12–25; cf. Matthew 21.18–22). Mark uses a ring to associate that incident with the cleansing of the temple:

1. Jesus addresses the tree: "May no one eat fruit from you ever again." (12–14)
   2. Expulsion of the dealers from the temple. (15–19)
3. The next day they discover the fig tree to have withered. (20)

The fig tree stands for Israel (on the basis of texts like Jeremiah 8.13, Hosea 9.10, Joel 1.7); hence the curse represents condemnation of God's fallen people.[4] The cleansing of the temple means the same thing: "Jesus' action is seen as an exercise of his Messianic authority, symbolizing God's judgment against the abuses of the Temple "(JBC). Mark's account is thus shaped in such a way as to bring two incidents of the same symbolic content into the closest possible narrative association. "The natural sequel to Jesus' triumphal entry would be his cleansing of the Temple . . . and the challenge of the Jewish authorities . . . Mark, however, interrupts this sequence, surrounding the story of Jesus' cleansing of the Temple by the cursing of the fig tree, both actions symbolizing God's judgment against Israel" (JBC).[5] The effect is diluted somewhat by the assorted sayings on faith, prayer and forgiveness appended at 11.22ff. This suggests, in turn, that the bracketing of the fig tree and the temple belongs to the pre-Marcan tradition and that the sayings were attached when the meaning of the curse was no longer understood.[6]

Mark's is also the only synoptic gospel to set Peter's denials in a ring. Matthew (26.69–75) and Luke (22.54–62) tell that story in a single piece, although each gives it a different place in the sequence of arrest and interrogation. Mark puts Peter outside by the fire just before Jesus faces the Sanhedrin (14.54). The notice is brief. Like many Homeric rings, it sets the stage and looks to the future but goes no further. When the crossexamination inside concludes (14.55–65), the scene shifts again to Peter in the courtyard and his denials follow (14.66–72).[7]

A final example.[8] Jesus goes to a house (apparently his own, 3.20), but such a crowd follows that he and the disciples cannot even take their meal. Now the ring:

1. His "relatives" or "those from his household" set out to take him in charge because they think he is mad.
    2. There follows a debate with the scribes on the source of Jesus' power to cast out devils. The scribes allege that he is possessed himself, hence his authority over unclean spirits. Jesus replies with the argument of a kingdom divided and ends with the unforgivable sin against the Holy Spirit.
3. Now his mother and brothers stand outside and send for him. This leads to Jesus' definition of his true kinsmen.

As with Peter in the last example, a brief notice sets the stage for development later. Peter is located in the courtyard by a fire; members of Jesus' household set out to take him in hand. But Peter and the kinsmen enter the narrative directly only after an intervening episode. The last ring is thematically integrated because Jesus' supposed madness (in part 1) "is equivalently an accusation of demonic possession" (JBC). This is the very subject in the debate with the scribes following. The association is therefore deliberate. Lane observes: "This section (22.30) follows naturally in the Marcan sequence through topical association—the listing of charges against Jesus. The conviction that he is deranged (verse 21) finds a more serious echo in the repeated accusation that he is possessed (verses 22 and 30). By framing the incident with the scribes this way Mark announces his intention that Ch. 3.22–30 be understood as a self-contained unit" (140).

These Marcan rings are oddly similar to certain ones in Homer— not those described in connection with the NL but another type that, like Mark's, starts with a brief introduction without action or consequence. Resumption and conclusion follow only after a separating inclusion. As one example among many,[9] consider Odysseus' interviews with his mother and Teiresias in *Odyssey* 11.

1. Odysseus sees his mother's ghost but he does not let her speak before he consults the seer Teiresias, 84–89.
    2. The interview with Teiresias, 90–151.

3. Odysseus converses with his mother, 152ff.

There is no practical reason for Anticleia's first mention at 84–89, but the two conversations make a contrasting pair. Teiresias' prophecy is dark and enigmatic, looking to the future and describing trials to come. And it is drawn on the large scale. The meeting with Anticleia is intimate and inward, turned to the past and into the family circle. It treats of loss and wasting distress. That tone is already struck, ever so lightly, in his mother's first appearance, before Teiresias unrolls the grand scroll of the future. As usual, then, the ring enlarges the contrasting narrative surfaces. Rings of this sort belong to a distinct subtype in the Homeric repertoire. Mark uses them as well.

I pointed out earlier that these rings are different from those of a more static, framing type or from refrains that connect beginnings and endings with verbal repetitions. This less dynamic sort is also present in Mark, for example at 6.7–13, where Jesus commissions the Twelve to preach and heal and sends them on their way. Now comes the story of the execution of John the Baptist (6.14–29), followed by a short notice of the return of the Twelve and Jesus' instructions to them to rest for a while (6.30–1). John's execution is simply enclosed by the commission of the Twelve; there is no suspension of the last, nor are they integrated by theme or detail.

Augustine's Confessions

One of the techniques observed in Homer and the NL both is refrain-like accumulation. An action or a detail or a theme recurs over a continuous stretch and builds to a climax: actions like Agamemnon's series of brother-pairs, or the waves of Trojan assault against the Greek fortifications; details like the interventions of Meriones one time after another at a certain stage of combat, or the repeated clusters of items at the first public association of Sivrit and Kriemhilt; themes, like Kriemhilt's memories on the day of her wedding with Etzel. The device is simple and spontaneous and capable of measureless variety. From the start of book 8 of the *Confessions*, Augustine builds a refrain on the subject of his sexual bondage that constrains the flight of his spirit to full self-abandon.[10]

First stage (chapter 1): his intellectual doubts have been satisfied. The world begins to grow mean in his sight, but the narrow way intimidates and he holds back: "As for my life in this world, everything was tottering, and my heart needed to be cleansed of the old yeast. And our savior, who is himself the way, was winning my assent, and I was loath to pass through its narrows." He decides, therefore, to approach one Simplicianus for advice and help.

Second stage (chapters 1–4): worldly honors have loosened their hold, but his captivity to women persists: "But I was still held in close bondage to womankind . . . Weak man that I was, I continued to choose the softer place, and because of this one thing I tossed and turned, lethargic and enervated with still other wasting cares. For I was being forced to adjust myself to the married state in still other ways that I was unwilling to endure. But I had given myself over and was being held to it." The introspection widens to consider the progress already made. Still he hesitates: "And I had found the good pearl, and I should have been selling everything I had and buying it, and I continued to hold back." So he goes to Simplicianus, who relates the story of Victorinus, an exemplum intended and received. Its implications are pondered at length.

Third stage (chapter 5): Augustine is inflamed by the example but remains held by the bonds of desire now grown to habit and servitude. This chapter explores his subjugation in a series of brilliant images (the chain, the sleeper). It will be surpassed only by the unforgettable struggle at the moment of conversion.

The effect, then, is this: the closer the man comes to his goal, the fiercer the struggle, the more tenacious the flesh's resistance. Religious and psychological truth conspire with literary effect. His move toward self-abandonment begins slowly in the first chapter (the world loses its appeal), and his hesitation is set in terms equally brief: "I was loath to pass through its narrows." The increasing strength of his resolve (set forth twice) is accompanied each time by depictions of his enslavement, these also escalating in length and elaboration. The refrain explores and deepens the issue in a series of enlargements, building to the finale.

Augustine's continual recourse to contemplative digression in the *Confessions* is well known. Sometimes these assume the shape of ring composition with a manner and effect not unlike Homer's own. Early in book 9, for example (chapter 8) he records the death of his mother: "We were returning together to Africa. And while we were at Ostia my mother passed away." With that the account is suspended. We are taken back in time to Monnica's childhood and rearing, her marriage and character. That story climaxes in the mystical transport of chapter 10. About five days after that, she falls ill. Her last conversations turn on the subject of her place of burial. She had always wanted to be laid to rest next to her husband but now she rises to an exalted indifference to the site of her grave. Then the story reaches back to its start and her death is told in full (chapter 11).

The ring is understated and effective. The location of Ostia, casually mentioned at the beginning, becomes the central issue in Monnica's last hours. The flashback on her life, held in straight temporal sequence (girlhood, marriage, death), rises to its zenith in the mystical experience shared by mother and son at the window. The insight of that moment inspires her satiety with life and disinterest in her place of burial. Her last words are on that subject: " 'Nothing,' she said, 'is far from God, and I do not need to worry that He will not know where to raise me on the last day.' " The ring is similar to the Homeric type: (1) the first brief notice of an event (Monnica's death at Ostia); (2) a résumé of her life; (3) her death described at length, with the excursus in the middle casting illumination over the end.

The vision at the window is itself fastened in a ring. That event begins with an explicit reminder of Monnica's approaching death ("as the day approached when she would depart this life") and with the compelling but unobtrusive symbolism of the setting. They gaze from a window, preparing themselves for a voyage over the sea after a hard journey: "The two of us were leaning out a window overlooking an enclosed garden in the house where we were staying, there in Ostia. We had sought privacy to prepare ourselves for the sea voyage after the toils of a long journey." The interlude ends with Monnica's return to the subject of her death. Her hopes in this life have been fulfilled, and now she longs for the end: "As for me, my son, nothing in this life gives me pleasure any more. I don't know what there is for me to do here, or why I should stay." The relation between the start and finish of the ring, and the function of the long middle part in connection with both, is the same as in the larger ring that encloses it.

Jeremias Gotthelf

I conclude this brief selection of comparisons with a somewhat longer excursus on Jeremias Gotthelf. This was the pen-name assumed by the Swiss German Albert Bitzius (1797–1854). He was a disciple of Heinrich Pestalozzi, an impassioned teacher of his nation, a political activist in his early years, later pastor at Lützelflüh, and prolific writer of novels and short stories. He was one of the most unusual personalities ever to put pen to paper, enormously gifted, an acute and staggeringly realistic observer of life. It is only in the twentieth century that the rank of this prodigious talent has become firmly established, and this mostly through the efforts of his countrymen. Still he remains little known and even less read outside his native country, and he is probably doomed to remain so. The first reason for this is language. Large parts of some of his best novels are cast in the Berner (Ementaler) dialect.[11] This made him inaccessible to the German-speaking public at large even in his own lifetime (by revising his manuscripts into standard German his publishers wrought havoc that no modern editing can entirely overcome), and even more so now. Satisfactory translation is next to impossible because of the ebullient metaphorical richness of the dialect itself and its deep fixity in time and place: backward rural districts in nineteenth-century Switzerland.[12]

The second reason is Gotthelf's iconoclasm with respect to the German literary tradition:

> Although Gotthelf's writings were assigned sometimes to the period of Realism, or sometimes even to that of the Biedermeier or Naturalism, the fact is they stood outside that tradition which derived from German Classicism and the Romantics. Gotthelf paid scarcely any serious notice to Goethe at all and to Schiller only in his early years. Literary appraisal that drew its values from German Classicism could make little headway with Gotthelf, whether in respect to style or to form and content. It is no accident that the founder and director of the Complete Edition, Rudolf Hunziker, was a classical philologist, that the first to reawaken modern interpretive interest was Walter Muschg (distinctly an outsider among academic Germanists), and that important contributions have been made to Gotthelf studies by non-Germans.[13]

A misunderstanding (going back to Gottfried Keller)[14] holds Gotthelf to be an artless writer, capable of great natural force and endowed with epic vision and overwhelming mastery of language, but disorganized and episodic, too given to discursive homilies and without firm control of his narrative. My intention here is certainly not to reexamine all that, but to call attention to some phenomena that contradict it, for Gotthelf uses many of the devices treated in the main texts of this study.

Uli der Knecht, like many of Gotthelf's novels, falls into two halves, in two locations: Uli's conversion to a sober life and preparation with the Bodenbauer, then his foremanship at the Glungge. The two parts stand as apprenticeship and fulfillment, training and performance.[15] Parallels and polarities emphasize the two as phases of a single process. Johannes as mentor, inspiration, and guardian in the first stands against Joggeli, the neurotic skeptic, tormentor, and obstacle in the second. Two sets of women, in open or hidden attraction to Uli (first Ursi and Stini, then Elisi and Vreneli), and vying with each other for his attention, set the stage for his double triumph: eventual tenancy of the Glungge and marriage to the woman who makes it possible.[16]

Within this large diptych other correspondences are also played out, sometimes spanning the two halves, sometimes with both inside just one of them. Whatever their distribution, Uli's story moves forward through repeated circumstances and crises. Important and instructive experiences happen more than once. Ideas are threaded through the narrative, pointing direction and drawing a moral. Similar episodes stand in congruence, reinforcing and reflecting each other, and marking the stages of Uli's ascent. As situations repeat themselves their content is enriched. They cast mutual illumination. Variation and change reveal development. And the "formularity," if we can call it that, of Gotthelf's fully developed sets is no less dense than in the epics.

Gotthelf brought the technique to *Uli* after experimenting with it in his *Bauernspiegel*. Meiss's two altercations at an inn mark his inner healing and growth to manhood. After Anneli's death he is at odds with God and man, riots in the tavern, deals blows and receives them, always the instigator, one against many, and feeling best with the bruises of combat upon him: "But I never slept better than with a half-dozen bruises on my head, like a plethoric after a blood-letting."[17] One day he spies the daughters of a hated former master dancing with their escorts. He calls out insults until their young men have no choice but to respond (319). As usual, he fights alone against a crowd, thrashes them all, takes his own share of damage, and leaves satisfied with his day's work.[18] But arrest and trial follow, then flight and years of military service with a Swiss regiment in France. It is there that he grows to maturity under the tutelage of Bonjour, his friend and mentor. After his return home, and in search of a place to remain, he again finds himself at an inn (424), this time with a throng of clerks, notaries, and procurators, secretaries and agents, parasitic bureaucrats exploiting the ignorance of honest citizens. Once again Meiss interferes. He calls out rebukes when their insolence becomes intolerable. This draws a furious response but he holds his ground, will not be intimidated, and finally sends the lot of them packing. The two episodes stand in firm concert (433): "So, after twenty years, another brawl, and I was clearly the instigator with my belligerent comparisons." These fights mark his departure and his return. But between his external circumstances in the two instances, between his tormented aggression in the first and his restraint in the second, his self-pitying rancor before and his defense of the right afterward— between these two poles lie his restoration and growth to wholeness. He left that first fight in stolid, pained content, never dreaming of consequences. Now he ponders his second triumph (434):

> So verweisete ich bei mir lange und machte endlich aus, dass ich recht gehandelt, aber nicht klug, dass ich an einem Orte, wo ich länger bleiben wollte, vorsichtiger zu Werke gehen, dass ich hier mein Spiel verdorben und weiter müsse, indem mit siebenundzwanzig Schreibern zu Feinden an einem Orte sich nicht wohl leben lasse, dass ich aber für einen Abend bloss als Durchreisender keine bessere Kur hätte anwenden und keinen besseren Weg hätte einschlagen können, um diesen Menschen ihre Erbärmlichkeit zu zeigen.

> I thought it over for a long time and finally decided that I'd done the right thing but not the smart thing. I needed to go to work more cautiously in a place where I wanted to stay a while. I'd spoiled my chances here and needed to move on, since life wouldn't be exactly pleasant with twenty-seven clerks for neighbors and enemies. But as long as I was just passing through for an evening, there was no better cure I could have applied and no better path I could have taken to bring home to these persons their utter wretchedness.

In *Uli* Gotthelf developed the device to a high art and used it again and again.

Uli drives a cow to market, first for Johannes, then for Joggeli (108, 193).[19] The two episodes stand as a pair, registering Uli's progress and comparing his two masters. Uli deals wisely and makes a handsome profit both times (109, 195). But this brings temptation: why not keep the winnings for himself (119, 196)? He manages to resist: the first time out of awe when admitted into the privacy of his master's house where the accounting takes place; the second time out of free reflection—he recognizes his self-serving excuses for what they are.[20] He also wants to keep his record clean, for how can he rebuke the unruly servants if he is no better than they (197)? Indeed, his success in resisting the same temptation earlier helps him now (197): "It occurred to him that he had already fought a similar battle before and that honesty had served him well." Uli has advanced: there is a more complex transaction the second time around, and his honesty wells from a firmer character. But as Johannes is the ideal master, Joggeli is his negative counterpart. The first gives Uli a chance to prove himself; he sets a fixed price for the animal and insists that his servant keep the profit (108: Uli's temptation comes because he sells much higher than expected). Joggeli refuses to set a price in advance and is actually laying a trap (194: this too will be repeated in another way with the miller).[21] The final accounting gives rise to some lively argument between husband and wife. Johannes continues to be generous despite his wife's short-sighted interference (121–23); Joggeli remains niggardly even in the face of Uli's honesty and over his wife's objections, and even tries to cheat by making Uli pay expenses (198). The two episodes are also embedded in larger problems. The first is set amid Uli's marriage prospects. Ursi and Stini have just retired in disgrace, and "ds Hubechbure Käthi" enters the picture as Uli returns from market. The second adventure is set amid Uli's efforts to persuade Joggeli to plan their work in advance. That agitation goads Joggeli to test his servant with the cows, and his opposition continues unabated despite Uli's performance.

Uli becomes involved in two fights, both of them in and around an inn. The first is a natural sequel to the *Hurnuss* contest between the Erdöpfelkofer and the Brönzwyler. The second is an attempt made on him by the rebellious hands at the Glungge after his arrival as foreman. The circumstances of the two are different, details and consequences no less so. Still an impressive accumulation of details binds them together, as well as one overriding similarity: two voices contend for the mastery of Uli's soul and he escapes the efforts of his enemies to do him harm.

Despite warning voices (Johannes, 54; Vreneli, 176), Uli is taken in both times by flattery and pretended friendship. Resli (55) fills his head with promises and prospects, and the hands at the Glungge lavish such cajolery that he wonders if these are the same persons who tormented him all week (177). Perilous designs stand behind these efforts. In the first, a plot is hatched to make Uli pay the damage costs arising from the brawl, while the rest go free (65); the plan in the second is to drink for an evening at his expense and then beat him senseless (175). Paying for the drinking is a bitter pill in both instances (60, 64, 175), and the careful notation of Uli's progress continues: Johannes gets him out of the first predicament (67), but he manages on his own the second time (179). Very important is the question of taking sides. Johannes delivers a stern rebuke on the subject: "Believe those who have your good at heart, not the scoundrels who say what you want to hear and then laugh at your fall" (55, 68, 69). That of course is precisely what Resli intends. Uli is dealt the same persuasion by the other servants of Joggeli (177): "Cast your lot with us, join us against the master."

The two crises, then, are associated by accumulated details (of which the fight at the inn is only one) and, more important, by a single dominant perspective: the danger of temptation into ruin by conniving enemies. Gotthelf establishes the relation by giving both episodes the same prelude.

I. Uli, plagued by fellow workers who mock and suspect his reformed conduct, ponders the story of paradise and the serpent (46). It comes to him that that story repeats itself for everybody. Two forces compete for us, but they come from the mouths of men. Part of us wants to do good, but something stronger draws us to the bad. It is with these thoughts in mind, yet despite them, that Uli falls under the influence of the dangerous Resli and with that becomes the intended victim of the first conspiracy.

II. All this now repeats itself in the second instance, but more intensely and with richer imagery (172). Uli returns from church, where the tongues of malevolent neighbors have dragged his new master through the dirt. Again he is reminded of the serpent and the garden (172). After lunch he retires to his room and begins to read the book of Genesis. Suddenly it all appears as if alive before him and in extravagant color: the golden tree, the glittering snake, the sweet fruit, the deliciously poisoned enticement, and then the fall with its grim and mysterious consequences. He is steeped in this reading when a servant throws open the door and summons him out.

There he is told that he owes them a night of drinking, and the second plot against him begins. Uli's imagination had just dressed the story of the temptation in mythical splendor. When he descends to the cowherd's room, where the attempt on him starts, the face of evil looks different: a set of filthy playing cards, the air filled with curses and obscenities. And so Uli is almost taken in again. Gotthelf is writing here with great virtuosity.

These repeated occurrences are rooted in the cyclic nature of human experience. Temptation, overcome once, returns again. Hard-won wisdom lapses, gains are thrown away, and victories are impermanent. Uli is spared none of this.

Sometimes scenes are correlated by inner polarity. The courting of Elisi by the drygoods salesman and Uli's winning of Vreneli are good examples. Elisi's mother participates in both. She is reluctant, duped, half persuaded and half suspicious in the first, and not much less foolish than her daughter. She becomes the wise and sovereign instigator in the second. The first courtship is all mendacity and pretense, disfigured on both sides by posturing and display, dissemblance and cloying extravagance. Compare with that the coming together of Vreneli and Uli, with their shyness and hard struggle against what they both want, but also with plenty of theatrics from Vreneli—these well up from feelings long hidden. It issues in the sweet and private sealing of their covenant next morning at the well.[22]

Sometimes Gotthelf lets ideas transcend themselves upon recurrence. They become purified, distilled, and resolved. An example are the two scenes where Vreneli resists the mistress' efforts to bring her and Uli together, and then where she and Uli ride to their wedding and approach the church. What relates the two are certain subjects of conversation. These are flung out in excitement and high temper in the first, then pass introspective review in the second. The first scene is filled with turbulence and humor, diplomacy and anger, fond hopes and hard clashes—and it ends in dreams come true. Straining against each other are the mistress' roguish and persistent mediation, Vreneli's ferocious resistance, her old resentments and secret affection for Uli. In the second scene, conflict is behind them, contention succeeded by concord, ideas are in perspective, and dialect is replaced by standard German.

Vreneli, in high dudgeon and in her ripe Ementaler, compares marriage to dying and wants none of it (335):

"Was, e schöni Sach! E arme Tüfel isch e Hochzytere," sagte Vreneli. "Hochzyt ha isch no viel ärger as Sterbe. Bim sterbe weiss me doch no öppe, ob me selig wird oder ob eim dr Tüfel nimmt, bim Hochzyta cha me gar nüt wüsse. We me meint, dr Himmel syg voll Gyge, su sys zletzt luter Donnerwetter. U we me meint, mi heyg dr Freinst, su isch es de zletzt, we me recht luegt, dr wüestisch Hung."

"What do you mean, a fine thing! A poor devil, that's what a bride is," said Vreneli. "Getting married is a lot worse than dying. When you die at least you have some idea whether you'll go to heaven or the devil'll take you. With marriage you can't know at all. Just when you think the sky is full of violins, it ends up sheer stormy weather. And when you think, I've got a real peaceful type, it turns out, when you take a close look, he's a real wild dog."

This is exuberent eloquence and it makes a fine show—but Vreneli's heart is in her rhetoric, not in the case she pleads, as the mistress knows (335):

du heschs o so wie äy Bettlere, wo geseit het, si möcht kei Büri sy, vo wege sie mög dKüchleni nit erlyde, das syg ere doch es Dolders Fresse, u wo me du grad druf im ene Cheller erwütscht het, wo sie e ganzi Bygete het welle stehle.

You're acting like the beggar woman who said she wouldn't want to be a farmer's wife because she couldn't stand the butter cakes—miserable slop as far as she was concerned, and then they caught her right after in a cellar where she was trying to steal a whole basket of them.

Uli returns to the comparison—with less flamboyance—on the morning of their wedding (400):

Es ist mir fast und doch nicht ganz wie beim Sterben: da geht man auch so einem Tor entgegen und weiss nicht, was dahinter ist, und dahinter kann die Seligkeit sein oder die Hölle. Und wenn man schon mehr oder minder glaubt, es sei die Hölle oder die Seligkeit, die einem wartet, so weiss man doch nicht, wie die Seligkeit ist und wie die Hölle ist, und beide sind sicher viel anders, als man glaubt, die Seligkeit viel süsser, die Hölle viel bitterer.

To me, it's almost like dying, but not quite. When you die, you also go through a kind of door, and you don't what's behind it. And either heaven or hell can be behind it. And even if you think you know more or less whether it's heaven or hell waiting for you, you still don't know what heaven is like or hell is like. And both are surely a lot different than you think—heaven a lot sweeter, hell a lot more bitter.

Back in the first scene, the mistress warns Vreneli to watch her tongue: words can have consequences for life (335):

> Gang mr doch mit sellige Rede, mi vrsüngt sih drmit gar gern. U we me scho e wenig kybig isch, sym Mul soll me doch geng e Rechnig mache. Mi weiss nie, was es eim gä cha, u we me de drin isch, su chunts eim wieder zSinn, was me gredt het, u sellige Wort chönne eym mengisch Tag und Nacht vrfolge, ärger as e Truppele wildi Tier, dass me kei Rue me het. U menge het ne nit angers wüsse z'ertrünne as dür e Tod.

> Go on, that's no way to talk. A person commits a sin before he knows it. And even if you've got a temper, you should rein in your tongue. You never know how it can turn out for you, and once you're stuck, then you remember what you said and words like that can pursue you many a day and night, worse than a pack of wild animals, so you never get any rest. And lots of people never have known how to escape except by dying.

Again Uli returns to the same subject (400):

> Ich habe einmal meine Grossmutter sagen hören, es sei von gar schwerer Bedeutung, was man am Hochzeitmorgen rede, und je näher man der Kirche komme, um so schwerer werde die Bedeutung. Da sollte man eigentlich an nichts anders denken als an den lieben Gott und seine Engelein, wie sie in Friede und Freude mit einander lebten und den Menschen alles Gute brächten und gönnten, und sollte nichts anderes reden als mit dem lieben Gott, dass er bei einem bleiben möchte am Abend und am Morgen, im Hause und auf dem Felde, im Herzen und im Wandel, und dass seine Engelein über einem wachen möchten jahraus jahrein, damit kein böser Geist Gewalt über einem bekäme und keiner zwischen beide hineinkäme. Sie hat manchmal gesagt, wie es ihr Angst geworden sei, als mein Vater und meine Mutter mit einander gelacht und im Spass gestritten und viel Weltliches geredet. Da sei es nicht lange gegangen, so seien die bösen Geister gekommen, beide seien früh in der Welt untergegangen, und wir seien arme Kinder geworden, allen Leuten im Weg und zweg zum Verderben.

> I once heard my grandmother say it's very, very important what you talk about on the morning of your wedding, and the nearer you get to church, the more important it is. You really shouldn't talk about

anything but the good Lord and his angels, how they live in peace
and joy together and like to bring everything that's good to people.
And the only talking you do should be with the good Lord, so that
he'll stay with you day and night, at home and in the field, in your
heart and in all you do, so his angels will watch over you year in and
year out, so no evil spirit will get you in its power or come between
the two of you. She used to say how frightened she got when my
father and mother laughed together and argued in fun and said lots
of worldy things. It didn't take long, she said, the evil spirits came
and both of them perished early in the world and we became poor
children, in everybody's way and ripe for ruin.[23]

In the first scene again, Vreneli, with her defenses weakening, insists
on her right to defend herself (335):

> "Base," sagte Vreneli, "ih han Ech nit welle höhn mache u dih o nit,
> Ueli, aber löyt mih rüeyig! Ih bin nüt as es arms Meitschi, u drum
> muess ih mih wehre, we mih öpper no zu öppis Mingerem mache
> will."

> "Aunt," said Vreneli, "I didn't want to make you mad, and not you
> either, Uli, but let me be! I'm just a poor girl, and so I have to defend
> myself when somebody wants to make me into something even
> less."

She reaffirms that before the church, in a changed tone but no less
firmly (401):

> Ich habe mich dir ergeben und will dir auch gehorchen, solange du
> mich lieb hast, und will tun, dass du mich alle Tage lieb haben kannst,
> will keine Zyberlegränne werden. Nicht dass ich mich auch nicht
> wehren würde, wenn du mich quälen, zu deinem Hund machen
> wolltest.

> I've submitted to you and I'll obey you, too, as long as you love me.
> And I'll act so that you'll be able to love me all the time, I won't
> become a whiner and a nag. Not that I wouldn't defend myself if you
> wanted to torment me and turn me into your dog.

This courtship reveals itself as a living process, organizing and pu-
rifying itself in the course of its growth.

Sometimes important ideas do not crystallize into corresponding
scenes but are made to chime like a refrain along a line of turning
points. One thinks, for example, of the role assigned to the medical
profession in the *Bauernspiegel:* the incompetent, indifferent, and

avaricious doctors at the deaths of Meiss's father and Anneli, and the neglect, with permanent consequences, he suffers during his own convalescence upon return. Other examples are the helping hands when things are desperate (Anneli, Mareili, Bonjour, the broker), and the understated but prophetic connection between his first post as *Kindermeitschi* and his last at the inn. Indeed, all the experiences of his childhood, and not least his education by Bonjour, prepare him for that final profession.[24]

The well plays a quiet but firm role in the love story of Vreneli and Uli, always early in the morning. Scenes from the Bible stand behind this, as do the realities of farm life. Vreneli, drawing water, overhears Joggeli's son importuning Uli to take a job with him (chapter 17). She tells the mistress, Joggeli hears of it, misunderstandings ensue, and Uli is embittered against his future bride. The mistress finally reconciles them (chapter 18). This is the first strong personal interaction between the two, and the mistress' intervention looks forward to her mediation, still far in the future, where she will bring them together in betrothal. They seal their promise at the well before sunrise (365), and again on the morning of their wedding.[25]

Many small details of this sort emphasize the recurrences and ascent in Uli's career. Before beginning work at the Glungge, he is so full of questions for Johannes that he will not let his master go (157): "He kept asking questions until Johannes finally stopped at an inn, drank a glass of wine with him and then sent him home almost by force." This repeats itself on a larger canvas when Uli and Vreneli, just married, spend the afternoon with Johannes and his wife, and the innkeeper and his wife as well, asking endless questions (413): "And the more they heard, the more eager Vreneli and Uli showed themselves to learn, and the more humble they became. They took in the experiences of their elders and fixed them in their memories, unencumbered as these were with useless things."

Correlated repetitions belong to Gotthelf's style and deserve more study. My purpose here has not been to carry that out, or even to classify all the forms it assumes, but to offer examples where it creates similarities to the epic manner. The likeness in execution and effect is impressive. Shared features set the pairs in natural correspondence, and the implications of the relationship speak for themselves. Nor has it been my aim to emphasize Gotthelf's epic qualities or his resemblance to Homer (although both are legitimately done). I mean instead to suggest that the devices in question are natural literary tools, serving the stylization that belongs to all literature. They are rediscovered and used by most writers at all times and in different genres. The techniques employed by the Greek and medieval epics along these lines are thus neither exclusively epic nor oral. They are probably more likely to appear in strongly marked form in literature of the spoken word where their contours stand out in sharp relief. And yet, as the example of Gotthelf shows, they are natural and effective in a purely written medium.

Conclusion

A COMPARISON of ring composition in Homer and the NL revealed differences: the figure has a wider use in the *Iliad* and the *Odyssey* and different specific applications. But the important comparison is more general, and so are the conclusions to be drawn from it. The story is articulated at the first levels of narration in the ordering of small incidents. Contrived arrangements create certain effects. We observe similar orderings on a still larger scale in both Homer and the NL. The Greek chieftains wounded in book 11 of the *Iliad* become figures in a defined sequence, each one contrasting with the rest and illuminating them. All of book 12 is built according to the same principle: graded repetition creates a line of reflecting mirrors. Then, on a still larger scale, books 11 and 12 are set in opposition, each with a gallery of portraits, one from the Greek side and the other from the Trojan. A close composition reveals itself from the foundation elements of narrative to the overriding structures of whole books and even beyond. And all this is built with formular elements.

The NL also has refined architectures on the large scale and they do not depend on numerical proportions. The epic falls into two distinct halves, with many components of each standing in interdependence with equivalents in the other. To pick a familiar example, both halves tell of an invitation to a festival that ends in disaster. In the first, Sivrit is asked with Kriemhilt to Wormez, and that leads to his murder. In the second half, Kriemhilt, now the wife of Etzel, invites her brothers and Hagen to a festival at her court where she has them killed. This is to avenge the assassination of Sivrit in the first part. That much is obvious.[1] But many smaller details in the two invitations, merging in correspondence or antithesis, add a commentary of their own. The NL is interwoven from start to finish by almost countless threads that join, associate, contrast, develop, and explain.

Most of these repeats—the building blocks of epic architecture—have the same formal stability as their relatives in Homer and elsewhere. Their fixed and undeviating lineaments belong to epic stylization, to the formularity that governs this poetry from its diction to its higher reaches. We have seen one example after another of how this utilitarian arsenal is pressed into the service of deep composition.

Given that, another conclusion forces itself—anticlimatic and obvious—but not without pertinence in today's climate of opinion. To begin with Homer, the artistry of the Greek epics draws them back from that alien strangeness where formulist studies have isolated them. The *Iliad* and the *Odyssey* belong, instead, within literature's conventional ambit and they respond, with certain adjustments, to familar and demanding criticism. Finnegan and Zumthor have discovered an indeterminate border between oral and written poetry. The Homeric epics show the same gliding contours inside their own space.

A favorite device of Homer is correlation, or contrapost. Things are placed in association—approximation or polarity—by shared details, structures, or placements. The pairs complement and enrich each other. But this is common to most literature. It belongs to the very definition of integrated narrative. Opening a book like Eberhart Lämmert's *Bauformen des Erzählens*,[2] we find a whole chapter on correlation, the art of associating things by repetition and mirroring. Quoting Wilhelm von Humboldt ("Nothing exists separately in language, every one of its elements reveals itself as part of a whole"),[3] Lämmert describes closely written *prose* like this:

> The single element sheds its limitation as mere point or extension and acquires something else in return, namely the power of a ray of light continually intersecting others or joining itself to them. It is only through these associative linkages that it ultimately acquires its real significance and attains its full reality. If we reduce narrative to single, self-contained units, we explain those parts only imperfectly.[4]

In this respect the *Iliad* and the *Odyssey* are like any ambitious literature. All the devices studied here are used to associate and focus in order to bring things into high relief. Of course, this manner has its own physiognomy in heroic poetry: block units with a stylized sameness and insistent repetition. These define epic and set it apart. They derive from a strongly normative tradition and from special circumstances of composition and delivery. But the purpose and effect remain the same as in any other literature: to distill, condense, refine, illuminate.

All this applies equally to the NL. It shows a similar manner, from small shapes to grand strategies of design. Here is Otto Holzapfel on the subject of epic stylization:

> And as for the larger epic formulas, images, themes, the stereotyped presentation of certain situations, and the structural formulas—those traditional devices that give longer action sequences a linguistic stability and allow them to be transmitted—they are not handed down by some automated process. They are distinctive features of a style that is as subject to evolution as any other and they are to be interpreted accordingly. It seems therefore fundamentally correct to speak of the "openness" of a text.[5]

I referred at the beginning to the theory that Homer belongs to a period of transition from oral to written poetry. Proponents insist that the quality and complexity of the *Iliad* and the *Odyssey* are conceivable only in the circumstances of leisure and reflection belonging to literate composition. Interestingly, speculation about the NL is moving in the same direction. Yes, it deals heavily in convention and formula, and it is doubtless rooted in a living oral tradition. Nevertheless, its conception and execution are such that they resist explanation in terms of an improvisational manner. Michael Curschmann has put it this way:

> Verbal expression and function, meter, rhyme, and a distinct vocabulary—these function economically together in what must be seen as calculated formular systems. The result, on the surface and over certain stretches, is the very stylistic habitus we expect from orally conceived poetry, especially in comparison with the courtly romances. That will, in fact, have been the author's intention. But closer examination reveals manifold interdependencies that can derive only from the conscious use of oral narrative style in a literate composition. Everything that we now know about the longevity and stability of oral narrative in poetic form compels the conclusion that this poet worked out of a living oral tradition. Thus, stories were still circulated "in the traditional manner," and the poet of the NL seized upon this same style. That was his aesthetic response to tradition, and he recast it in the medium of the Nibelungen-strophe. His speech was no oral diction encountered everywhere within certain linguistic borders and

available for use by everybody. It is the specific language of the NL
itself. Oral style pressed into the service of literate composition: that
is the relation of this poetry to earlier tradition.[6]

This resembles speculation about Homer. And yet the *Iliad* and the
Odyssey do not fall completely into line. Their formula systems sometimes reveal an awesome complexity and rigor. The medieval epics
are, of course, heavily formular as well. Special studies of *Roland* and
the NL leave no doubt on that score.[7] But Homer's formular networks
seem to me to be more complicated and refined, more extensive and
more economical. The sheer intricacy of these systems puts the *Iliad*
and the *Odyssey* at a remove from the others and makes it harder to
imagine how they were actually composed and written down. As I
observed earlier, I do not think we are in a position to understand
this yet. Therefore, as we ease Homer back into the familiar literary
tradition, it will be well to keep the enigma of his style in mind. This
strange difference attaches to it, although it is related on familiar levels
to literature everywhere.

In sum, then: Homer and the poet of the NL emerge as careful
artists, and not just in the grand design of their epics and in their
moral depth and heroic spirit. We also discover the creative personality of both in the way they composed at the gound level, in the
shaping of small scenes and in the integration of the same into larger
constellations. Both poets did this in a traditional manner. It has been
a long time since Maurice Bowra catalogued the large consistencies
of the epic genre: a race of heroes, emphasis on warfare, deeds larger
than life, close attention to armor, clothing, and the trappings of
station. Now we see that these affinities continue into the finer dimensions of style: architectonics, symmetry, parallelism, correlation.
These resemblances are interesting in themselves. It is also useful to
define them because that helps us to read the epics with a sharper
eye for intention and effect. It refines our definition of epic style and
allows us to classify epic more precisely in relation to literature at
large.

The observations presented here cannot tell us many things we
want to know: how were the epics composed? written down? trans-
mitted? But they tell us much about how the poems actually work
and how tradition and invention are variously represented there. The
evidence points away from formular mechanics and improvisation
and toward meditated craft, toward individual excellence and away

from stylized anonymity. If the poems were composed by word of mouth, then our concept and definition of the oral style need to embrace this level of artifice and achievement.

One last thing: this study labors in a field that should be under more intense cultivation. There are many comparative studies of Homer and medieval epic in respect to oral theory and formula count, but few that compare texts in terms of wider yet precise definitions of style. There is far too little of that even between *Roland* and the NL. More study along those lines would teach us much about how these poems work at the elementary stages of story line, how they are assembled at the levels of scene, episode, and movement. And that effort would call for the inclusion of more languages than I have been able to draw on.

Notes

Abbreviations

BOOKS

Brault: G. J. Brault, *The Song of Roland. An Analytical Edition* (University Park and London, 1978). Vol. 1, Introduction and Commentary; Vol. 2, Text and Translation.

Fenik: B. C. Fenik, *Typical Battle Scenes in the Iliad* (Wiesbaden, 1968).

Finnegan: R. Finnegan, *Oral Poetry: Its Nature, Significance and Social Context* (Cambridge University Press, 1977).

Gräf: H. Gräf, *Der Parallelismus im Rolandslied,* diss. Würzburg (Wertheim a.M., 1931).

Griffin: J. Griffin, *Homer on Life and Death* (Oxford, 1980).

Heldensage: *Zur germanisch-deutschen Heldensage,* sechzehn Aufsätze zum neuen Forschungsstand, hrsg. K. Hauck (Wissenschaftliche Buchgesellschaft, 1961, Wege der Forschung, Band XIV).

Heusler: A. Heusler, *Nibelungensage und Nibelungenlied* (Dortmund, 1955).

Hoffmann[1]:   W. Hoffmann, "Die Fassung C des Nibelungenliedes und die 'Klage,' " *Festschrift Gottfried Weber* (Bad Homburg, 1967; Frankfurter Beiträge zur Germanistik, hrsg. H. O. Bürger und K. von See, Band I), 109–43.

Hoffmann[2]:   W. Hoffmann, *Kudrun. Ein Beitrag zur Deutung der nachnibelungischen Heldendichtung* (Stuttgart, 1967).

JBC: *The Jerome Bible Commentary.* 2 vols. (bound as one), ed. R. E. Brown, J. A. Fitzmeyer, and R. E. Murphy (Prentice Hall, 1968).

Lane: W. L. Lane, *The Gospel According to Mark* (The New International Commentary on the New Testament, vol. 2, Grand Rapids, 1974).

Leaf: W. Leaf, ed., *The Iliad.* 2 vols. (London, 1900–1902); repr. A. M. Hakkert (Amsterdam, 1960).

Mergell: B. Mergell, "Nibelungenlied und höfischer Roman," Eu-
                     phorion 45 (1950), 305–36; repr. in *Nibelungenlied und Ku-*
                     drun (below), 3–39.
MHV: *The Making of Homeric Verse. The Collected Papers of Milman*
                     Parry, ed. A. Parry (Oxford, 1971).
Michel: Ch. Michel, *Erläuterungen zum N der Ilias* (Heidelberg, 1971).
Nagel: B. Nagel, *Das Nibelungenlied. Stoff-Form-Ethos* (Frankfurt
                     a.M., 1965).
Neumann: F. Neumann, *Das Nibelungenlied in seiner Zeit* (Göttingen,
                     1967).
Nibelungenlied   hrsg. H. Rupp (Wissenschaftliche Buchgesellschaft,
und Kudrun: Darmstadt, 1976, Wege der Forschung, Band LIV).
Panzer: F. Panzer, *Das Nibelungenlied. Entstehung und Gestalt* (Stutt-
                     gart/Köln, 1955).
Reinhardt: K. Reinhardt, *Die Ilias und ihr Dichter* (Göttingen, 1961).
Rychner: J. Rychner, *La Chanson de Geste. Essai sur l'art épique des*
                     jongleurs. Société de Publications Romanes et Françaises
                     (Genève-Lille, 1955).
Schadewaldt: W. Schadewaldt, *Iliasstudien.* (Wissenschaftliche Buch-
                     gesellschaft, Darmstadt, 1966); repr. from *Abhandlungen der*
                     philologisch-historischen Klasse der sächsischen Akademie der
                     Wissenschaften, Band XLIII, Nr. VI, Leipzig, 1943.
Siefken: H. Siefken, *Überindividuelle Formen und der Aufbau des Ku-*
                     drunepos (München, 1967).
Von der Mühll: P. Von der Mühll, *Kritisches Hypomnema zur Ilias* (Basel, 1952).
Wachinger: B. Wachinger, *Studien zum Nibelungenlied. Vorausdeutung,*
                     Aufbau, Motivierung (Tübingen, 1960).
Weber: G. Weber, *Das Nibelungenlied: Problem und Idee* (Stuttgart,
                     1963).
Wilamowitz: U. von Wilamowitz-Moellendorf, *Die Ilias und Homer* (Ber-
                     lin, 1920).
Zumthor: P. Zumthor, *Introduction à la Poésie Orale* (Paris, 1983).

JOURNALS

AfSnS: *Archiv für das Studium der neueren Sprachen*
AJPh: *American Journal of Philology*
CR: *Classical Review*
DU: *Der Deutschunterricht*
GR: *Germanic Review*
GRM: *Germanisch-Romanische Monatschrift*
HScPh: *Harvard Studies in Classical Philology*
JHS: *Journal of Hellenic Studies*
LEC: *Les Etudes Classiques*
LH: *Lettres d'Humanité*
MA: *Le Moyen Age*

M&H: *Medievalia et Humanistica*
TAPA: *Transactions of the American Philological Association*
WW: *Wirkendes Wort*
ZfdA: *Zeitschrift für deutsches Altertum*
ZfdPh: *Zeitschrift für deutsche Philologie*
ZffSL: *Zeitschrift für französische Sprache und Literatur*

Preface

1. See e.g. Finnegan and Zumthor.
2. Two welcome exceptions in the matter of texts are A. B. Lord's edition of Avdo Mededović's *The Wedding of Smailagić Meho* (Cambridge, Mass., 1974), and A. T. Hatto's *The Memorial Feast for Kökötöykhan* (New York, and London, 1977). This last is a Kirghiz epic; Hatto offers a text and parallel English prose translation.
3. MHV 266 and esp. 314.
4. J. Notopoulos, "Homer and Geometric Art," *Athena*, 1957, 73.
5. B. Van Groningen, *Paratactische Compositie in de oudste Griecksche Literatur* (Amsterdam, 1937); J. Notopoulos, "Parataxis in Homer: A New Approach to Homeric Literary Criticism," *TAPA* 80 (1949), 1–23; B. E. Perry, "The Early Greek Capacity for Viewing Things Separately," *TAPA* 68 (1937), 403–27.
6. For a review of these efforts, MHV 266, lv, and Griffin xiii–xiv.
7. Griffin, xiv and passim.
8. E.g. J. Latacz, "Homer," *DU* 6 (1979), 5–23; H. Erbse, *Beiträge zum Verständnis der Odyssee* (Berlin, 1972), 177–89.
9. J. A. Russo, "Is 'Oral' or 'Aural' Composition the Cause of Homer's Formulaic Style?" *Oral Literature and the Formula*, ed. B. A. Stolz and R. S. Shannon (Ann Arbor, 1976), 31–54, esp. 40–47.
10. See esp. Zumthor, 21 and 36.
11. Zumthor insists that a distinction between written and oral literature can ultimately be made. He cites e.g. the preponderance of parataxis in the oral mode (136–37) and gives more weight to that than to formulas (125): "C'est moins sur ces marques elles-mêmes (formules) que devra s'interroger une poétique de l'oralité, que sur les rapports instables d'où résulte, au niveau des concaténations d'éléments et de leur effets de sens, l'économie particulière du texte *dit*."
12. "The Criticism of an Oral Homer," *JHS* 90 (1970), 93, 94.
13. Nagler, *Spontaneity and Tradition: A Study in the Oral Art of Homer* (Berkeley, 1974); Nagy, *The Best of the Achaeans: Concepts of the Hero in Archaic Greek Poetry* (Baltimore, 1979).
14. The *Iliad*'s battle scenes are composed mainly in terms of conventional scenes and action sequences. See Fenik, *Typical Battle Scenes*.
15. Zumthor on the definition of oral style (141): "Selon l'opinion la plus répandue chez les ethnologues (et les rares poéticiens au courant de leurs travaux), le trait constant et peut-être universellement définitoire, de la poésie

orale est la récurrence de divers éléments textuels: 'formules' au sens de Parry-Lord et, plus généralement, toute espèce de répétition ou de parallél- isme. Aucun de ces procédés, certes, n'est le propre exclusif de la poésie orale: Jakobson voyait en eux le fondement de toute langage poétique . . . I'l n'empêche qu'un lien étroit, et sans aucun doute fonctionnel, les attache à l'exercice de la voix."

Iliad 11

1. Details in Fenik, 82–89.

2. All this from Wilamowitz, 185. The closest formal parallel to 11.86–90 (indicating the time of day by reference to familiar events) is in the *Odyssey* at 12.439. General descriptions before the start of single combats are a regular feature by themselves, e.g. 4.446, 8.60, 13.125. The function of the simile at 66–70 is familiar, as is the manner of indicating time. See Fenik, 79–82.

3. Lines 78–83 were absent from Zenodotus' text and athetized by Ar- istarchus and Aristophanes. Wilamowitz (184) discards lines 74–77 with them. But little summaries of the sort are not uncommon; cf. 5.506, 13.345, 15.593.

4. J. B. Hainsworth, "The Criticism of an Oral Homer," *JHS* 90 (1970), 95, offers essentially the same outline of Agamemnon's aristeia and compli- ments its "clarity, balance and proportion."

5. Compare 12.182 and 20.395.

6. He almost caught Aeneas in the same way: 20.188.

7. Schadewaldt, 47, 50.

8. Compare 4.160–2. The passage in book 6 presents problems. See the Excursus.

9. The unlike dispositions of the two men receive a final emphasis in book 24 (653, 686): it would be disastrous for Priam to be discovered in camp by the Greek general.

10. Antimachos received gold as a reward for his support. This is a theme in the *Iliad*. Performances for special bounty are usually conceived in pre- sumption and collapse in disaster. Athena lures Pandaros into breaking the truce with prospects of glory and splendid gifts from Paris (4.95). Dolon aims far above his station in demanding the horses of Achilles (10.303, 319). Com- pare Nestor's modest offer on the Greek side and the moralizing scholia *ad loc*. Othryoneus, who promised to drive the Greeks away in return for the hand of Cassandra, comes to a bad end (13.363). Hector's promises at 17.229 are equally vain, and things go no better for Teucer after Agamemnon prom- ises him a special share of the booty from Troy if he kills Hector with one of his arrows (8.273).

11. At 186.

12. Schadewaldt, 51.

13. Fenik, 55, 86, 213. See also Wilamowitz, 187. Cf. Von der Mühll, 193.

14. At 6.297; 5.69.

15. According to Pausanias (10.26, 7–8), Lesches (*Ilias Parva*, Test. 14, Al- len) said this: Antenor's son, Helicaon, was wounded during the sack but was recognized and saved by Odysseus and Menelaos—this because of the

hospitality shown them by his father. Pausanias adds that he could not find Laodice, daughter of Priam and wife of Helicaon (*Iliad* 3.121), listed by any poet among the captive Trojan women. He conjectures that she was also spared for Helicaon's (Antenor's) sake. On Antenor in post-Homeric legend, see W. Kullmann, *Die Quellen der Ilias* (Wiesbaden, 1960), 177.

16. *Archelochos* and *Akamas*: paired with Aeneas at 2.823 and 12.99 and associated with Poulydamas in an exchange of slayings at 14.442–505. *Laodamas*: slain at 15.516, with Poulydamas retaliating immediately. *Polybos*: appears with two of his brothers (Agenor and Akamas) along with Hector, Poulydamas and Aeneas at 11.56 (two sets of three's). *Agenor*: the most important Antenorid; he is in the constellation mentioned just above at 11.56; summoned by Aeneas along with Deiphobos and Paris at 13.489; with Poulydamas and Aeneas at 14.425 (joined by Sarpedon and Glaukos); one of a series of Trojans slaying Greeks at 15.329—Hector, Aeneas, Poulydamas, Polites, Agnenor, and Paris; again with Poulydamas, Aeneas, and Hector at 16.535.

17. 11.146; 11.261; 13.202; 14.496. The act always occurs in moments of fury and as a vengeance. At 14.496 Peneleos beheads Akamas (a son of Antenor) in revenge for the slaying of Promachos and Akamas' boasting about it (476). 13.202 is even closer in spirit to the scenes in book 11. Teucer decapitates the corpse of Imbrios and spins the head "like a ball" through the ranks until it rolls dead at Hector's feet. The anecdote paints Imbrios as a sympathetic man of high standing. Teucer commits the act in anger over the death of Amphimachos, who was slain not by Imbrios but by Hector.

18. Interestingly, a scholion preserves Nicanor's interpretation of *stēthesi pamphaīnontas* in line 100. Their bared and hairless chests gleam in the sun, which shows their youth. See Griffin, 105.

19. Wilamowitz (195) saw a contradiction between the Agamemnon of book 11 and the same man in books 1, 14, and 19. But he failed to grasp the sophistication of the *Iliad's* character drawing. Aggression and cowardice, brutality and self-abasement, insolence and timidity sit easily together in this complex and interesting character.

20. Hippomachos, another son of Antimachos, is killed by Leonteus at 12.188. He dies fighting in the train of Asios, just where we would expect to find him.

21. On the pathos of the two lines, Griffin, 105.

22. See Griffin's useful survery, 123. His comments on Priam the great sufferer are just right (113, n. 20): "Priam is *the* old man and father whom we see suffer in the poem . . . and the accumulation of disasters upon him can be made visible and tangible in terms of pathos. We know Priam: other pathetic fathers are, by contrast, bloodless."

23. For details, Michel, 83–91.

24. On simile placement and subject matter, see W. Scott, *The Oral Nature of the Homeric Simile* (Leiden, 1974), 12–95.

25. So Kullmann, *Die Quellen der Ilias*, 277 and n. 1; "Die Eigentümlichkeit, auf vorausgesetzte Sagen dadurch anzuspielen, dass man von den Söhnen der vorausgesetzten Hauptpersonen redet, ist für die Ilias charakteristisch."

26. The closest analogue is in the *Odyssey,* 4.335.

27. This usage is described by R. Hampe, *Die Gleichnisse Homers und die Bildkunst seiner Zeit* (Tübingen, 1952), 5.

28. See C. Moulton, *Similes in the Homeric Poems* (Göttingen, 1977, Hypomnemata, Heft 49), 96–99 on all the similes applied to Agamemnon.

29. Some of these connections were observed by Wilamowitz (195), all of them by Moulton (*Similes,* 46) and by T.B.L. Webster, *From Mycene to Homer* (London, 1960), 232.

30. Wilamowitz (192) compared 11.489 where Aias slays a group of the enemy and then receives a simile (so Hector here). The comparison is unobjectionable but not very useful. This is actually a frequent pattern (Fenik, 84). The sequence at 297–309 is more complex and has a closer analogue at 15.618.

31. Reinhardt, 252.

32. Hector's defeat is taken as a contradiction of Zeus's promise at 186 (e.g. by Von der Mühll, 195), but this is to view things in too narrow a focus. Events are worked through with retardation and laid out on a large canvas. Full analysis of this by Schadewaldt, 1–29, 54–5, 108, 110.

33. G. Schoeck, *Ilias und Aithiopis, kyklische Motive in homerischer Brechung* (Zürich, 1961); Ph. Kakridis, "Achills Rüstung," *Hermes* 89 (1961), 293, n. 1.

34. So Reinhardt, "Das Parisurteil," *Tradition and Geist* (Göttingen, 1960), 30: "Paris triumphiert wo Hektor unterliegt. Zu Hektors ganzer Tragik ist auch dies hinzuzurechnen." Bowmen are worsted in direct confrontation with spearmen at 8.320 (Hector and Teucer) and 13.581 (Menelaos and Helenus). But Paris is always successful with his bow: here, at 11.505, 11.581, 13.660.

35. Diomedes' earlier wounding at the hands of Pandaros (5.95) makes an interesting comparison. That arrow had to be drawn out too, and the placement of the wound might also have cyclic connections (Schoeck, *Ilias und Aithiopis,* 77). But Diomedes remains prudent and calm. It is Pandaros who plays the fool (192, 209), and Diomedes is given the chance to avenge himself (290). I have dealt with Diomedes in book 11 earlier: "Stylization and Variety: Four Monologues in the Iliad," *Homer: Tradition and Invention* (Leiden, 1978), 75.

36. See Fenik, "Stylization and Variety," 71–74.

37. Ibid., 76.

38. "Hektor und Andromache," *Die Antike* 11 (1935), reprinted in *Von Homers Welt und Werk* (Stuttgart, 1959). References are to this printing.

39. Ibid., 212: "Wir blicken zuerst auf den äusseren umgebenden Rahmen und verspüren sofort die Hand eines Dichters, der ordnet, gliedert, baut. Das Gespräch zwischen Hektor und Andromache ist die dritte, ausgedehnteste der drei 'Szenen,' die den in die Kampfhandlung der Ilias eingelegten 'Akt' *Hektor in Troia* bilden: Hektor vor seiner Mutter Hekabe (6.242–285), Hektor bei Paris und Helena (312–368), Hektor und Andromache (369–502). Vor dieser Szenen-Dreiheit steht ein kurzer Eingang (237–241), am Ende ein Nachspiel (503–529). Zwischendrein schiebt sich hinter die Hekabe-Szene die Erzählung vom Bittgang zu Athene, dem die Göttin die Gewährung weigert (286–311). Das Ganze ist ein strenger Bau und doch absichtslos wie nur ein Stück Leben."

40. Ibid., 213–14: "Zur Begegnung mit Hekabe kommt es, weil Hektor den Bittgang veranlassen soll, der ihn in die Stadt bringt. Doch die Szene gibt mehr. Die sorgenschwere Stimmung klingt neu auf in der mütterlichen Fürsorge (254): 'Mein Sohn, was liessest du den Kampf und bist hergekommen? Ja, die Achaier zermürben unsere Leute, da wolltest du von der Höhe der Burg die Hände zu Zeus erheben. So will ich dir Wein bringen zur Spende dem Gott und dir zur Stärkung.' Und weiter: Die erste Begegnung zeigt Hektor als Sohn, die zweite als Bruder und Schwager, die dritte als Gatten und Vater—drei Verwandschaftsgrade, drei Stufen seelischer Bindung. Und in allen drei Beziehungen ist Hektor der gleiche: der nicht verweilende, den es wieder zum Kampf hinaustreibt. Für diese männliche Haltung Hektors hat der Dichter ein wunderbar einfaches Symbol geschaffen. Hektor weist den Wein zurück, den ihm die Mutter bietet, 'auf dass er ihm den Drang nicht hemme und er seiner Kraft vergässe.' So wird er in der nächsten Begegnung es ablehnen niederzusitzen, wozu Helena ihn freundlich nötigt. Und diese Abwehr weiblicher Sorge um ihn wird schliesslich in der Andromache Szene sich vertiefen. Noch unmittelbar bereitet die zweite Stufe, der Aufenthalt Hektors bei Paris und Helena, die Begegnung mit Andromache vor. Hart vor dem Hauptgebilde legt der Dichter ein Gegenbild ein, damit das Hauptbild desto kräftiger dastehe. Vor das Paar Hektor-Andromache tritt das andere Paar Paris-Helena in umgekehrtem Verhältnis: der willensschwache (523), wankelmütige (352) Mann neben der starken, ehrbewussten, ihres unwürdigen Daseins überdrüssigen Frau—der Held neben der nur liebenden Gattin, der Mutter seines Sohnes. Der Kontrapost ist eines der festesten Stilmittel in der baumeisterlichen Hand des Iliasdichters. Er zwingt den Blick in Bestimmte Richtung und erspart dem Dichter das Reden. Und der Dichter meistert dies Mittel mit so unauffälliger Sicherheit, dass niemand die künstlerische Absicht merkt, der er doch unterliegt."

Excursus: *The Adrestos Incident*

1. See *Lexikon des frühgriechischen Epos*. The word is much more common in the *Odyssey* than in the *Iliad*, e.g. 2.231, 5.9, 7.310, 8.348, 14.84 and 433, 15.71, 21.294, 22.46. Leaf *ad loc.* tries to soften the word but manages only to blur his own meaning: "*aisima* does not in fact imply an absolute moral standard . . . beyond what is implied in due retribution . . . for misdeeds." But whether this is "due retribution" is the very thing in question.

2. The scene on Olympus at the start of book 4 was interpreted brilliantly by K. Reinhardt, "Das Parisurteil," *Von Werken und Formen* (Godesberg, 1948), 11–36, and printed again in *Tradition und Geist* (Göttingen, 1960), 16–36. He argues that the scurrilous tale of the beauty contest is transformed and suppressed. The goddess' anger is elevated from spite (*spretae iniuria formae*) to a dark and enigmatic persecution. It is the change from *Märchen* to epic.

3. In *Odyssey* 14.276 we hear how a captured marauder threw himself on the mercy of the Egyptian king. He was not only spared but protected by his captor from the angry populace. Attempts to kill him after he had been accepted are called "evil deeds" (284) and unwelcome to Zeus, the guest god.

4. There is a curious resemblance between Axylos, the generous host living "by the road," and Rüedeger, a man of the same qualities living in a similar location (NL 1639.1): "Der sitzet bî der strâze/ und ist der beste wirt."

5. See M. Parry, "The Homeric Gloss: A Study in Word-Sense," MHV 240–50, esp. 246–50; F. Combellack, "Some Formular Illogicalities in Homer," TAPA 96 (1965), 41–65.

Iliad 12

1. So E. T. Owen, The Story of the Iliad (Toronto, 1946), 119: "Thus casually the poet wakens . . . the sense of transitoriness of the interests for which men strive with such intensity . . . and gives an ironic coloring at the outset to the picture of Hector's triumph." Apollo's destruction of the wall is described in the same spirit at 15.361.

2. The simile has been criticized (e.g. by Wilamowitz, 211) because the animal is killed while Hector is not. But see Moulton, Similes in the Homeric Poems, 47 and n. 54. Discrepancies of this sort are common and, in fact, belong to the manner of Homer's similes. Book 11.474, compares Odysseus to a stag that dies while Odysseus does not. Book 21.573 makes Agenor like a panther that will not give way when wounded: Agenor will run away.

3. On simile strings in book 12, see Moulton, Similes in the Homeric Poems, 64.

4. The catalogue of Trojan contingents is in normal position, just before a new stage in the fighting. Compare 8.261, 11.56, 16.168. Wilamowitz (212) observes that Asteropaios (102) is out of place because he has no part in the teichomachia. He was, in fact, probably added just to round off the number and maintain consistency. Observe that when he is named in a catalogue of Trojan allies at 17.217 he enters into the subsequent fighting (352). As for the rest, the Trojan chiefs named here actually maintain the offensive up through book 14: Hector, of course, throughout; Paris in 13; Poulydamas throughout; Alkathoos, Agenor, Helenus and Deiphobos in 13; Asios in 12 and 13; Aeneas in 13; Archelochos and Akamas in 14.

5. General descriptions at the onset of a new battle or a fresh phase of one already in progress belong to a standard manner: 4.446, 8.60, 13.125, 14.388, 15.263, 16.562, 17.262, 20.31.

6. See Leaf on 252; Von der Mühll, 205.

7. E. Bethe, Homer. Dichtung und Saga I: Ilias (Leipzig-Berlin, 1914), 134; Wilamowitz, 216. On Asios as an intrusion, see Leaf's introduction to book 12 and his notes on 12.112 and 13.384; Wilamowitz, 213 and 224; Von der Mühll, 216. Behind these opinions is the conviction that the Achaean wall is a later addition (since it is ignored in subsequent books), hence Asios, whose activity in 12 consists only of his attempt to storm the barricade, must belong to the same stratum. Denys Page opened a new offensive in the teichomachia of the scholars with his History and the Homeric Iliad (Berkeley, 1963), 315. This drew counterattacks from O. Tsagarakis, "The Achaean Wall and the Homeric Question," Hermes 97 (1969), 129–35, and M. L. West, "The Achaean Wall,"

CR 83 (n.s. 19, 1969), 255–60. Bethe in *Homer*, 133, had added the interesting but incorrect argument that Asios' defiance of Poulydamas badly disrupts the confrontation between Hector and his counselor. Asios belongs to a constellation of oppositions.

Iliad 13

1. I think there is no escaping the conclusion that Hypsenor is killed and that his "heavy groaning" at 423 where he is carried off the field is an unmitigated discrepancy. For an explanation, Fenik, 132. Wilamowitz (48, n. 1) correctly refused to twist the Greek into something it cannot mean. Schadewaldt (103, n. 1) and Michel (88) were less prudent, trying to make "he loosened his knees from under him," 412, mean only that Hypsenor was "felled" but not mortally wounded. This does not convince. Book 18.31 is the most feeble of parallels. In fighting contexts "to loosen a man's knees" means to kill and nothing else. Not only does Deiphobos assume that Hypsenor is dead (no sure evidence by itself, of course—compare Pandaros at 5.101), but Idomeneus does, too (447). His boast "Three of you killed for one of us" (447) expresses a proportion and theme that would be crippled if Hypsenor remained alive. Schadewaldt and Michel make much of the fact that the man is not explicitly said to have been killed. But the same could be said of Peisandros at 11.143. In fact, J. T. Sheppard (*The Pattern of the Iliad*, London, 1922, 95, n. 3) tried to accommodate this by taking 11.143 to mean that Agamemnon hurled the man from his chariot but failed to kill him (a Peisandros fights Menelaos at 13.601). One could remove the famous Pylaimenes discrepancy in the same way. When he falls at 5.576 there is no direct word that he actually died. He appears again at 13.658, very much alive. Such cases are numerous. A check of "Melanippos" in the concordance will provide another illuminating example.

2. Diverse objections to Idomeneus' speech (e.g., how did he know of Othryoneus' promise?) are unimpressive and correctly dismissed by Michel (84). The *Nibelungenlied* supplies an interesting parallel, both in the type of episode and its treatment by critics. Blœdelîn promises Kriemhilt to take vengeance on the Burgonden in return for marriage to the widow (former betrothed?) of Nuodunc along with his lands and castles (1904). He is then slain by Dancwart, who mocks him for the payment he strove for (1927.3–1928.2): "daz sî dîn morgengâbe,/ sprach Dancwart der degen,/ zuo Nuodunges briute,/ der du mit minne woldest pflegen./ Man mac si morgen mehelen/ einem andern man,/ wil er die brûtmiete,/ dem wirt alsam getân." Dancwart could not have known of Kriemhilt's promise, but the value of his knowing compensates for its impossibility. See de Boor, *ad loc.* and Nagel, 402. The second half of strophe 1928 contains a feeble attempt to explain the discrepancy: "ein vil getriuwe Hiune/ het im daz geseit,/ daz im diu küneginne/ riet sô grœzlîchiu leit." De Boor, trenchantly: "ein schwächlicher Versuch zum Ausgleich, widerspricht aber der ganzen Grundhaltung der aventiure, die auf ahnungslosen Überfall der wehrlosen Knechte gestellet ist." The pedantic effort recalls, in turn, *Odyssey* 12.389, where Odysseus

explains how he knew who brought Helios word that his cattle had been eaten.

3. Emphasized by W. Friedrich, *Verwundung und Tod in der Ilias* (Göttingen, 1956), 22, and Michel, 94.

4. Praised by the scholion for its onomatopoetic effect.

5. Friedrich, *Verwundung und Tod*, 19.

6. Fenik, 24. Other occurrences at 5.166, 12.310, and 17.483.

7. Meriones' activity continues in the sequel. Friedrich, *Verwundung und Tod*, 56: "Da er schon in der Vorbereitung der Doppelaristie eine bedeutende Rolle spielte, wechselt sein Name regelmässig wie ein Rondothema mit denen der anderen griechischen Helden: Meriones—Idomeneus—Meriones—Antilochos—Meriones—Menelaos—Meriones."

8. Sometimes the association of names astonishes, as at 15.419–91 (a self-contained series of slayings). On the wall with Priam in book 3 are Panthoos, Thymoites, Lampos, Klytios, Hiketaon, Oukalegon, and Antenor. Of these, Lampos, Klytios, and Hiketaon are Priam's brother (20.237). Sons of these three are slain during that stretch of fighting in book 15 (Kalytor, son of Klytios; Dolops, son of Lampos; Melanippos, son of Hiketaon), while sons of Priam (Hector), Panthoos (Poulydamas), and Antenor (Laodamas) figure prominently. Only Thymoites and Oukalegon (who is never heard from again) do not lose sons at 15.419–591. Of the eight Trojan involved in that fighting, only two (Kleitos and Kroismos) are not from families represented on the wall.

9. Pylaimenes had been slain at 5.576, and his reappearance here is a famous scandal—famous mainly because commentators have not noticed all the other examples. See above, note 1.

10. E.g. Leaf *ad loc.* Wilamowitz, 225, conjectured that it might be the original finish of an Idomeneus poem now lost. The suggestion has nothing to recommend it.

11. Michel, 112: "dass die Troer anstelle einer Wiedergutmachung den Kampf mit dem Ziel der Vernichtung der Achaier fortführen—ist unbegreiflich; dass Zeus, der das Gastrecht wahrt, die Frevler derart unterstützt—ist unbegreiflich; dass es überhaupt Menschen gibt, die des Kampfes nicht überdrüssig werden, wenn doch schon die angenehmen Dinge Sättigung bringen—ist völlig unbegreiflich!"

12. G. Strasburger, *Die kleinen Kämpfer der Ilias* (diss., Frankfurt, 1954), 75; Fenik, 148.

13. This regrouping of material from a central story into minor images of itself is characteristic of the *Iliad*. Carroll Moulton has called attention to an interesting example in book 17: "The Speech of Glaukos in *Iliad* 17," *Hermes* 109 (1981), 1–8.

Introduction, Part II

1. Eggers, "Vom Formenbau mittelhochdeutscher Epen," *DU* 11 (1959), Heft 2, 81–97. See also R. Kienast, "Zur Tektonik von Wolframs Willehalm,"

Festschrift für F. Panzer (Heidelberg, 1950), 96–115; K. Lachmann, *Zu den Nibelungen und zur Klage* (Berlin, 1836) and Mergell, 327. See note 3 below for another example. For a review of these and other efforts, Nagel, 97–104 ("Gliederungsversuchen").

2. It began on the classical front with P. Maury's "Le Secret de Virgile et l'architecture des Bucoliques," *LH* 3 (1944), 74–147, ascended to LeGrelle's "Le premier Livre des Géorgiques, poème pythagoricien," *LEC* 17 (1949), 139–235, and culminated in G. E. Duckworth's monumental and astonishing *Structural Patterns and Proportions in Vergil's Aeneid: A Study in Mathematical Composition* (Ann Arbor, 1962). Duckworth gives a full explanation of the golden ratio on pages 37–39. On the golden section in medieval German poetry: H. Koch, "Über den goldenen Schnitt als Formprinzip in der frühmittelalterlichen Dichtung der Germanen," *AfSmS* 175 (1939), 1–15; H. Eggers, "Der goldene Schnitt im Aufbau alt- und mittelhoch-deutscher Epen," *WW* 10 (1960), 193–203.

3. E.g. Sister Mary Frances, S.N.D., "Architectonic Symmetry as a Principle of Structure in the Nibelungenlied," *GR* 41 (1966), 157–69. Nagel's warning is important (101): "So zeigt sich, dass letztlich doch *inhaltliche* Kriterien für die Gliederung massgebend sind."

4. See Nagel's sober review, 72.

5. Maurer, Über die Formkunst des Dichters unseres Nibelungenliedes," *DU* 6 (1954), Heft 2, 77–83; reprinted in *Dichtung und Sprache des Mittelalters. Gesammelte Aufsätze* (Bern, München, 1963), 70–79, and again in *Nibelungenlied und Kudrun*, 40–52. See also his "Über den Bau der Aventiuren des Nibelungenliedes," *Festschrift Kralik* (Horn, 1954), 93–8 (this last is much shorter and useful only if the article on "Formkunst" is unavailable).

6. Cf. Eggers, "Formenbau," 52.

7. Maurer, "Formkunst" (in *Nibelungenlied und Kudrun),* 52: "Es ist wohl unnötig, noch einmal zu betonen, dass es bei den Analysen nicht darauf ankommt, ob der oder jener Abschnitt um eine Strophe länger oder kürzer wird. Die harmonische Ausgewogenheit, die gewollte und erreichte Harmonie der Glieder bleibt, auch wenn sich Gruppen von 27 und 28, von 20 und 21 Strophen entsprechen."

8. Wiehl, "Über den Aufbau des Nibelungenliedes," *WW* 16 (1966, Heft 5), 309–23.

9. Nagel, 10.

10. Nagel has already called for something like this (85): "Das NL ist vielfältiger untergliedert, als die rein formale Gliederung in Strophen und Aventiuren erkennen lässt. Deshalb müssen auch jene Erzähleinheiten in den Blick gerückt weden, die nicht so augenfällig abgegrenzt sind, aber dennoch relativ selbständige Bauelemente darstellen." It was Wachinger who first pointed the way (67): "Das also verstehen wir unter Symmetrie: nicht spiegelbildliche Anordnung blosser Grössen, sondern spiegelbildliche Entsprechung von Stil, Inhalt und Funktionen von Strophengruppen, die nicht unbedingt auch im Umfang gleich sein müssen."

11. See Eggers' helpful musings on the subject.

12. Mergell, 315.

13. See notes 1 and 2 above.

Symmetry

1. The repetition serves as a refrain and hence acquires a patterning force. *Sît* appears elsewhere in such clusters: 18.2, 18.4, 19.3 (C 17.2, 17.4, 18.3), this also a solemn look into the future with Kriemhilt; again in the introduction of persons: 5.4, 6.4, 7.3 (C 4.3, 5.4, 6.4). The usage is thus clear. In strophes 21–26 (C 20–25) C omits *sît* in 22 (C22) but establishes a refrain of its own with the triple repetition of *des* at (C) 22.4 and 24.4 (cf. 21.4). Characteristically, C's *des* at 22.4 makes more explicit the verse's connection with the preceding than B's paratactic *sît* (22.4).

2. We will see a similar leaping back and forth in time below (also in reference to a youth's growth to manhood) at *Kudrun* 162.

3. Hoffmann[1], 120.

4. Nagel has called attention to the regular one-strophe exchanges in dramatic dialogue, e.g. at 1941–1943 between Dancwart and the Huns, at 329–334 in the deliberations over Gunther's courtship, or at 1460–1472 in the debate over Kriemhilt's invitation. "In dieser Weise hat der Dichter die isolierende Wirkung der Strophenform in den Dienst einer dialogisch-dramatischen Technik gestellt."

5. See S. E. Bassett, "The Second Necyia Again," *AJPh* 44 (1923), 44–52; Fenik, *Studies in the Odyssey* (Wiesbaden, 1974), 148.

6. The reasons for this diminishing number are unclear to me. Perhaps it has to do simply with the relative complexity of the respective objects. A shield invites more description than a spear, a spear than a stone.

7. On the arming scenes in the *Iliad*, see W. Arend, *Die typischen Szenen bei Homer* (Berlin, 1933), 92, and J. Armstrong, "The Arming Motif in the Iliad," *AJPh* 79 (1958), 337–54. Prünhilt's great strength also recalls the heroes of the *Iliad*. This is of course a widespread motif in folktale and epic. If we feel that the NL is violating even this permissive canon, we should take note of an episode in the epic of India, the *Ramayana*, where the bow to be strung by the hero needs 5,000 men to carry it out; cited by D. Page, *Folktales in Homer's Odyssey* (Cambridge, Mass., 1973), 108.

8. There are important (and divergent) analyses of this scene by Mergell, 321; W. Wapnewski, "Rüdigers Schild," *Nibelungenlied und Kudrun*, 134–78; and J. Splett, *Rüdiger von Bechelaren. Studien zum 2. Teil des Nibelungenliedes* (Heidelberg, 1968), 70–106.

9. Alois Wolf has called attention to how dialogue in the NL turns inward, revealing human dimensions: "Gerade der Schild, eines der unentbehrlichsten Requisiten der germanisch-mythischen Vorstellungswelt, dient dem Menschlichen, an ihm entzündet sich ein Heldentum, das ganz von Innen getragen ist, an ihm offenbart sich zutiefst Menschliches." In "Zur Gestaltung und Funktion der Rede in germanischer Heldendichtung," *Literaturwissenschaftliches Jahrbuch der Görres Gesellschaft*, N.F. 3 (1962), 25.

10. Masser, "Von Alternativestrophen und Vortragsvarianten im Nibelungenlied," *Hohenemser Studien zum Nibelungenlied,* unter Mitarbeit von Irmtraud Albrecht, hrsg. von Achim Masser (Dornbirn, 1981; *Montfort Heft* ¾, 1980), 302/128–303/129.

11. For more examples, Fenik, *Studies in the Odyssey,* 355 .

12. Heusler might have underestimated the flexibility achieved by dialogue in the NL. He observed that while falling short of true stichomythy, it did manage to advance beyond the stiffness of the alliterative period ("Der Dialog in der altgermanischen erzählenden Dichtung," *ZfDA* 46 [1902], 237): "Das deutsche Volksepos geht wohl äusserst selten, das Nibelungenlied nirgends, bis zur Sichomythie. Aber in der nicht spärlichen Verwendung einzelner Redekurzverse hat es die Zähflüssigkeit der stabreimenden Zeit überwunden." As examples of *Redekurzverse* he cites 830.4, 840.1, 853.4, 874.1, 887.1, 1412.4, 1413.1. But my last example from aventiure 18 shows how manipulation of the strophe itself, and contrast from scene to scene, creates much animation.

13. Cf. G. T. Gillespie, "Spuren der Heldendichtung und Ansätze zur Heldenepik in literarischen Texten des 11. und 12. Jahrhunderts," *Studien zur frühmittelhochdeutschen Literatur,* hrsg. L. P. Johnson, H. H. Steinhoff and R. A. Wisbey, Cambridge Colloquium, 1971 (Berlin, 1974), *Publications of the Institute of Germanic Studies of the University of London,* vol. 19, 257: "Der Donauübergang der Burgunden im NL ist weit mehr als Überquerung einer geographischen Grenze: er versinnbildlicht klar und deutlich den Übergang in den Bereich des unvermeidlichen Todes und erinnert stark an die Fahrt der Seelen über den Styx." Compare Wachinger, 38 and note 1: "Von der Ankunft an der Donau bis zur Ankunft bei Pilgrim begegnen den Burgundern ein Hindernis nach dem anderen . . . alle zeigen, wie die Burgunder gegen alle Hindernisse, die schon als solche von schlechter Vorbedeutung sind, sich den Weg in den Untergang erkämpfen."

14. Wachinger, 46–47, reconstructs Hagen's reasons for his silence.

15. Wachinger (55) identifies the two stages somewhat differently: "Die Reise der Nibelungen zerfällt, wie wir gesehen haben, in eine Etappe der Hindernisse (Hauptstation: Donauübergang) und eine Etappe der entgegenkommenden Freundschaft (Hauptstation: Bechelaren). Beide Etappen sind unmittelbar auf die Endkatastrophe bezogen, aber in ganz verschiedener Weise. Der Donauübergang ist ihr zugeordnet als Vorausdeutung: Hindernisse sind schlechte Vorzeichen, Kämpfe geben den Vorgeschmack von der späteren Saalschlacht. Der Aufenthalt in Bechelaren aber als heiteres, glanzvolles und friedliches Idyll ist in der beliebten scharfen Antithese auf den düsteren Hintergrund bezogen."

16. Panzer thought Lamprecht is the direct source here for the NL: "Das Motiv ist in den deutschen Alexander V. 2643 ff. übernommen und die Erzählung des Nibelungenliedes Str. 1581–83 deckt sich auch im Einzelnen bis in den Wortlaut hinein so weit mit der Darstellung des alten Alexandergedichtes, dass dies zweifellos die Vorlage gewesen sein muss, der der Dichter des Liedes folgte." "Nibelungische Problematik. Siegfried und Xanten, Hagen

und die Meerfrauen, Magyaren und Hunnen." *Sitzungsberichte der Heidelberger Akademie der Wissenschaften*, phil.-hist. Kl., 1953–54, Nr. 3, 22.

Correlation

1. Nagel, 117–36; Nagel, *Staufische Klassik* (Heidelberg, 1977), 507.
2. Nagel, *Staufische Klassik*, 509.
3. Neumann has directed similar strictures against Weber, 131.
4. Cf. Wachinger, 77.
5. The same detail marks their arrival at Rüedeger's castle, 1318.1. It is in fact common: *Kudrun* 1118 and Wolfram, *Parzival* 37.10, 38.14, 61.3, 69.21.
6. W. Schröder, *Nibelungenstudien* (Stuttgart, 1968), 117; cf. Hoffmann[1], 127 and 135.
7. S. Beyschlag ("Das Motiv der Macht bei Siegfrieds Tod," *Heldensage*, 207) argues that Gunther is actually playing the statesman (compare Etzel at 1894 and the kings together at 1967). But Sigmunt's description simply arouses other expectations (although these are fulfilled in the long run - see Weber, 43, and Wachinger, 33). Gunther also cuts a sorry figure when the declaration of war from Saxony paralyzes him. Beyschlag whitewashes liberally (207): "die Kriegserklärung der Sachsen und Dänen zeigt ihn als den überlegenden, sorgenden Fürsten, der sich nicht ohne weiteres in ein kriegerisches Abenteuer stürtzt." But the text creates a different impression. Cf. 147.4, 153.1–3, and in general Gunther's total dependence on Sivrit. Strophe 174 is downright humiliating. In short, Gernot urges peace and comes off well; Gunther prevaricates and looks bad.
8. Panzer, 308.
9. Nagel, *Staufische Klassik*, 520.
10. Nagel, 69.
11. Nagel, *Staufische Klassik*, 520.
12. For an incontrovertible example, Wachinger, 53. See his conclusions as well, 143–5.
13. Mergell, 309: "Auch ist Siegfrieds Forderung keineswegs nur die Eingebung eines flüchtigen Augenblicks, sie ist auch nicht bloss im Hinblick auf die Erwerbung Kriemhilds ausgesprochen. Sondern es geht Siegfried um die Herstellung eines echten Einklangs von Sache und Person, von Herrschaft und Besitz. Dem *ellen* des Landesherrn soll, nach seinem Willen, der Landes*fride* verdankt werden. Mit dieser Auffassung ist Siegfried der vollendete Gegenspieler zum Burgunderhof, wo ein altüberlieferter, in herkömmlichen Formen erstarrter Kulturzustand erreicht ist, der den ursprünglich personenhaften Bezug aller Dinge fast hat vergessen lassen. Mit Siegfrieds Ankunft aber wird—nicht erst durch sein Handeln, sondern allein schon durch sein Dasein—ein latenter Zwiespalt von Tradition und Tatgesinnung, von Statik and Dynamik, von Mangel und Überfluss (oder wie immer man diesen Gegensatz begreiflich zu fassen sucht) offenbar. Diesen Gegensatz empfindet unser Dichter als ein Problem des Lebens selbst, als Ausdruck des Lebensgefühls seiner Zeit."

14. Version B and A read at 114.4: "daz widerredete Hagene/ unde Gêrnôt zehant." C (114) corrects to: "daz wider redet aleine/ der herre Gêrnôt zehant." Hoffmann[1] (121) sees here an effort to remove Hagen from the ranks of the brave. C was also probably after a more consistent text (as often). Gernot speaks alone here, as he does after each face-off. Hagen is silent until 121.

15. The number twelve is conventional, but no less pointed for that. C changes 118.2 to "jâ enzimt dir niht mit strîte/ deheinen mînen genôz bestân. Thus Sivrit's fist shaking is softened into emphasis on rank. Hoffmann[1], 118, lists other examples of C's efforts toward a more courtly text, especially in matters of standing and protocol.

16. Compare Karl's answer to Oliver in the *Rolandslied* (1325) when the latter volunteers to serve as envoy and spy to the court of Marsilie: "ze boten wil ich dîn niht:/ du bist ze gæhe mit der rede,/ unde Ruolant mîn neve,/ mit zornlîchen worten./ daz ist mir ze vorchten:/ si stœrent grôze êre."

17. Wapnewski, "Rüdiger's Schild," *Nibelungenlied und Kudrun*, 166.

18. Some effort is made to mitigate the discrepancy. At 907.4 Hagen rides up close to note the marker's position. We might presume that was enough. But at the murder he "struck him through the cross" (981.2). Special pleading might allow this to mean "he struck him through the spot the cross had marked," but anyone satisfied with that sophistry is welcome to it. Besides, the act loses immediacy and symbolic force if the spear does not pass through the actual sign.

19. De Boor, *Nibelungenlied*, xxxii; cf. his note on 898.1.

20. There is no translating the word *triuwe* with its full range of meanings, e.g. "fidelity," "good faith," "trust," "belief," "love," even "covenant" or "agreement" in older German. Fundamentally it means the moral obligations binding persons who belong together. Latin *fides* is very close.

21. See H. Burger, "Vorausdeutung und Erzählstruktur in mittelalterlichen Texten," *Typologia Litterarum (Festschrift Max Wehrli*, Zürich-Freiburg i. Br., 1969), 139: "So haben die Personen ihre je eigenen unterschiedlichen Möglichkeiten der Gewissheit über Zukünftiges—wobei die Stufung von absoluter Sicherheit des prophetischen über das des heroischen Ablaufs gewisse Bewusstsein Hagens bis zur rein innermenschlichen, infolgedessen ungewissen Ahnung reicht."

22. The depiction of Kriemhilt in this scene is both masterful and problematical: see Wachinger, 35.

23. Hoffmann[2], 250.

24. Siefken, 13, 166, 23.

25. But it is by no means a contemptible effort: Hoffmann[2], 289; Siefken, 166.

26. Siefken, 130.

27. Ibid., 146 and 98.

28. Hoffmann[2], 39: "Es gehört zu den kunstvollen Fügungen der Dichtung, dass Hetel im Kudrunteil eben das Schicksal ereilen wird, vor dem er Hildes Vater . . . bewahrt: nämlich bei der Verfolgung der Entführer der

eigenen Tochter das Leben zu verlieren." Hilde, of course, conspired in her own abduction; Kudrun did not.

29. Siefken, 123, n. 1: "Diese auffallende Parallelität des Erzählens in der Hilde—und in der Kudrunhandlung muss zusammengesehen werden mit der oben gezeigten Parallelität der Verfolgungsschlachten. Es ergibt sich damit ein gewichtiges Argument für die These, die Kudrunhandlung sei aus dem Gerüst der Hildehandlung entstanden und füsse nicht auf eigener Sagen."

30. On the discrepant versions of Hagen in *Kudrun*, Hoffmann[2], 34.

31. For a good survey of the motif "far from home" in Homer, see Griffin, 106.

32. Hoffmann[2], 304: "Diese menschenbildliche Konzeption aber ist das, was zugleich der ideele Kern des Gesamtwerkes ist: dass Leid den Menschen nicht verhärten muss, sondern überwunden werden kann, dass nicht Untergang und Zerstörung—und innere Zerstörtheit—am Ende stehen müssen, sondern dass der Wille zur Vergebung und Versöhnung Harmonie schaffen kann."

33. Wolfram uses it the same way at *Parzival* 630.6: "swer rehte kunde schouwen,/ von Lôgrois diu herzogîn/ truoc vor ûz den besten schîn."

34. Submission in Pelrapeire is not given Klamide as an option, although Chrétien has it (2684), briefly and not in direct discourse. When Parzival vanquishes Orilus, his demands follow a similar pattern (266.7): "I will spare your life if you allow this lady (Jeschute, Orilus' wife) back into your grace." "No, I cannot, her guilt is too great. Ask anything but that. My brother has two kingdoms. Pick whichever you want for yourself. But as for this lady, I cannot be reconciled with her." "Then go to Arthur and submit to a lady who was beaten because of me," etc. But here the figure carries a different content. Wolfram weaves a maze of irony and hidden associations. Orilus never mentions his own name or his brother's (Lehelin). Good for him that he does not, for one of Lehelin's two kingdoms was taken by him from Parzival's family. At the same time, the lady that Orilus must submit to is his own sister. Yet all this remains undiscovered for now. Parzival, in fact, is enmeshed in ties to almost everybody he meets without knowing it. Webs are even spun between him and the armor worn by Orilus (260.28): a spear from Gahaviez, a helmet made by Trebuchet (cf. 253.29) in Toledo (land of Kailet), leg guards from Anschouwe, his horse's mail from Tenebroc (home of the grail maiden Clarischanze, 232.25 and 806.23), and the animal itself from Brumbane, a lake in the grail country.

35. Cf. W. Schmidt, "Formprinzipien deutscher Kunst im Mittelalter,"*Festschrift F. Panzer,* hrsg. R. Kienast (Heidelberg, 1950), 153: "Die eigentlich schöpferischen Kräfte sind nicht darauf verwandt worden, neue Formen zu finden, sondern die vorhandenen, übernommenen, weiterenwickelten zu Trägern letzter seelischer Ausdrucksmöglichkeiten zu erheben."

Ring Composition

1. The major studies of ring composition in Homer are : W.A.A. van Otterlo, "De Ringcompositie als Opbowprincipie in de Epische Gedichten

van Homerus," *Verhandelingen der koninklijke Nederlansche Akademie der Weten-schappen*, Afd. Letterkunde, Nieuwe Reiks, LI, no. 1 (Amsterdam, 1948), 1–95; J. Gaisser, "A Structural Analysis of Digressions in the Iliad and Odyssey," *HScPh* 73 (1969), 1–43; D. Lohmann, *Die Komposition der Reden in der Ilias* (Berlin, 1970).

2. See Moulton's excellent analysis, *Similes in the Homeric Poems*, 56–58.

3. Version C makes the king's offer even more explicit by changing 311.3 "wir gern stæter suone;/ des ist uns recken nôt" to "wir gern stæter suone/ und geben michel guot" (C 313.3). This is one of C's frequent efforts toward clarity. That is, it prepares better than B's text for Gunther's description of their offer to Sivrit (314).

4. Some verbal echoes underline the point: "ê daz ir sceidet hin" (Gunther to his guests, 310.1) and "ê daz wir wider rîten / heim in unser lant "(Liudegast and Liudeger to Gunther). C produces even more: 312.1 and 313.2; 312.3 and 313.3.

5. Hoffmann[1], 121 and 125.

6. Compare B 982.2 and C 991.2; B 984.4 and C 993.4. Hoffmann[1], 122.

7. 994.4: "mich riuwet niht sô sêre / sô vrou Kriemhilt mîn wîp." Cf. *Iliad* 6.450–4 (Hector to Andromache): "But the suffering of the Trojans to come, of Hercuba herself or Lord Priam, or my brothers, none of that touches me as does yours."

8. Prünhilt's disquiet goes to the roots of her being. Her obsession with Sivrit's rank is only a surface symptom, an attempt to translate inner void into terms comprehensible to others and herself. Nagel has, I think, inter-preted this correctly, even though these things emerge only implicitly from the circumstances and never become a direct issue ("Widersprüche im Ni-belungenlied," *Nibelungenlied und Kudrun*, 419): "Viewed objectively, minne is the absolutely overpowering compulsion of destiny. In the eyes of the lover, minne appears as a freely chosen inner bond, as constancy of the heart. It has scarcely been noticed before now—in fact not even realized—that the poet of the NL has depicted Siegfried's love for Kriemhild as just this kind of minne destiny, and that the personal problems in the relationship between Siegfried and Brünhild spring from this very source. Only the fatal, trans-forming power of minne could nullify natural causality and neutralize the affinity that binds Siegfried and Brünhild together. Tragedy, and indeed not guilt-tragedy but fate-tragedy, was the inevitable consequence, since a minne destiny of the sort strikes only one of the predestined partners and allows him to find fulfillment in a newly defined goal. The other, remaining outside and unreleased, must necessarily fail to achieve what she was born for. On the one side, then, there is Siegfried, happy and fulfilled. Set against him is Brünhild. Despite the externals of rank and power she remains unsatisfied, unable to find peace of mind as her thoughts circle endlessly around Siegfried (and Kriemhild)."

9. Uote's friends and Gunther's men ride out to greet the visitors before they arrive (782). Prünhilt must be reminded to receive them.

10. Observe the same order when Kriemhilt and Etzel come together for the first time. She is lifted from her horse first (1349.1), then Etzel dismounts

(1349.2–3). The poet is meticulous about such matters, and his audience will have been alert to them.

Prolepsis

1. Wachinger, "Zusammenfassung vor dem Abschnitt," 8–10.
2. Masser, "Von Alternativestrophen und Vortragsvarianten im Nibelungenlied," *Hohenemser Studien zum Nibelungenlied*, unter Mitarbeit von Irmtraud Albrecht, hrsg. von Achim Masser (Dornbirn), 1981 (Montfort Heft ¾, 1980), 307/133–308/134.
3. Ibid., 304/130–305/131.
4. Fellmann, "*Style Formulaire* und epische Zeit im Rolandslied," *GRM* n.F. XII (1962), 337–61.
5. All translations from *The Song of Roland* are Brault's.
6. Fellmann, 339: "The anticipation at 2022f. causes no monotonous repetition of the same thing in laisse CLI. Instead, a general summary is followed by complete development of the idea in a scene. Moreover, a stylistic feature characteristic of the Song of Roland makes the surprise effective. There is no unbroken continuity of wording between laisse CLI and the verses just before. Instead, the laisse starts completely afresh with *Or veit Rollant*, so that the same situation appears under a different aspect."
7. Ibid., 338.
8. Ibid., 343.
9. Brault (I, 315) interprets somewhat differently. To quote him in full: "One notes, however, a curious interlacing of events in this passage:

1. Charles travels from Saragossa to Aix; stages along the way are indicated (v. 3683: Nerbonne; v. 3684: Bordeaux; v. 3689: Blaye), but speed is emphasized (c. 3696).

2. Charles arrives at Aix (v. 3697).

3. In his palace at Aix Charles summons his judges from every corner of the empire (vv. 3698–3703).

4. Arriving at his palace at Aix, Charles encounters Alda (vv. 3705 ff.).

5. That night, there is a wake for Alda and she is buried the following day (vv. 3731–3732).

6. Charles is at Aix; Ganelon is flogged and awaits his trial (vv. 3734–3741).

7. Charles summons his judges (v. 3743).

8. The judges assemble at Aix (v. 3744).

9. The trial of Ganelon is held on Saint Sylvester's day (vv. 3745 ff.)."

"The chronology," Brault continues, "is evidently 1,2,4,5, viewed as consecutive actions. Items 3 and 7 are one and the same event and occur later, simultaneously to 6. Items 8 and 9 take place at approximately the same time and are the culmination of all these activities. Item 3, then, appears to be the only incident narrated out of order, and this flashforward serves to highlight the occurrence. The framing of Alda's death with two separate allusions to the summoning of the judges underscores the inseparability of the two events." So far Brault. But his outline and interpretation blur slightly the facts of the text. His number 4 above reads: "Arriving at his palace at Aix." But the French actually says (and in Brault's own translation): "The emperor has returned from Spain,/ he comes to Aix." Again, his number 6: "Charles is at Aix." The French reads: "The emperor has returned to Aix." Brault's outline thus removes the obtrusive feature, namely the repetition of finite verbs reporting Charles's return. He also omits from his numbers 3 and 4 all mention of verse 3704, the proleptic "Now begins the trial of Ganelon." Yet the differences between Brault's outline of the scene and my own are slight. His number 3 (plus the omitted verse 3704) are the only items out of strict chronological order. They are, as he says, an anticipation of upcoming events. The repeated notices of Charles's return are a majestic refrain, emphasizing the import of the moment, and they do not interrupt the progression of things.

10. After Segremors, Keie rides out to challenge Parzival in a parallel encounter. Note the *absence* this time of prolepsis (293.28): "Keie sîner jost enthielt,/ unz er zem Wâleise sprach:/ 'herre, sît iu sus geschach," etc.

11. Curschmann, "The Concept of the Oral Formula as an Impediment to Our Understanding of Medieval Oral Poetry," *M&H* n.s. 8 (1977), 63–76, esp. 72ff. And again, "Nibelungenlied und Nibelungenklage, Über Mündlichkeit und Schriftlichkeit im Prozess der Episierung," *Deutsche Literatur im Mittelalter. Kontakte und Perspektiven*, Hugo Kuhn zum Gedenken (Stuttgart, 1979), 95.

12. Ibid., 72.

13. Ibid., 73.

Accumulation

1. Other examples are at the end of aventiure 5 (C 327–28), with marriage advice to Gunther from his counselors; at the close of 13 (C 821–22), preparing for the quarrel between the two queens; after 905 (C 913), setting the stage for the hunt; after 1112 (C 1124–25), leading to Kriemhilt's agreement to be reconciled with Gunther.

Chanson de Roland and Rolandslied

1. The most thorough exposition is by Gräf, the best and most influential by Rychner (68ff.). Also see Brault I, 47 and 75.

2. Brault I, 49. "Turoldus" is the name found on the Oxford manuscript. Majority opinion now considers him the author, not just the copyist. See Brault I, 4, and n. 18, p. 340.

3. All these are treated by Gräf: French and Saracens (16); the two conferences (7); the gathering of peers (8: "Spiel und Gegenspiel findet durch

die Schaffung analoger Situationen und ihre gleiche Darstellung in zwei sich folgenden Bildern eine wirksame Betonung."); Roland-Oliver (30: Gräf's chart on p. 34 reveals the remarkable parallelism of the two scenes between Roland and Oliver on the sounding of Oliphant); Roland-Ganelon (26); Charles-Paligan (18).

4. For the patterns of assonance, Rychner, 90; on the other binding details, Brault I, 172.

5. Full details and discussion in Brault I, 190.

6. The scene itself is made parallel to Ganelon's conversation with Blancandrin during the ride to Saragossa (starting at laisse 28).

7. L. Pollmann finds still another dimension in these repeats ("Von der *Chanson de Geste* zum höfischen Roman in Frankreich," *GRM* n.F 16 (1966), 2–3: "Wenn beispielweise Marsilius im *Rolandslied* dreimal den gleichen, nur durch die Erfordernisse der von laisse zu laisse wechselnden Assonanz leicht variierten Worten sein Erstaunen zum Ausdruck bringt über Karl den Grossen, der alt und weisshaarig, der seines Wissens schon mehr als hundert Jahre alt ist und doch des Kampfes nicht müde wird, dann kann man darin einen *progrès psychologique et dramatique*; sehen, aber es ist zugleich mehr als dies: das im Gegenüber mit dem Unerklärlichen instinktiv den Ritus suchende Staunen des Heiden lässt Karl den Grossen eine neue, phänomenale Wirklichkeit gewinnen, die des Geheimnis gewussten Sakralen. Das Staunen und der Bestaunte haben Zeit, im Rhythmus dieser periodisch wiederkehrenden Formulierung als sie selbst zur Geltung zu kommen, sich in ihrem Wesen zu spiegeln."

8. J. J. Duggan offers a convenient summary: *The Song of Roland: Formulaic Style and Poetic Craft* (Berkeley, 1973),98.

9. Rychner: "Mais cette cohésion dramatique est unique" (40); "c'est la forte cohérence du Roland qui étonne; elle est aussi l'exception" (47).

10. Keller, "La place du Ruolantes Liet dans la tradition rolandienne," *MA* 71 (1965), 215–46, 401–21. For an earlier view, Ph. Aug. Becker, "Das Rolandslied," *ZffSL* 61 (1937), 1–22, 129–56. Becker believed there was a revised text of O, commercially multiplied and distributed, and that was what Konrad used. Becker failed to grasp the fluid transmission of heroic poetry and the multiplicity of versions.

11. W. Besch, "Beobachtungen zur Form des deutschen Rolandsliedes," *Festgabe für Friedrich Maurer* (Düsseldorf, 1968), 129.

12. For details and description, Brault I, 135.

13. Note the triple repetition: "Respunt li reis" (17, 18) and "Li empereres respunt par maltalant" (19).

14. Emphasized by R. B. Schäfer-Maulbetsch, *Studien zur Entwicklung des mittelhochdeutschen Epos*, I (Göppingen, 1971) 144.

15. But other connecting details abound: Saracen insult and French reply correspond closely in all three duels (4020–44, 4227–46, 4385–4402); the first and third encounters set the religions in conflict; all three challenges begin the same way: "bistu hi, Ruolant?" (4021); "bistu hie, Olivir?" (4227); "bistu hi, Turpin?" (4385). There are many other correspondences.

16. On this last phenomenon, see Pollmann, "Von der *Chanson de Geste zum höfischen Roman*". Antje Missfeldt has compared Konrad's division of episodes into segments (as marked by initial capitals) with Turoldus' use of the laisse to the same end: "Ein Vergleich der Laisseeinheiten in der Chanson de Roland (HS. O) mit der Abschnittstechnik in Konrads Rolandslied,"*ZfdPh* 92 (1973), 321–38. She discovers much correspondence between the two in the divisions themselves and in the ways they are marked at the start and finish. But she finds that Konrad tends to remove the more rigid parallelisms and to loosen sequences of laisses that Turoldus holds to a strict correspondence. Thus (333): "Der starre Ablauf paralleler Strophen und ihre genaue Ausrichtung nach einem bestimmten Schema widerstreben Konrad offensichtlich: er bemüht sich, diese Laissen umzugestalten, um den Zwang einer festgefügten Abschnittsumgrenzung, die den Laissenkonturen entsprechen würde, zu entgehen. Er füllt die Abschnitte unregelmässig." Konrad tries to follow *Roland's* divisions where he has to (338): "Zum anderen,—in seiner Eigenschaft als Dichter seines Landes und seiner Zeit—, an den Stellen, wo er das Prinzip der Wiederholungs—und Parallelabläufe umgestalten muss,—das wirkt sich im Aufbau durch eine andere Unterteilung als im afrz. Lied aus. Angestrebt wird eine in erster Linie fliessende, auf Sukzession ausgerichtete Erzählweise." These useful findings need to be modified on two counts. (1) The marking of narrative segments by initials is subject to error and omission in transmission. One has to do with an indeterminate quantity (as she recognizes, p. 322). (2) Many of Konrad's finer structures remain only adumbrated if one marks them solely with capitals. The instrument Missfeldt has chosen to work with thus measures these things only imperfectly, however useful it is in the discovery of others. Still her contention remains true that Konrad aimed for a smoother narrative with *less salient* articulation.

17. Konrad does the same, 5037: "Die haiden waren do gelegen, inoch lebeten ir zwene," etc.

18. Schäfer-Maulbetsch, *Studien zur Entwicklung des mittelhochdeutschen Epos*, 145, divides similarly but emphasizes the alternation of duels and mass engagements.

19. The increase in the number of Christians slain is so steady that one cannot help suspecting textual corruption at 4849. The numbers from the fourth through the sixth entry (the sixth being the break in the sequence) are: 108 (4587), 308 (4762), and 108 again (4849). The repetition of 108 increases suspicion.

20. One notices small touches: Blanscandiz brings up Roland's name first (1839). Marssilie does not need to—by the second meeting Genelun is ready to do that himself (2264).

Beyond the Epic

1. JBC *ad loc.*
2. Lane, 189.

3. Observe the temporal movement from 1 to 3: 14.1 and 14.12; Lane, 491.

4. See Lane, 399. Understanding of the symbolism seems to have faded at some point, leading to confusion in Mark's explanation of Jesus' motives. The tree is in leaf, and Jesus approaches to see if it is bearing. On discovering "only leaves," he pronounces the curse, as if in disappointment at finding nothing to eat. But we are told expressly that "it was not the season for figs," something Jesus would have known for himself. The symbolic act thus became overlaid with a naturalistic decor. In Matthew (21.21ff.) that process has continued. Jesus looks for figs because he is hungry, curses the tree at finding none, and it withers at once. The miracle then becomes the occasion for a homily on the power of faith.

5. Lane, 400: "In this context the fig tree symbolizes Israel in Jesus' day, and what happens to the tree the terrible fate that inevitably awaited Jerusalem. The explanation was already put forth by Victor of Antioch, in the oldest existing commentary on Mark, that Jesus had 'used the fig tree to set forth the judgment that was about to fall on Jerusalem.' This is certainly the evangelist's understanding of the episode, for in the Gospel of Mark Jesus' action in the Temple is firmly embedded within the fig tree incident. The a-b-a structure of Ch. 11:12–21 (fig tree–cleansing of the Temple–fig tree) serves to provide a mutual commentary on these two events."

6. In the OT passages referred to above (Jeremiah 8.13, Hosea 9.10, Joel 1.7), where the fig tree stands for Israel, the vine is named with the fig and means the same thing—indeed it is the better known symbol of the two. Interestingly, Mark sets the parable of the vineyard and its wicked husbandmen in close association with the curse of the fig tree at 12.1. Matthew does the same (21.83) and even inserts another vineyard tale in the parable of the two sons (21.28). The vineyard parable goes back most directly to Isaiah 5.1 (also a pronouncement of judgment on Israel). This clustering of judgmental texts (cleansing of the temple, parables of the vineyard) argues for taking the curse of the fig tree as meaning the same.

7. Lane, 532, also explains this intercalating as characteristic of Mark's style. John (18.16) frames Jesus' first hearing with the account of Peter as well, but differently. The first denial (18.16–18) comes before Jesus is questioned by Annas (18.19–24). When the scene ends, and before Jesus is led to Pilate's praetorium, Peter is shown making his last two denials (18.25–7).

8. The JBC (on Mark 5.21–43) cites Mark 6.7–31 as another encapsulated narrative (the sending of the Twelve; cf. Lane, 137 and 206), but that does not seem to me a good example. By the time the apostles return at 6.30 their mission is complete and we hear only the briefest report of it. What marks the other rings is the bare notice or start of something, then its suspension, and finally its resumption and conclusion.

9. More cases and discussion in Fenik, *Studies in the Odyssey* (Wiesbaden, 1974), 88–91.

10. Text by M. Skutella (Stuttgart: Teubner, 1969).

11. He did not, of course, write in pure dialect, an orthographical impossibility if nothing else. Werner Günther describes his language like this: "Ein stilisiertes, in der Lautung dem Hochdeutschen angenähertes Berndeutsch, ein im Tonfall und syntaktisch der Mundart angeglichenes Hochdeutsch." This from "Gotthelfs Grösse," *Form und Sinn. Beiträge zur Literatur und Geistesgeschichte* (Bern–München, 1968), 130–1.

12. One small example from *Uli der Pächter*, chap. 7 (all quotations from Gotthelf are taken from the edition of Walter Muschg, *Jeremias Gotthelfs Werke*, in zwanzig Bänden, Basel: Verlag Birkenhäuser, 1948–49): "Wir haben im Berndeutsch gar herrliche Worte, die verschiedenen Sorten und Abarten des Geschwätzes zu bezeichnen: dampen, dämperlen, klapperen, stürmen, schwadronieren, poleten, hässelen, gifteln, schnäderen, ausführen, kifeln, rühmseln, usw." Nor does it lie in the realm of possibility to translate, say, the massive abuse exchanged by Mädi and "ds Zyberlihoger Lisi" in chap. 18 of *Anne Bäbi Jowäger*, I. For an excellent introduction and survey of Gotthelf's dialect, the uses he puts it to and the luxuriance of its vocabulary, see Werner Günther's *Neue Gotthelf-Studien* (Bern, 1958), esp. the chapter on language and style (208–56).

13. Karl Fehr, *Jeremias Gotthelf* (Stuttgart, 1967), 94: "Gotthelfs Schriften wurden zwar der realistischen, manchmal sogar der biedermeierlichen oder der naturalistischen Epoche zugeordnet, standen aber in Wahrheit ausserhalb jener Tradition, die von der deutschen Klassik und Romantik herkam. Gotthelf hat sich kaum je ernsthaft mit Goethe und nur in jungen Jahren mit Schiller auseinandergesetzt. Die literarische Wertung, die ihre Massstäbe von der deutschen Klassik bezog, konnte mit den Schriften Gotthelfs sowohl nach Stil wie nach Form und Inhalt wenig anfangen. Es ist kein Zufall, dass der Begründer und Leiter der Gesamtausgabe, Rudolf Hunziker, ein klassischer Philologe war, dass der erste Erwecker der modernen Deutung, Walter Muschg, ein ausgesprochener Aussenseiter unter den akademischen Germanisten war und dass wichtige Beiträge zur Gotthelf–Forschung von Nichtdeutschen geliefert wurden."

14. Keller's reviews appeared in the *Blätter für literarische Unterhaltung* between 1848 and 1855. For a convenient summary and evaluation, see Werner Günther, *Jeremias Gotthelf. Wesen und Werk* (Berlin–Bielefeld, München: Erich Schmidt Verlag, 1954), 240.

15. Fehr, *Jeremias Gotthelf*, 50: "Mit Uli der Knecht bahnt sich überdies eine für viele spätere Werke typische Struktur des Romangeschehens an, nämlich die Aufgliederung in zwei Entwicklungsstufen. Im vorliegenden Fall wird sie so motiviert, dass sich das im ersten Bauernhof Erworbene in einer anspruchsvolleren und verantwortungsschwereren Umgebung bewähren muss."

16. Vreneli does not pursue Uli, but she respects and worries about him from the start. And we discover near the end that she had indeed loved him secretly for long (363): "Uli, den es so lange schon in verschwiegenem Herzen geliebt."These four women also represent variations on the opposition of frugality and charm: Stini possesses only the first, Ürsi only the second, Elisi neither, and Vreneli both.

17. For the source of Gotthelf citations, see above, note 12. Translations are mine.

18. This behavior has deep roots. Troubles start for Meiss and Anneli at an inn, where too much wine, jealousy, and anger lead to a brawl where Meiss fights like an enraged beast against a crowd (286). He almost strikes her by mistake in his fury; she drags him outside and leads him away; she tries to persuade him to go home; his anger flares up again and so she lets him spend the night with her. With that, disaster begins to build: Anneli becomes pregnant, Meiss is refused compensation that he counted on, payment is suddenly demanded for debts he never knew he had, the pastor refuses to marry them until these obligations are met, and Anneli and her baby die wretchedly in childbirth. Meiss returns to drinking and fighting, repeating the self-destructive acts that brought him to such misery. Vengeance, self-hatred, self-punishment, expiation and renewal of guilt, flight from pain and into it: cause and effect join in a pernicious circle.

19. Gotthelf likes to make a trip to market the occasion of decisive turns in the action, and of danger, opportunity, or of sudden mysterious luck. The stage is set for Uli's move to the Glungge at market (chap. 11). One thinks of the epic *Märitgang* of Anne Bäbi Jowäger (chaps. 8 and 9), frustrating for her but quietly, and with nobody guessing it, ending in the first encounter with Jacobli's future bride. Uli drives another cow to market in *Uli der Pächter* (chap. 22). Again he finds mystery and surprising luck: an encounter with Hagelhans, an excellent sale, and he passes a test without knowing it.

20. The farmhouse family room *(Stübli)* becomes the subject of a comparison with the salon, that product of conspicuous consumption at society's higher levels. Gotthelf describes the farmhouse with bemused irony and respect. "Er [Uli] kam und trat mit einer Art Respekt in dieses Heiligtum, in dieses Kämmerlein, das Allerheiligste des Hauses." "Darum trat er diesmal ein wie in einen geheimnisvollen Hain, in dem einem Dinge begegnen konnten, die noch kein sterbliches Auge gesehen." This excursus on the farmhouse shrine comes before a scene where its owners display honesty and good will. The characters and setting express an ideal. Another spirit reigns at the Glungge, and Uli's entrance into the farmhouse there passes without comment. Gotthelf's touch in such matters is so sure that one takes it for granted.

21. Incidents spin off doublets of themselves in a kind of spiral. Joggeli tests Uli twice, once with the cow and later with the miller. This second trial makes Uli almost pack up and leave. Then he almost leaves a second time when the new son-in-law appears. Examples are numerous.

22. It would be instructive to study the many ways in which Uli is contrasted with Elisi's husband, even in details like their treatment of animals (cf. 281 and 411), or the fleeting mention that Uli "verstehe sich nicht auf das Tuch und sei noch allemal betrogen worden" (89; cf. 284, 302, 322). In respect to the courtships, the motif of a "trip" binds them together (this doubtless grounded in the circumstances of rural life). First comes Uli's forced and humiliating journey with Elisi to visit her brother and sister-in-law, where

she makes advances and sets his thoughts in that direction (chap. 19); then Elisi's fatal excursion to the spa (chap. 21); and finally the perambulation of the mistress with her two charges (chap. 24). The last two are even associated by their titles. These trips have something in common with the excursions to market (above, note 19). They take persons out of their every-day circumstances and bring crisis or opportunity, stimulus and new problems that are then worked out back in the family. The center stage is home and farm. Contact with the world outside that magic circle brings the issues that quicken its life and advance the plot. Many of Gotthelf's novels are charged by the tension between these two poles. The "outside" fuels the narrative with fresh problems; these bring hearth and home into commotion, moving its life forward and developing its character. As usual, this is no artificial construct by Gotthelf, but something grounded in the real life of the rural population he writes about. The dynamics of this interchange would make a useful study in themselves.

23. The notion occurs frequently, e.g. in *Anne Bäbi Jowäger*, II, chap. 1. Mädi and Sami get in an argument soon after Jacobli and Meyeli arrive home after their wedding. Hansli puts a stop to it (19): "Sami . . . wollte das Gefecht fortsetzen, aber Hansli sagte, er hülf, si wette yche, selligi Wort am e sellige Tag trage nüt ab. Man sollte immer acht geben, was man rede, aber bsungerbar a sellige Tage, da bedeutete alles etwas, un öppis Wüests werd chum öppis Guets bidüte, darum düechte es ihn witziger, sie schwiegen."

24. The second half of *Der Bauernspiegel* (starting with Meiss's induction into the military) is by consensus less successful than the first, but fundamental themes hold them together.

25. Gotthelf repeats this scene at the start of *Uli der Pächter* (11). Uli ruminates on the challenges facing him at the well early in the morning. Vreneli startles him with a sudden embrace: "Plötzlich wurde er umschlungen; hochauf fuhr er, als ob es wirklich Schlangen wären." (That small scene contains, *in nuce*, the essential crisis of the entire novel and its solution.) Cf. *Uli der Knecht*, 365: Vreneli "war mit unhörbarem Tritte an Uli getreten, schlug es rasch beide Hände vor dessen Augen. In gewaltigem Schreck zuckte der starke Mann zusammen." And again, on the morning of their wedding, at the same place and hour (396): "ging er zum Brunnen. Da umfingen ihn wieder schalkhafte Hände, und Vreneli brachte ihm den holden Morgengruss." We do not see this side of Vreneli until after the wedding, but it is there from the start (chap. 12): "Draussen nahm ihn ein munteres, schönes Mädchen in Empfang, nussbraun an Haar und Augen, rot und weiss an den Backen, kusslicht die Lippen, blendend die Zähne, gross, fest aber schlank gebaut, mit ernsten Mienen, hinter denen der Schalk lauerte, aber auch die Gutmütigkeit."

Conclusion

1. Nagel, *Staufische Klassik* (Heidelberg, 1977), 509.
2. Stuttgart: Metzler Studienausgabe, 1968.

3. "Es gibt nichts Einzelnes in der Sprache, jedes ihrer Elemente kündigt sich als Teil eines Ganzen an."

4. "Der Einzelzug verliert damit seine absolute Punkt—oder Strecken-haftigkeit. Er erhält dazu die Mächtigkeit eines Strahls, der ständig andere kreuzt oder sich mit anderen bündelt. Er wird endlich erst durch dieses verschränkende In-Bezugtreten zu seiner eigentlichen Bedeutsamkeit er-hoben und erhält damit seine volle Realität. In jedem Fall erschliesst also eine Ausgliederung und sukzessive Abgrenzung von Einzelheiten diese selbst nur unvollkommen."

5. Holzapfel, "Homer—Niebelungenlied—Novalis. Zur Diskussion um die Formelhaftigkeit epischer Dichtung," *Fabula* 15 (1974), 34: "Auch längere epische Formeln, Bilder, Motive, stereotype Darstellungen bestimmter Situ-ationen und Strukturformeln, die grössere Handlungsabläufe mit traditi-onellen Mitteln sprachlich fixieren und tradierbar machen, sind vor allem als Stileigentümlichkeiten zu interpretieren, die auch dem möglichen Wandel des Stils unterworfen sind, und nicht als Ergebnisse eines Überlieferungs-mechanismus. So scheint es grundsätzlich richtig zu sein, von der 'Offenheit' eines Textes zu sprechen."

6. "In, man muss schon sagen, kalkulierter Automatik wirken sprach-licher Ausdruck, Funktion, Metrum, Reim und eine ganz bestimmte Lexik ökonomisch zusammen. Oberflächlich betrachtet ist das Ergebnis—besonders im Vergleich zur gleichzeitigen höfischen Erzählung—streckenweise ganz das, was man als stilistisches Verhalten einer mündlich konzipierten Dichtung erwartet. Das dürfte genau der Absicht des Dichters entsprechen: die viel-fältigen Interdependenzen, die näheres Zusehen aufdeckt, setzen die be-wusste Literarisierung eines mündlichen Erzählstils voraus. Nach allem, was wir inzwischen über die Langlebigkeit und Festigkeit mündlicher Erzählung in poetischer Form wissen, wird kaum noch jemand bestreiten, dass dieser Dichter aus einer noch lebendigen mündlichen Tradition heraus arbeitete. So wurde der Stoff 'traditionellerweise' bekannt gemacht, und der Dichter des 'Nibelungenliedes' griff diesen Stil auf—als seine ästhetische Antwort auf die Tradition—und bildete ihn im Medium der Nibelungenstrophe um. Seine Sprache ist keine allerorts im gleichen Sprachraum so anzutreffende und beliebig anwendbare mündliche Sprache, sondern 'Nibelungisch.' . . . Stili-sierung der mündlichen Dichtungsform - das scheint mir der übergeordnete Gesichtspunkt in Hinblick auf das Verhältnis dieser Dichtung zur voraus-gehenden Tradition." The above is from Curschmann, "Nibelungenlied und Nibelungenklage. Über mündlichkeit und Schriftlichkeit im Prozess der Ep-isierung," *Deutsche Literatur im Mittelalter. Kontakte und Perspektiven* (Hugo Kuhn zum Gedenken), hrsg. Ch. Cormeau (Stuttgart, 1979), 85–119; quota-tion from pp. 93–94. This view is supported by Wachinger, "Die 'Klage' und das Nibelungenlied," *Hohenemser Studien zum Nibelungenlied*, unter Mitarbeit von Irmtraud Albrecht, hrsg. Achim Masser (Dornbirn, 1981; *Montfort Heft* 3/4, 1980), 265–91.

7. After their transfer to the study of medieval literature, the methods of Parry and Lord were developed further and generated a considerable lit-

erature. In lieu of an extensive bibliography, the reader is referred to the review by K.H.R. Borghart, *Das Nibelungenlied. Die Spuren mündlichen Ursprungs in schriftlicher Überlieferung* (Amsterdam, 1977). One will find an extensive bibliography, statistical tables on formulas in the NL, and an excellent survey of "the question," including attention to oral poetry studies in other western European literatures. Also very useful is the collction of republished essays by the Wissenschaftliche Buchgesellschaft; *Oral Poetry: Das Problem der Mündlichkeit mittelaltlicher epischer Dichtung,* ed. N. Voorwinden and M. De Haan (Darmstadt, 1979). For *Roland,* see J. J. Duggan, *The Song of Roland: Formulaic Style and Poetic Craft* (Berkeley, 1973).

Index

MARTIN CLASSICAL LECTURES